Guardians of Finance

Guardians of Finance

Making Regulators Work for Us

James R. Barth, Gerard Caprio Jr., and Ross Levine

The MIT Press
Cambridge, Massachusetts
London, England

MIT Press books may be purchased at special quantity discounts for business or sales promotional use. For information, please email special_sales@mitpress.mit.edu or write to Special Sales Department, The MIT Press, 55 Hayward Street, Cambridge, MA 02142.

This book was set in Sabon by Graphic Composition, Inc., Bogart, GA. Printed and bound in the United States of America.

Library of Congress Cataloging-in-Publication Data

Barth, James R.
Guardians of finance : making regulators work for us / James R. Barth, Gerard Caprio Jr., and Ross Levine.
    p.   cm.
Includes bibliographical references and index.
ISBN 978-0-262-01739-8 (hbk. : alk. paper)
1. Financial crises. 2. Financial crises—Prevention. 3. Finance—Government policy. 4. Financial institutions. 5. Banks and banking. 6. Global Financial Crisis, 2008–2009. I. Caprio, Gerard. II. Levine, Ross. III. Title.
HB3722.B374 2012
332.0973—dc23
                                                                    2011038519

10 9 8 7 6 5 4 3 2

Contents

Preface

By 2008 the global financial crisis threatened the world economy. As asset prices plummeted and investors lost confidence in major financial institutions, governments around the world rushed to shore up their financial systems. The US government took over the multi-trillion dollar mortgage finance giants, Fannie Mae and Freddie Mac, as they were going bankrupt. Governments in about two dozen industrial economies deemed it necessary to provide financial support to many of the world's largest financial institutions, including American International Group, Bank of America, Citigroup, Goldman Sachs, JP Morgan, Union Bank of Switzerland, Northern Rock, and Royal Bank of Scotland.

The global crisis is much more than a financial disaster: it is an economic and social calamity that has had devastating and lasting effects on the lives of millions of people around the world. The unemployment rate in the United States was about 4.5 percent in 2006 to 2007. It more than doubled to over 10 percent in 2010 and still remained about 9 percent in mid-2011. Workers in European countries also suffered, with unemployment rates rising from about 7.5 percent in 2007 to 10 percent in 2011. Alarmingly, youth unemployment rates reached 40 percent in some countries. Economic opportunities available to many individuals were constrained by crippled financial systems. Bank credit, which when employed effectively provides the means for entrepreneurs to grow existing businesses or start new ones, dried up in 2008. In Europe, net bank lending (new loans less the repayment of the principal on existing loans) declined to zero, while in the United States, it turned negative.

The fiscal burdens imposed on governments by the crisis will be felt for many decades. As governments nationalized the losses of failing financial institutions and economies slid into recessions, national debt soared to alarming levels. In the United States, federal debt held by the public nearly doubled, jumping from about 35 percent of gross domestic product in 2001 to almost 70 percent in 2011. The fiscal fallout has been similar in many other countries. In Spain, the national debt also doubled, rising from less than 40 percent in 2007 to about 80 percent of national output in 2011; the debt burden in Ireland has been even worse. All of this additional debt means that current and future citizens are going to pay more in taxes and receive less in social services during the coming decades.

The adverse consequences resulting from the global crisis are all too evident in various statistics. Investors often rush to invest in gold when they are worried about the future; the price of gold was about $400.00 an ounce in 2002 but rose to above $1,500 an ounce by mid-2011. The major rating agencies downgraded the sovereign debt of many major countries, and even downgraded US government debt in 2011. The cost of insuring the payment on the outstanding debt of several European countries, notably Greece, Ireland, Italy, Portugal, and Spain, and several US states, such as California, Illinois, Michigan, and New York jumped markedly after 2008, in some cases rising four- or fivefold.

The widespread financial collapse has severely undermined faith in the institutions that were created by governments to ensure the safety and soundness of financial systems. Whether through official supervision, sound regulatory rules, or effective markets, the major regulatory agencies were charged with creating an environment that would foster an efficient allocation of resources, promote economic growth, enable the pursuit of economic opportunities, and reduce the likelihood of a systemic crisis like the one that occurred and from which so many continue to suffer.

What went wrong? Did a combination of bad luck, a few policy mistakes, and some overly ambitious financiers lead to the collapse of the global financial system? Or did core institutional deficiencies in the system associated with selecting, implementing, and reforming financial policies help cause this and other crises? If the latter, have we corrected those weaknesses and, if not, are those defects setting the stage for the next, perhaps even larger, crisis?

This book is about the role played by the Guardians of Finance—the major financial regulatory institutions—in aiding and abetting the global financial crisis. During the ten to fifteen years during which this crisis was brewing, what were such "Guardians" as the Federal Reserve, Securities and Exchange Commission, and Federal Deposit Insurance Corporation in the United States doing? What about financial regulators in other countries? Did the Financial Services Authority in the United Kingdom, the Irish Financial Regulator, the Financial Supervisory Authority in Iceland, the Office of the Superintendent of Financial Institutions in Canada, and regulators in many other countries encourage or discourage the excessive risk-taking associated with the economic devastation through which millions of individuals are suffering? In the most recent crisis, and in earlier crises, governments have usually responded by adding more regulations and more regulators. Given that the severity of crises has been growing over time, isn't it time to reconsider the fundamentals—the core institutions associated with financial regulation?

In this book we evaluate the role of major financial regulators in leading us from crisis to crisis, analyze their behavior, and suggest ways of reforming the Guardians of Finance so that they work for society at large—and not just for a few financial elites.

Acknowledgments

Authors depend on discussions with, feedback from and advice given by many in the course of putting together a manuscript, and we are no exceptions. In addition to valuable suggestions from three anonymous referees, we received numerous comments, source materials, and/or suggestions on the manuscript from Maria Carkovic, John Chant, Chuck Friedman, Charles Goodhart, Stephen Grenville, Stephen Haber, Patrick Honohan, Philip Lane, Eric Lewin, Charles Littrel, Rick Mishkin, Lindsay Mollineaux, Dan Nolle, and Larry Promisel. We also benefited from excellent advice and editorial services at MIT Press from Jane Macdonald, Janice Pieroni, and Emily Taber, as well as Dina McNichols, Jim's former Milken Institute colleague.

Jim was fortunate roughly ten years ago, thanks to Jerry, to spend a semester visiting the World Bank, where he met Ross. This has led to a stimulating and productive collaboration examining various aspects of bank regulation. This book is the most recent product of our joint research. He has benefited from conversations with several of his colleagues at Auburn University, especially Dan Gropper and John Jahera, as well as his colleagues at the Milken Institute, including Glenn Yago, Tong Li, Triphon Phumiwasana, Wenling Lu, and Apanard Angkinand. He is also grateful to Dan Brumbaugh, who not only first introduced him to the problems of bank regulation but co-wrote numerous papers that have influenced his thinking about these problems. Helpful comments, even when taking issue with some of the conclusions, were provided at a seminar at the US Comptroller of the Currency a few months before the book was finalized.

Jerry began thinking about this book while supported by a Fulbright grant to visit at Trinity College, Dublin, during the unfolding of the Irish crisis in 2009; he thanks the Institute for International Integration Studies at Trinity, as well as the World Fellowship from Williams College and the Fulbright Program, for making that visit possible. He benefited from comments from the PhD seminar he taught on Financial Crises at Trinity, and from those he received at conferences at the Finlawmetrics Conference at Bocconi University; the VII Colloquium on "Financial Collapse: How Are the Biggest Nations and Organizations Managing the Crisis?" organized by the Associazione Luiss-Guido Carli and Fondazione Cesifin "Alberto Predieri" in collaboration with the editors of *The Journal of Financial Stability*, October 2, 2009, Ravenna; The World Bank; Queens University, Belfast; The Central Bank of Ireland; The Brookings Institution; and the University of Maryland.

Ross had the good fortune of presenting bits and pieces of this book at many seminars and conferences, including at the Bank for International Settlements, Brown University, Claremont–McKenna College, the Federal Reserve Banks of Boston and Chicago, Kansas City Federal Reserve's conference in Jackson Hole, Wyoming, the Fuqua School of Business, the Geneva Institute, George Washington University, the Hoover Institute, the International Monetary Fund, the London School of Economics, and the World Bank. Unsurprisingly, some regulatory individuals and others at these conferences had objections. And indeed we have revised and honed our views through these helpful interactions. Furthermore Ross deeply appreciates the numerous helpful conversations with his colleagues and students at Brown, including Oded Galor, Juan Carlos Gozzi, Peter Howitt, Eric Lewin, Glenn Loury, Lindsay Mollineaux, David Weil, and Yona Rubinstein, each of whom sometimes disagreed vehemently with various points but none of whom gave up on setting Ross right.

We are indebted to our families. Ross thanks Steve who kept forcing him to explain things better and Norman who urged him to put the big picture together in a book. His wife Maruja was an intellectual companion, talking about the big themes, the organization of chapters, the phrasing of sentences, the rewriting of sentences, the reorganization of chapters, and the reconsideration of big themes. The book would not be the same without the clarity or her insights. And Ben and Rebecca were enthusiastic supporters, patiently hearing more about financial regulation than teenagers should have to bear over dinner.

Jerry thanks his wife Jeanne for putting up with far too many nights and weekends of work on this manuscript, not to mention so many "thrilling" conversations given over to explanations of the regulation of finance on far too many occasions!

Jim dedicates this book to his daughter Rachel for always "pushing" him to write for a broader and less technical audience and to his brother Robert for providing motivation to write another book for him to read.

Despite all of this support, we take responsibility for the views expressed here. Any errors likely result from not listening sufficiently to one or more of the people who tried to help us.

1

Introduction

. . . the recent financial crisis was not a natural disaster. It was a man-made economic assault. People did it. . . . And, it will happen again unless we change the rules.
—US Senator Carl Levin[1]

An Accident?

It was a terrible, terrible accident—something awful to watch unfold. This is the narrative told by many of the world's most influential policy makers and financiers to explain the financial crisis. It was a terrible accident precipitated by an unforeseeable confluence of events that conspired to bring down the global financial system. A global savings glut, integrated international capital markets, and poorly designed macroeconomic policies fueled large capital flows. In several major economies, those flows in turn triggered lower interest rates, weaker loan standards, a boom in toxic financial innovations, and an unsustainable explosion of credit.[2] The inevitable crisis was a "perfect storm," in which fate brought together all of these events in a way no one could anticipate.

The story is told and retold by a chorus of luminaries who include Treasury Secretary Timothy Geithner and his predecessors in the position, Henry Paulson and Robert Rubin. Ben Bernanke, Chairman of the Federal Reserve Board, and his predecessor, Alan Greenspan, are in the choir, as are numerous other current and former officials and observers from around the world. Greenspan has likened the financial crisis to a "classic euphoric bubble" and a "hundred years flood."[3] Those outside the United States—such as the late Brian Lenihan, the former Finance Minister of Ireland, and then French Finance Minister (now IMF Managing Director)

Christine Lagarde—were quick to concur, suggesting that their country's "accidents" were made worse by US policy choices. Building on the bubble image, others have painted a picture of financiers behaving like lemmings following each other off the risk-return cliff in the massive rush to market increasingly complex financial products. One of them, Charles O. Prince, the former CEO of Citigroup, is frequently cited for his remarks on the eve of the crisis: "When the music stops . . . things will be complicated," he said. "But as long as the music is playing, you've got to get up and dance. We're still dancing."[4] In this version of events, policy makers were confronted with floods, bubbles, and suicidal financiers, and there was not much they could do. The crisis happened *to* them.

When policy makers are not blaming unpredictable events and uncontainable forces, they frequently claim that they could have prevented the crisis, or at least dampened its severity, if only their agencies had been granted more and broader powers. Ben Bernanke, Henry Paulson, and Christopher Cox, the former head of the SEC, repeatedly argue that they had insufficient "tool kits" to combat increasing financial market fragility. These policy makers also argue that it was sometimes unclear who had supervisory authority over systemically important financial institutions.[5] This view also fits the "accident" narrative: with insufficient legal authority and insurmountable regulatory gaps, it was impossible for policy-makers to prevent the crisis.[6] As argued by Treasury Secretary Geithner,

If we could have done it any differently, we would have done it differently. Instead, we had no other choice. That is the basic lesson.[7]

This extraordinary statement—"we had no other choice"—is at best incomplete, and an unsympathetic reader might describe it as deceptive or at least self-serving. Granted, once the crisis exploded, the damage was inevitable. Once Bear Stearns, Lehman Brothers, American Insurance Group (AIG), the government-sponsored housing finance entities (Fannie Mae and Freddie Mac), and other major banks and investment banks had failed or been bailed out by authorities around the world, serious and widespread economic fallout was unavoidable. But this does not mean that policy makers couldn't have *prevented* such a devastating crisis; it does not imply that they could not have taken prudent actions in the decade or so before the crisis to lower the risk and severity of the "accident."

This accident view is not all wrong. Large international capital flows and macroeconomic policies did fuel speculative investments. Financial innovations and deceptive practices did facilitate excessive risk-taking, fraud, and the exploitation of uninformed investors. There were regulatory gaps. Real estate prices soared and then plummeted in many parts of the United States and around the world. Many troublesome developments taking place during the decade before the crisis were difficult to discern through the deluge of daily events.

But the accident explanation is woefully incomplete. In the decade or so before the crisis, policy makers watched closely as international capital flows lowered interest rates and narrowed credit spreads, and set off the East Asian crisis in 1997. They monitored the unprecedented boom in housing prices in the United States, Iceland, Ireland, the United Kingdom, Spain, and elsewhere. They documented the credit boom and surge of fraudulent mortgage lending practices in the United States, and the growing reliance on short-term financing by banks in many countries. They closely analyzed, reviewed, and debated the explosive use and abuse of derivatives, which are financial instruments whose prices depend on the value of other assets. They enacted policies that allowed and encouraged bankers to lower the capital supporting their assets and then engage in ever more risky activities.

Things just don't add up to the perfect storm view. Several European countries with a single financial regulator and little financial innovation suffered a financial crisis, suggesting that new financial instruments and regulatory gaps were not essential ingredients. Following expert reports, authorities in Iceland, Ireland, and the United Kingdom now reject the accident view and admit that systemic defects with regulatory systems helped cause the crises. Describing the events of 2007 to 2009 as an accident misses essential features of what transpired during the ten to fifteen years before the crisis.

By wrapping the accident narrative around themselves as insulation against blame for the current crisis, policy makers impede the development of reforms that might prevent the next crisis. The world is now dealing with wreckage from the colossal failure of financial regulation, where "regulation" refers to the full range financial policies, rules, enforcement procedures, and official supervisory practices associated with shaping financial market activities. Only by identifying the full range of factors giving rise to the crisis—including flaws with regulatory institutions themselves—can one develop comprehensive and meaningful reforms that enhance the functioning of financial markets and institutions to the betterment of societies.

This Book

The purpose of our book is to document major financial regulatory failures during the ten to fifteen years before the most recent crisis and propose reforms that would improve the financial regulatory system. It is not about the crisis period and who did what after it broke out; nor is it only about the United States. It is about how systemic weaknesses with the governance of financial regulation—the system associated with designing, implementing, assessing, and reforming financial policies—contributed to crises around the world and how to fix those defects.

We extract the more general and essential causes of the crisis by providing a longer run perspective and by looking beyond the US financial system. In analyzing the decade or so before the cascade of financial institution insolvencies and bailouts, and hence before policy makers shifted into "emergency response" mode, we examine a comparatively calm period during which the authorities had ample time to learn about the evolving impact of their policies and make adjustments to address emerging problems. By looking beyond the United States, we use a richer array of experiences to identify common deficiencies in the institutions associated with selecting, implementing, and evaluating financial policies. Although the US financial system is the epicenter of the global financial crisis and hence a focus, it has unique elements. For instance, while US regulators blame financial innovation and the alphabet soup of regulatory bodies operating in the United States, many crisis countries, some of which suffered much worse damage than the United States, did not have any of these characteristics. Did so many countries suffer their worst crisis since the Great Depression with no common elements? In this book, we identify the common elements underlying breakdowns in regulatory systems in countries around the globe.

The Guardians of Finance Did Not Work for Us
Rather than characterize the crisis as an accident, we show that financial regulators—the Guardians of Finance—repeatedly designed, implemented, and maintained policies that helped precipitate the global financial crisis. The Guardians embraced policies that permitted, and too

frequently encouraged, the executives of private financial institutions to undertake socially harmful, though privately profitable, investments. We do not believe regulators intended to cause the crisis, or even that they acted with malice. But we do provide abundant evidence that they recklessly endangered the global economy.

Regulators ignored warning signs of increasing financial system fragility, signs that should have been quite clear in light of the 130+ financial crises around the world since 1980.[8] Regulators did little when leading commercial banks moved over half of their assets off balance sheets, when the largest financial institutions dramatically reduced owner-contributed equity capital through the purchase of opaque credit default swaps, when their own inspectors repeatedly identified problems in financial institutions, when banks grew their assets at unprecedented rates, and when they learned that their own policies were encouraging reckless behavior by financiers. We do not claim that any single policy maker put all the pieces together and predicted the depth and breadth of the crisis. Rather, we show that regulators working within the narrow confines of their own institutions systematically chose policies that increased the fragility of that component of the financial system for which they were responsible, and they maintained those policies even as they learned about the adverse consequences of their decisions.

The crisis was not simply the result of an uncontainable bubble, it was not only due to the incompetence and impotence of regulators, it was not just a mistake, and it does not primarily reflect regulatory gaps. There was a systemic failure of the system associated with selecting, implementing, assessing, and reforming financial regulations. The crisis did not just happen *to* policy makers. It happened because of them.

Although we recognize that a multitude of factors contributed to the crisis, we focus on one, crucial precipitating factor: the Guardians of Finance adopted policies that induced financiers to take excessive risk; they often knew their policies were destabilizing the financial system many years before the crisis; and the Guardians too often chose not to reform their destabilizing policies, even though they had the power and time to do so.

Why Do the Interests of the Guardians Deviate from Those of the Public?
Why didn't the Guardians work for us? To address this question, we first ask, what *incentivized* regulators to behave the way they did? We then

document the failings in the governance of financial regulation that *allowed* regulators to behave in the ways that they did.

What motivated the Guardians to make the decisions they made? Perhaps there is no single answer. One line of reasoning argues that the Guardians of Finance were captured by a flawed ideology that led to a series of regulatory debacles. For example, Ayn Rand's "acolytes"—Alan Greenspan and Christopher Cox—made policy decisions based on a superficial understanding of free markets. By assuming that private financial institutions would operate prudently, *despite* incentives to do otherwise, these Guardians helped guide the world directly into a "perfect storm." Although we do not believe that one ideology fully accounts for the crisis, ideologies matter. We later document how defective ideologies helped destabilize financial systems.[9]

Many stress that corruption and the "revolving door" between financial institutions and regulatory agencies pervert financial regulation. For example, the prominent MIT economist Simon Johnson and former McKinsey consultant James Kwak note that as people move from private financial institutions to regulatory positions and back again, there is a question of whose interests these people are serving when they are regulators.[10] Robert Rubin was the co-head of Goldman Sachs, then Secretary of the Treasury, and then a senior official at Citigroup. Henry Paulson was CEO of Goldman Sachs and then Secretary of the Treasury. Gerald Corrigan was president of the New York Federal Reserve and is now a senior official at Goldman Sachs. William Dudley was a partner and managing director at Goldman Sachs and is now president of the New York Federal Reserve Bank. David Mullins was vice-chairman of the Board of Governors of the Federal Reserve System (subsequently in this book, "the Fed") and then resigned to become a partner in the infamous hedge fund Long Term Capital Management.[11] More generally, every single president of the New York Federal Reserve, except the first one, Benjamin Strong (who held that job after serving as president of Bankers Trust and then died in office) and Timothy Geithner (who went on to become Treasury Secretary, but whose career is not yet over), went on to work for a private financial institution after leaving public office. And, the co-founder and editor of *Institutional Risk Analytics*, Christopher Whalen documents how members of the New York Federal Reserve, including those in the Division of Supervision and Regulation, frequently move directly from their regulatory offices to highly lucrative positions within the firms that they used to regulate.[12] It is hard in view of this situation not to question the integrity of financial regulation; even if all regulators are trying to act honorably, the appearance of conflicts of interest weakens the public's faith in the sector and in government regulation.

Although we detail many more examples of the revolving door between private financial institutions and official regulatory agencies, we do not fully embrace the revolving door explanation of questionable regulatory behavior. On the one hand, our personal and professional experiences from working with regulators and within regulatory institutions suggest that regulators are highly skilled individuals who have devoted themselves to public service. So this explanation just doesn't feel right to us. Moreover none of the revolving door examples demonstrates that any individual behaved in a corrupt or unethical manner. On the other hand, we understand the power of incentives. Clearly, regulators are inextricably connected to the financial services industry. Clearly, the revolving door spins rapidly and regulators are not completely independent of private financial institutions.

Beyond the revolving door, financial institutions spend enormous amounts of time and money on lobbying politicians both to enact sympathetic laws and to pressure regulatory agencies to interpret and implement those laws in sympathetic ways. The Academy-award winning film, *Inside Job*, argues that the financial services industry has corrupted the design of financial regulations by politicians and the execution of those policies by regulators. Research by academics and individuals at the International Monetary Fund shows that financial institutions get much of what they want from their lobbying expenditures, as campaign contributions change the voting behavior of legislatures on crucial financial policy issues.[13] According to this view, the financial service industry's influence over politics helps account for why the Guardians do not always work for us.

Why Do the Interests of the Guardians Deviate from Those of the Public? Is It "Home Field" Advantage?

Psychology provides an additional explanation for why the incentives of regulators differ from those of the public. The Guardians are people like everyone else and therefore subject to a powerful human trait: conformity. Psychologists find that social influences affect beliefs and behavior. The Guardians might adopt the views of the professional community in which they operate most frequently and comfortably—namely the financial services industry.

Consider the home field advantage in sports, which is persuasively described in the book, *Scorecasting*, by Tobias J. Moskowitz, a finance professor at the University of Chicago, and L. Jon Wertheim, senior writer for *Sports Illustrated*. Across all the sports that they study, including soccer, basketball, cricket, rugby, hockey, football, and baseball, the home team wins a disproportionately large proportion of the games. For example, in more than 100 years of major league baseball and college football, not once have the road teams collectively won more games than the home teams. In professional soccer leagues around the world, home teams win well over 60 percent of the games.

The home field bias is not explained by player performance. Moskowitz and Wertheim show that there is no evidence that crowd support boosts player performance, that home players exploit unique characteristics of the home field, or that the rigors of traveling to away games hurts player performance.[14] If player performance does not account for the home field advantage, what does?

The bulk of the home field advantage is explained by the systemic biases of officials, referees, and umpires. Moskowitz and Wertheim show that officials are not biased for a particular team; they are always biased for the home team. They conform to the views of the home crowd. Soccer referees add more extra time to the end of games when the home team is losing, especially when the match is close. Baseball umpires call fewer strikes against home batters than away batters, especially at crucial junctures in close games. Home teams in all sports receive fewer meaningful penalties, especially in the critical parts of close games. Moreover crowd size matters. Official bias is greater in high-attendance games.

For regulatory officials, the "home crowd" *is* the financial services industry. People from the financial services industry "surround" regulatory officials; they meet with regulators daily. It is the financiers who will immediately jeer and taunt officials if they do not like their "calls." Since regulators might have recently worked for the financial services industry and might soon be going to work there, it would be natural for regulators to identify fairly closely with the financial services "community" that envelops them. In contrast, the general public has a hard time even buying tickets to this game. They do not interact with regulators on a daily basis; they are not part of this community. Moreover the general public simply does not have the information and expertise to follow what is happening in financial regulation on a regular basis and to assess the broad ramifications of those regulatory policies. The public has a difficult time coordinating and communicating their views—"cheers"—to balance the influences of the financial services industry. This home field advantage induces a systematic bias among financial regulators, especially on crucial issues and at crucial junctures.

This behavioral view of official bias does not imply that officials are corrupt; rather, it implies that officials are only human. People are social animals, who want to fit in with their communities:[15]

Psychology finds that social influence is a powerful force that can affect human behavior and decisions *without the subjects even being aware of it*. Psychologists call this influence conformity because it causes the subject's opinion to conform to a group's opinion.

Critically, the behavioral view does not imply that officials succumb to social pressure and reluctantly change their *stated* opinions to match those of the group; rather people genuinely *believe* the opinions of the group. As emphasized by Moskowitz and Wertheim, psychological studies show that people's actual perceptions change because they operate within a social milieu. Thus officials, referees, and umpires truly believe they are making the right calls on the field of play and that they are acting in the public interest when making regulatory decisions. They would furiously, and genuinely, reject any intimation that they were biased against the visiting team or in favor of the financial services industry.

From this perspective, regulatory bias is a natural human manifestation of the current institutional structure of financial regulation in which the financial services industry enjoys a decisive home field advantage. To create a regulatory system that works for the public, we must reform the institutional structure of financial regulation to account for this particular aspect of human nature. In this book we propose just such an institutional reform to reduce, if not totally eliminate, regulatory bias.

Why Doesn't the Public Compel the Guardians to Act in the Public Interest?

Regardless of what shaped the interests of the Guardians, why is the public unable to govern them effectively? If regulators made systematic mistakes, why didn't the public and its elected representatives force them to adjust? If regulators were captured by a flawed ideology, why didn't others effectively challenge that view? If money distorted politics and regulation, where was the public to set things straight? If regulators were conforming to the opinions of the financial services industry, why didn't the public form a countervailing check? In other words, although regulators are not independent advocates of the public good, why did—and do—the public and its elected officials *allow* regulators to behave in ways that are inconsistent with the public interest?

Part of the answer is simple: the opaqueness and complexity of finance prevented—and prevents—the public and its elected officials from obtaining informed, expert, and independent assessments of financial regulation and, therefore, from governing financial regulators. Without such sound assessments, the public cannot know what regulators are doing or evaluate the repercussions of regulatory actions. Hence the public cannot even begin to compel regulators to act in the public's best interests. It does not get any simpler than this: How can the public and its elected representatives govern the regulatory authorities when the regulatory authorities have a monopoly on both the information and expertise necessary for assessing their own performance?

Around the world, including in the United States, there is no institution that (1) is independent of short-run political influences, (2) is independent of the allure and influence of private financial markets, (3) has the power to demand and obtain information about regulatory decisions and financial market conditions, (4) contains the expertise to evaluate that information, and (5) has the prominence to deliver such an assessment effectively to the public and their elected representatives. There are few effective checks and balances on the Guardians of Finance.

Policy makers are not addressing this dangerous state of affairs. Major regulatory reforms—including the Dodd–Frank Wall Street Reform and Consumer Protection Act of 2010 and the Basel Committee on Banking Supervision's proposed framework for improving bank regulation, Basel III—steer clear of *the* central financial regulatory challenge: how to get regulators to act in society's best interest. There is a hint that some European countries recognize that systemic failures in the institutions associated with financial regulation contributed to the crisis, but emerging proposals do not address the fundamental institutional problem of getting the Guardians to work for the public.

The current strategy of giving existing regulatory agencies more and broader discretionary power—without enhancing the governance of those agencies—is playing dice with the global economy's future. If countries do not fix the systemic problems with the Guardians of Finance, more and more costly crises will likely ensue, thwarting economic prosperity and limiting economic opportunities.

A Proposal to Make the Guardians Work for Us

We propose a "Sentinel" to improve the process for selecting, implementing, evaluating, and reforming regulation; the name, Sentinel, comes from a telling quote at the start of chapter 8 by James Madison, who anticipated the problem that public officials might not always look out for the public's interests. The Sentinel's sole power would be to acquire any information necessary for evaluating financial regulation. As the public's sentry over financial policy, its sole responsibility would be to assess continuously and report at least annually on the state and impact of financial policies. The Sentinel would have no direct regulatory authority and would not reduce the statutory power of any existing regulatory agency. It would contribute to the financial regulatory system by providing an informed, expert, and independent assessment of financial regulation. It would *allow* informed debate without having the power to determine policy. It would break the monopoly of information and expertise currently held by unelected, unaccountable, and largely unchallenged regulators.

We design the Sentinel to be both politically independent and independent of financial market influences, though we recognize that this is no easy task. These are unique and essential characteristics. In capitals around the world, lobbyists both shape legislation and coerce politicians to put pressure on regulators with respect to the interpretation and implementation of those laws. In regulatory agencies, the allure of lucrative jobs in the private sector is ever present and former industry leaders frequently run those very agencies. Regulators and industry experts interact on a regular basis, raising concerns about conformity and regulatory bias. We structure the Sentinel both to be independent of short-run politics and to minimize, if not eliminate, the revolving door. Since the Sentinel would not have direct regulatory responsibilities, its staff would not be in constant, daily contact with financiers. These features will partially insulate the Sentinel from the financial services industry, making it a more positive force in enhancing financial regulation for the public at large.

Do we really need another institution? Yes, definitely. No other existing entity currently has the incentive, power, or capabilities to provide an informed, expert, and independent assessment of the full constellation of financial sector policies. All of these must be combined. Transparency alone is not enough. Even if all information were released to the public, which it is not, that would be insufficient. It takes a multidisciplinary team of financial economists, lawyers, accountants, regulators, and individuals with private-sector experience to assess financial regulation. This team must be independent of the more narrowly focused influences of the financial services industry and short-term politics.

The Sentinel would improve financial regulation. As an additional group of experts reviewing and reporting on financial regulations, it would reduce the probability and costliness of regulatory mistakes. As an informed, expert institution, it would reduce the ability of regulators to obfuscate regulatory actions and the likelihood that one or two leading regulators with a simplistic ideology could unduly influence financial regulators. As a prominent institution, the Sentinel's reports, available to legislators, the executive branch, and the public, would reduce the influence of special interests on the public's representatives and the importance of the revolving door on regulators. Furthermore it would reduce the home field advantage enjoyed by the financial services industry. In sports the official bias vanishes when there is effective monitoring. For example, in baseball, the home field advantage in called strikes and balls disappears when umpires know that their calls are being digitally monitored. Even the *same* umpire becomes less biased when he knows about the monitoring. Thus conformity and official bias diminishes with greater transparency.[16] The Sentinel, by enhancing monitoring and transparency, will play a similar role: It will reduce regulatory bias before it manifests itself in official decisions.

One way to see the value of the Sentinel is to imagine taking it away. Consider a country with a Sentinel that has the power to demand information, the expertise to evaluate that information, and both the prominence and independence to make its judgments heard. As an entity whose sole objective is to evaluate the state of financial regulation from the perspective of the public, it informs the public about financial regulation. While regulators sometimes dispute the Sentinel's analyses and even reject its recommendations, the Sentinel fosters, and permits, an informed debate. Now consider eliminating such an institution. Consider writing an editorial arguing for the elimination of this institution and instead placing enormous discretionary power over the implementation of laws governing the allocation of capital in the hands of unelected, largely unmonitorable, officials with close ties to the financial services industry. We believe it would be difficult to make such an argument—though we are sure that some well-paid lobbyists would still try.

We are under no illusions that the Sentinel would solve all problems. The Sentinel is not enough. Regulatory institutions around the world, groups of experts, such as the Squam Lake Working Group on Financial Regulation and the Warwick Commission, and numerous individual researchers are working hard to design better regulations and to propose laws that would reduce the ability of the financial services industry to distort the political and regulatory process associated with establishing, interpreting, and implementing financial policies. The success of these efforts is *necessary* for enhancing the operation of financial markets. The Sentinel is not a substitute for them; rather, it will complement these efforts. While no cure-all, the Sentinel would *improve* the regulatory apparatus.

Financial Regulation Matters

After one of the worst financial crises in history, the title of this section seems beyond dispute. Of course, both finance and regulation of finance matter. The recent crisis disrupted the lives of people around the world. Unemployment rates soared and national debts have reached alarming levels as governments bailed out wealthy financiers by socializing their losses. Past crises have also been costly, especially for the poor. For instance, the fiscal costs of the financial crises of the 1970s to 2001 averaged 13 percent of GDP, and one crisis in three was quite large, with a fiscal cost over 20 percent of GDP. A few—Argentina in the 1980s and Indonesia in the 1990s, cost about 50 percent of GDP, and the costs of the current Irish banking crisis seem likely to top that figure. But these sums hide the human tragedy of crises: for what Indonesia spent on its crisis, it could have tripled its health and education spending in perpetuity! Poverty rates had been declining dramatically in Thailand, Korea, and Indonesia up to 1996, but with the crisis of 1997, those rates jumped and took several years to once again approach their former levels. Argentina also saw a graphic rise in poverty in its crisis of 2001 to 2002: formerly middle-class workers were living in slums and foraging for food. The United States has also seen its poverty climb in the current crisis and long-term unemployment, previously rare, has become a serious social issue. In Ireland, homelessness and rising emigration are turning the pages back to sadder chapters of Irish history.

But the importance of finance is not simply due to financial crises.[17] How can one explain how a group of tiny Northern Italian city states became the center of the Renaissance in the 14th to 16th centuries without at least some part of their success attributable to the financial revolution that began there? Or how tiny Holland became a world power and fended off the forces of mighty Spain without understanding the role of finance? Similarly it is difficult to fully explain England's emergence as a world power and the birthplace of the industrial revolution without taking into account the impact of its financial revolution.[18]

Ample research shows that finance affects national rates of long-run economic growth and the equality of economic opportunities. Finance influences who can start a business and who cannot, who can pay for education and who cannot, and who can attempt to realize one's economic aspirations and who cannot. The financial system shapes whether capital flows to those with the best ideas and entrepreneurial initiative or to those with the most accumulated wealth and political connections. Research shows that financial policies that stimulate improvements in the operation of banks disproportionately help lower income individuals, reducing income inequality and accelerating overall economic growth. Financial institutions influence the effectiveness with which firms deploy capital after receiving external credit. Although economics is said to be the only field in which two people can share a Nobel Prize for opposing views, the evidence demonstrating the beneficial effects of well-functioning financial systems is impressive and varied.[19]

We emphasize the positive side of finance because some might erroneously conclude from the devastating effects of the crisis that it is necessary to repress finance, that is, impose a series of simple but drastic controls on what financial institutions and markets can do—limits on interest rates, ownership and activities of banks, how credit can be allocated, and other forms of government intervention. We recognize that finance can be a force for much damage when done poorly. But financial markets are not merely casinos where the rich come to place their bets, and financial institutions are not simply crisis prone warehouses for storing wealth. The financial system allocates capital, monitors the use of that capital, and provides mechanisms for managing risks. Finance is not all that matters for growth and poverty alleviation, but its impact is significant. It is exactly the central importance of finance for economic prosperity that motivates our examination of what went wrong with financial regulation and our recommendations for how to make the system work better.

Some Final Introductory Remarks

In presentations at regulatory agencies around the world, some current and past regulators reject the notion that regulators, at least in their own countries and agencies, would ever behave in a manner inconsistent with the public interest. An overwhelming body of evidence suggests that the financial services industry unduly influences financial policy, whether it is through campaign contributions, the close professional and personal connections between regulators and financiers, ideological capture, or the conforming behavioral influences of the home crowd—the financial services industry—on regulators. In a democracy we do not assume that government officials behave like angels, and we should also not assume that the Guardians of Finance are immune to the psychological influence of conformity. Therefore we should not grant unelected, unaccountable officials a monopoly over the information and expertise necessary for making policy decisions. Instead, we should create a system of checks and balances and auxiliary institutions to promote transparency and healthy debate. We are not biased against regulators; we want to reduce regulatory bias.

Might we be accused of "cherry-picking" examples of regulatory failure without balancing them with examples of regulatory successes? This is partially true. Our goal is not to comprehensively assess the performance of financial regulatory agencies around the world. Rather, we choose examples of major policy decisions, across different regulatory agencies, from around the world to illustrate *systemic* failures with financial regulation.

On really big decisions, an array of regulatory agencies got it wrong—and they maintained their bad policy choices over many years as information accumulated about the destabilizing repercussions of their policies. Even if an objective assessment shows that the regulators were right 95 percent of the time, too frequently they repeatedly blew key calls. As in sports, the home field base is particularly strong at decisive junctures of crucial games. The same was, and is, true of financial regulation. When it really matters, the financial services industry—not the public—gets the call. That is the focus of our examples and our reform recommendations.

Are we "Monday-morning" quarterbacking by identifying regulatory failures after the fact? Of course we are. Part of developing a strategy for winning the next game involves understanding why we lost the last. Our goals are to identify systemic defects with the financial regulatory apparatus and make recommendations on how to fix them. We are not arguing that, "we told you so." Rather, we show that the Guardians *themselves* frequently knew about the destabilizing effects of their policies, or should have known given the information and expertise within the regulatory agencies. Part of the reason that we, and others, could not have predicted the crisis is that we did not have the information, nor did we have teams of economists, regulators, accountants, and lawyers to assess that information. The Sentinel would break the dangerous monopoly on information and expertise within regulatory agencies, whose views are too frequently influenced by the entities they regulate.

Similarly those who direct their ire at "greedy" bankers and "dishonest" credit rating agencies will complain that we blame regulators. We blame many and harshly critique many of the actions of the leaders of Moody's, Standard and Poor's, Fannie Mae, Freddie Mac, and many other institutions; we document the pernicious ramifications of their conduct throughout the book. We identify a number of governance failures in financial organizations and believe that significant reforms are needed—reforms that in order to work will require both stockholders and creditors to suffer losses. But we focus on the functioning of the regulatory system. There is a qualitative difference between a government official and a private-market participant. The government official is *supposed to* act in the public interest, while the private financier's responsibility is to the firm—its shareholders and employees. Hence we focus on weaknesses in the financial regulatory system.

Others may reject the Sentinel as naïve, arguing that the financial services industry is so powerful that it has completely captured the executive, legislative, and judicial branches of governments, so it will capture the Sentinel too. This is too extreme; the Sentinel can help. Political systems are neither perfect, such that they reflect the pure public interest, nor are they perfectly flawed, such that they reflect the exclusive interests of the financial services industry. There is room for the Sentinel to enhance financial regulation. As developed in a series of influential papers and books by the Stanford University political scientist Stephen Haber, the connection between politics and finance is complex.[20] It differs across countries with different political and financial systems. It changes over time within countries, as some constituencies gain power, others lose power, and political and financial systems evolve. The changing and complex relationship between politics and finance underlines the value of an institution devoted to providing an informed, expert, and independent assessment. Interestingly, as we note in chapter 8, some European countries are beginning to establish Sentinel-like agencies, though not exactly along the lines that we specify. The Sentinel will not fix all problems, but it will improve the process for making regulatory decisions.

Moreover—and perhaps most important—this book will challenge people from both ends of the political spectrum, those with an unquestioning faith that markets correct the distorting effects of government policies and overcome market imperfections and those with a deferential confidence in the good intentions and abilities of government officials. We reject both views as logically and practically wrong. Centuries' worth of evidence suggests that we should not rely on the angelic motivations of government officials or their superior skills in manipulating the levers of power to promote the public interest. Experience also demonstrates that markets are highly imperfect. Markets certainly do not undo the pernicious effects of bad policies, and there is no logical reason for believing that removing one regulation, even one that is offensive when considered in isolation, from a complex mixture of regulations will necessarily improve the financial system. As Adam Smith and James Madison taught us a couple of centuries ago, we should be wary of powerful private- and public-sector groups.

Our focus on the straightforward failures of financial regulation may upset those seeking clever explanations for how a global economic catastrophe mushroomed without anyone seeing it. Some develop innovative theories of herd behavior and regulators brainwashed by cascades of favorable information. Perhaps. But other, less clever, but more systemic forces were at play. Regulators enacted and maintained policies that encouraged excessive risk-taking even as they learned that their decisions were steadily increasing the fragility of the system. It was also a regulatory-induced disaster.

Road Map

The remainder of this book is organized as follows. Chapter 2 explains why it is so difficult to get financial regulation right, why simplistic ideological prescriptions, whether from the right or left, are dangerous, and why it is crucial to adopt a prudent, adaptive approach to regulation that focuses on the incentives facing financial market participants. In chapter 3 we show how changes in financial market conditions over the past couple of decades made it both easier and more desirable for financial institution executives to increase risk-taking. Along with chapter 2, this chapter explains why and how many private firms undertook investments that produced short-run bonuses for executives at the expense of long-run solvency.

The core chapters of the book, chapters 4, 5, and 6, demonstrate that regulators selected and maintained policies that contributed to the collapse of the global financial system. Chapters 4 and 5 show that the Guardians of Finance in the United States and several other countries—notably, but not solely, Iceland, Ireland, and the United Kingdom—knowingly endangered their economies in the ten to fifteen years before the recent crisis. While many officials around the world would like to blame the United States, we argue that crises in European countries were mostly home-grown affairs and were merely made worse or had the timing affected by events in the United States. Chapter 6 illustrates that systemic defects with the institutions associated with selecting, implementing, evaluating, and reforming financial regulations are not new. The savings and loan (S&L) crisis of the 1980s was supposed to be the last financial crisis for the United States, as authorities put in place a system in which supervisors were compelled to intervene as banks weakened, and even to close them down before the banks' losses had completely depleted their capital. Yet the system did—and does—not work. Systemic institutional problems require systemic institutional solutions.

After showing that current reform efforts ignore the core institutional deficiencies underlying financial sector crises in chapter 7, chapter 8 sketches the institutional contours of the Sentinel and explains how it would help induce the Guardians of Finance to work for the public, improving the overall operation of financial systems. This book is not the final word on how to design a Sentinel, but so far regulatory reform efforts have studiously been avoiding institutional reforms that would enhance the governance of the Guardians of Finance. Our hope is that this book is at least the beginning of the important discussion on an absolutely critical aspect of improving financial regulation. Society deserves no less.

2
Regulating Finance Is Hard to Do

The truth is rarely pure and never simple.
—Oscar Wilde, *The Importance of Being Earnest*, 1895

Introduction

Financial regulation is extraordinarily hard to do. The economics is complex. The politics is tricky. And the economic and political ingredients are constantly changing as economies evolve, financiers innovate, lobbyists lobby, and older political constituencies weaken as new ones emerge. This chapter, by describing the economics and politics of financial regulation, explains why regulating finance is so hard to get right and stresses that societies sorely need—and can obtain—effective financial regulation, not simplistic dogmas or theories that do not work.

Four cornerstones underlie our view of financial regulation. First, there are sound economic reasons for regulating finance. Thus eliminating regulations and regulators (i.e., the Guardians of Finance) is not a desirable option. Second, since finance affects the allocation of scarce capital, politicians everywhere have always—and will always—intervene in the operation of financial systems. Thus eliminating regulation is not a feasible option. Third, government officials do not necessarily use their powers to promote the best interests of the public. Thus giving ever more and broader power to unaccountable and unmonitored regulators, without some way to ensure that these powers will be well utilized, is an undesirable option. Fourth, the economic and political complexity of financial regulation means that the public and its elected representatives cannot easily and directly evaluate the performance of financial regulators, which impedes their ability to compel the Guardians to act in the public interest. Thus the existing institutional system—which relies too heavily on simply hoping that the Guardians of Finance will always decide to act in the public interest—has proved to be very costly.

The ever-present financial policy challenge is to create an institutional structure that induces the Guardians of Finance to behave at all times in the public's best interests. The essential first step in meeting this challenge is acknowledging the economic and political complexity of regulating finance. Only by acknowledging this complexity will economies reject simplistic ideological approaches to financial regulation that either put undue faith in the perfection of markets or in the angelic intensions and exceptional abilities of government officials. In dynamic, complex economies, such static, simplistic approaches to financial regulation are inherently flawed and hence potentially dangerous. By simultaneously emphasizing both the complexity of financial regulation and the importance of a vibrant, innovating financial system for economic prosperity, this chapter highlights serious defects with the current institutions associated with enacting, implementing, assessing, and reforming financial policies.

Shareholders versus Debt Holders: The Essence of Regulatory Complexity

Inherent Tensions

The inherent battle that exists between shareholders and debt holders within a limited liability corporation provides a clear vantage point for discussing the complexity of financial regulation. With limited liability, shareholders can only lose what they invested in the corporation; debt holders of a bankrupt corporation cannot seize the homes or other assets of the shareholders to satisfy the corporation's financial obligations.

Shareholders and debt holders battle over risk. While both want the corporation to succeed, shareholders tend to prefer more risk than debt holders, holding other features of the corporation the same. If the corporation earns any amount equal to or less than the promised fixed payment to the debt holders (plus operating expenses), the debt holders receive all the profits, and the shareholders earn nothing. However, if the corporation earns more—even much more—than the promised fixed payment to debt holders (plus operating expenses), then the debt holders still get only the promised fixed payment. The "upside" for debt holders is limited to the promised fixed payment to them. In contrast, shareholders get all of the additional earnings after paying operating expenses and debt holders; their "upside" is unlimited. While it is not certain that every owner in all situations prefers a riskier investment, the nature of the payoffs to shareholders and debt holders suggests that owners tend to prefer higher risk projects than debt holders.[1]

Shareholders therefore tend to want the corporation to make riskier investments with correspondingly higher expected rates of return than debt holders. Debt holders simply want to get paid back all of the time and do not care about the potential for the corporation to earn enormous profits some of the time. Shareholders, however, receive virtually all the extra benefits from a successful, even if risky, investment.

Shareholders and debt holders can, however, reach a carefully monitored truce. Debt holders have designed several defensive strategies for deterring stockholders from inappropriately increasing the riskiness of a corporation's projects. For example, bonds and loans often include covenants mandating that corporations (1) use the funds only for specific projects, (2) refrain from inappropriately increasing the overall riskiness of the corporation's projects, and (3) maintain a healthy amount of collateral that can be used to pay off the debt holders if a risky project fails. Large debt holders, particularly banks, frequently demand periodic financial statements, seats on the company's board of directors, and regular discussions with the company's executives to monitor corporate behavior. Shareholders and debt holders coexist, even though they have inherently different views about the preferred amount of risk. Owners still, in general, search for ways to increase risk by, in most cases legally, circumventing the covenants and scrutiny of the debt holders, while debt holders work to foil these efforts. One might think of a tug-of-war, with one side pulling for more risk and the other side pulling for safer investments.

Within a financial corporation, changes in regulations can easily disturb this anxious balance and cause risk to explode. Any policy—or expectation of policy—that reduces the incentives for debt holders to constrain risk-taking will provide greater latitude for shareholders to increase risk-taking: If those pulling for safer investments "let go," there could be a dangerous lurch toward more risk. For example, if the government convinces debt holders that regulatory authorities are going to keep the corporation from increasing risk, the debt holders will not work as diligently to limit risk-taking. Why should they? It is a costly activity and the government is doing it for them. Similarly, if the government assures debt holders that it will pay the corporation's debts if the corporation fails, the debt holders will work less energetically, if at all, to prevent owners from increasing risk. Why should they? If the firm does not pay them, the government will.

Disturbing the Balance of Power

While chapters 4 and 5 provide detailed accounts of how financial regulators upset checks and balances within financial institutions by reducing incentives for debt holders to monitor and limit risk taking of financial firms, it is worth mentioning some key examples here. When the US Securities and Exchange Commission (SEC) announced that it was going to supervise risk-taking behavior of the largest investment banks, potential purchasers of debt from those investment banks then did not have to scrutinize the portfolios of those banks as carefully. The SEC was on the prowl. Similarly, since debt holders were virtually certain that the government would bail out Bank of America, Citigroup, and other huge financial conglomerates because they were "too big to fail," the debt holders faced fewer incentives to monitor these banks. If things turned sour for the banks, the government would pay the bank's debts to avoid the economywide reverberations of their bankruptcy. When the US government signaled, through a variety of actions, that it was insuring the debts of housing giants Fannie Mae and Freddie Mac, this eased the need for purchasers of their bonds, including China, which was reportedly in regular contact with the US Treasury Department about the safety of various US dollar denominated investments, to write and enforce restrictive covenants. Why should they? The government would pay if Fannie and Freddie could not. This is exactly what happened in 2008, when US taxpayers assumed responsibility for about $2 trillion worth of Fannie and Freddie debt obligations when the two institutions were placed in conservatorship by its regulator.

When regulation weakens incentives of private investors to constrain risk, what will substitute for these private constraints on risk-taking? Before regulation changed incentives, the "self-correcting" market mechanisms were the covenants and monitoring techniques developed by debt holders to control risk. Now, what serves as a constraint? Leaving it to the market under these circumstances is not a reasonable, or well-reasoned, option because regulations weakened incentives of private investors to limit risk.

There are two reasonable public policy responses. One is to eliminate policies that reduce incentives of debt holders to constrain risk, restoring equilibrating tensions between shareholders and stockholders. But such a response might be unfeasible or undesirable. If powerful political motivations produced the regulation that protects debt holders and reduces their incentives to monitor risk, then getting rid of that regulation might not be viable. If there are good economic reasons for protecting debt holders (which we discuss below), then eliminating these regulations might be downright harmful.

A second reasonable response is to employ additional regulations to reduce risk-taking. One form of additional regulation focuses on encouraging private sector investors to monitor the actions of financial institutions. For example, regulations that force banks to issue noninsured securities to large debtor holders create a class of creditors with the incentives and ability to monitor risk taking (assuming, of course, that the government does not bail out these debtholders). Another example of regulations focused on enhancing market monitoring involves capital. Regulators frequently force owners of financial institutions to invest more of their own wealth in the bank, which increases their financial exposure to the bank and hence mitigates some of the risk-taking incentives.

A second form of additional regulation focuses on boosting direct government oversight of financial institution risk taking. Again, consider the same three examples of financial regulations that reduce incentives for debt holders to monitor and contain risk. When the SEC enacted policies that reduced private sector monitoring of investment banks, it could have implemented procedures to thwart an escalation of risk. When financial institutions are perceived to be too big to fail, regulators could limit risk-taking by them. When investors believed that the government would insure the debts of Fannie and Freddie, the government could have established constraints on the institutions' portfolios, rather than encouraging them to take on more risk. If the first option—removing regulations that interfere with private sector monitoring of and constraints on financial institution risk—is politically infeasible or economically undesirable, then establishing additional regulations might be the best and perhaps only option for limiting excessive risk.

A delicate balance of regulations might emerge to limit risk, and upsetting this balance by eliminating one regulation, even one that is unappealing when considered in isolation, could destabilize the entire financial system.

By ignoring this simple, essential message, the Guardians of Finance contributed to the most recent economic crisis, and past ones too. Consider the same three examples. In 2008, when the SEC announced that it was supervising investment banks, with the result that the purchasers of investment bank debt did not monitor them as closely as before the SEC policy change, then we should not have been surprised that investment bank shareholders successfully boosted risk when the SEC failed to stop them. When everyone expected the government to bail out too-big-to-fail banks, with the result that debt holders had no incentive to monitor those banks, then we should not have been surprised that banks boosted risk once the Federal Reserve eased its constraints on bank risk-taking. When the purchasers of Fannie Mae and Freddie Mac bonds were correctly convinced that the US government would insure those debt obligations, the bondholders did not have any incentive to constrain the risk taking of those multi–trillion-dollar financial institutions. Consequently, when Congress then weakened regulatory oversight of Fannie Mae and Freddie Mac, as it did to encourage and indeed require these institutions to support less creditworthy borrowers, we should not have been surprised that Fannie and Freddie managers successfully took greater risks.

The *combination* of regulatory policies affects the incentives of private financial market participants. Relaxing a single regulation, such as the regulatory limit on risk-taking, amid other regulations that dissuade debt holders from constraining risk can have calamitous repercussions because under these conditions, the debt holder does not monitor risk and neither does the regulator. Selecting financial regulations based on their independent appeal, rather than on how they jointly combine to affect the incentives of private market participants, leads to disaster.

Hot and Sour Soup

A simple analogy might help. Consider a very different, complex mixture. Think about designing the recipe for hot and sour soup. Getting it right involves blending and balancing a complex fusion of spicy, sweet and sour flavors. It involves much more than assessing the appeal of each ingredient individually. Consuming a tablespoon of hot chili oil would be revolting, but eliminating it from hot and sour soup would ruin the delicate balance of flavors. Similarly, orange juice is delicious, but not in hot and sour soup. Selecting ingredients based on their independent appeal is not an effective strategy for producing good soup. It's all about balance.

Like a successful hot and sour soup, sound financial regulation involves an assessment of how individual regulations blend together to affect the behavior of financial markets. It is misguided to assess whether a regulation should be enacted or repealed without considering how the regulation interacts with other factors shaping the incentives of financial market participants.

Like all analogies, this one has its limitations, but it helps illustrate a major theme: selecting, implementing, and reforming financial regulations is too complex to be compatible with simplistic ideologies. From one end of the spectrum, some claim that the fewer financial regulations, the better. This doctrine, however, is both poorly conceived and dangerous as a practical guide to policy-making. Eliminating one distasteful regulation from a complex blend of regulations will not necessarily improve the financial system. An opposing ideological dogma holds that adding appealing financial regulations will promote public welfare; this simplistic approach is also demonstrably flawed. Regulations that appear desirable when examined in isolation may have harmful effects when combined with other factors shaping financial market incentives. Just as orange juice would ruin hot and sour soup, empowering the Guardians of Finance without adequate checks and balances on their behavior can ruin the economy. The proper design of financial regulation depends on the degree to which institutions oblige the Guardians of Finance to work for the public.

Three Approaches to Financial Regulation

Given this perspective on how regulations affect the behavior of financial institutions, we now discuss the three major approaches to financial regulation—the laissez faire, public interest view, and private interest views. We use this discussion to (1) frame major debates on financial regulation, (2) describe the economics and politics of widely used financial regulations, and (3) highlight the danger of making complex financial regulatory decisions based on a simple ideology.

Laissez Faire

The laissez faire approach to financial regulation argues that governments should "let it be." They should not interfere in the operation of financial markets and institutions. There should be no deposit insurance, no capital regulations, no supervisory oversight of financial institutions, and no government-sponsored support for housing or other activities. This view has acquired some popularity and was the intellectual inspiration for some decisions made by top regulators in the United States, Iceland, Ireland, the United Kingdom, and other crisis countries.

Laissez faire is founded on two well-known assumptions: that both the legal system and markets are perfect. Thus under the first assumption, if a firm promises to pay you 40 percent of its profits in one year, you can enforce that contract easily. In the extreme this "do-it-yourself" view assumes that individuals and firms can negotiate, write, and enforce complex contracts with all sorts of intricate contingencies *costlessly*. There are no lawyers' fees and no delays in negotiating, litigating, or settling contracts.

The perfect markets assumption also implies that there are no costs to acquiring information, no difficulties with processing that information, and that we all have the same information; there are no "informational asymmetries." With perfect markets JP Morgan has no more information about its clients than you can readily obtain publicly, and you can easily know as much as Goldman Sachs about the pricing of such financial instruments as credit default swaps—not to mention that you can get lawyers every bit as good as those who work for Goldman or any other intermediary. Within financial firms, everyone has the same information too; executives cannot extract more from the firm than shareholders want to pay them because each shareholder has information about the productivity of each executive. In this world, mortgage brokers could not fool borrowers about the type of mortgage loan that they were getting or about its risks.

The assumption of perfect markets does not mean that people are omniscient. Even with perfect markets there is risk; projects fail, and people lose money.

But with perfect markets there is no need for consumer protection or antifraud regulations to protect individuals. The economic rationale for such regulations is that the public is unable to see through the misleading practices and scams of deceitful financial institutions. With perfect markets, however, consumers have as much information as banks—and regulators—about financial markets, so each individual can make informed decisions. And with perfect legal systems consumers can write contingent contracts that will automatically compensate them if the financial institution misbehaves in a predesigned and easily verifiable manner. Under the laissez faire assumptions there is no economic justification for having a range of policies designed to protect uniformed individuals because there are no such individuals.

Moreover the perfect markets assumptions mean there are no economic forces that favor large, complex financial institutions over individuals. There are no fixed costs of production and no economies of scale, so the average cost of production does not fall as production increases. With perfect markets, if Bank of America provides bad services or charges too high a price, anyone can start a bank instantly and drive Bank of America out of business. There are no economies of scope either, so there are no advantages to bundling services, such as cable television and Internet service or bank lending and securities underwriting, to be offered by a single firm. With perfect markets, if Bank of America makes a loan to a firm, this does not provide it with any advantages over you or anyone else in helping the firm sell its bonds or equities. There are no economic forces favoring the formation and endurance of large financial conglomerates, or for that matter any intermediary, as individuals can to it all themselves just as efficiently.

With perfect markets there is nothing special about a large financial institution failing either. In economic terminology, there are no externalities, where an externality is a cost or benefit incurred by a party who did not participate in the action that produced the cost or benefit. In the real world, if someone talks loudly on a cell phone in a restaurant, others incur a cost. Cars pollute air that others breathe. When someone plants a beautiful garden, the garden benefits others who did not pay for it. When a financial institution fails, this might adversely affect nonfinancial firms and productive workers who have nothing to do with this financial institution. The laissez faire view assumes that such externalities do not exist to any meaningful extent.

This is a huge assumption: one of the major economic reasons for constructing a vast regulatory apparatus to ensure the safety and soundness of financial institutions is the fear that if a large financial institution fails, it will have potentially catastrophic ramifications on the economy. Fear of both contagion—where the failure of one bank causes the failure of other banks—and spillovers—where the failure of a financial institution causes nonfinancial corporations to fail as they lose access to finance with adverse effects on employment—are central arguments for financial regulation. With perfect markets and legal systems, however, these core reasons for financial regulation and government interventions melt away.

To illustrate the power of assuming the existence of perfect markets and legal systems, let's consider two popular interventions: deposit insurance and regulatory restrictions on bank risk. We first give an economic justification for these policies, and then show how perfect markets and legal systems undermine these justifications.

One rationale for deposit insurance is that most depositors know little about the financial condition of their bank due to informational asymmetries. It is just too difficult to acquire and understand information on the quality of the bank's assets. Therefore any rumor that makes depositors nervous about the soundness of their bank could cause them to withdraw their money. Even if the bank were very sound, nervous depositors would all "run" to the bank to get their money out. This "bank run" could cause a healthy bank to fail since banks lend out most of the deposits and retain little cash, assuming that people typically only withdraw a very small fraction of their deposits at any one time.

A run on a bank can be a positive development: if that bank is making bad loans, the run by depositors takes away its ability to do more harm by paying higher interest rates to attract more deposits to make more bad loans. The run would both punish bankers for making bad loans and serve as a signal to other banks about a failed investment strategy.[2]

However, a bank run can produce large, negative externalities. Like pollution, bank runs hurt people beyond the bank and beyond depositors "running" to remove their savings. First, if a healthy company's bank fails, the company may not have the cash to pay its workers and suppliers, resulting in its own failure and the subsequent unemployment of its formerly productive workers. Thus people would be hurt who had nothing to do with the bank or the bank run. Second, the run on one bank could have a contagious effect. It could make depositors in other banks nervous about their own banks and induce them to make their own "runs," causing many perfectly sound banks to fail at once simply because depositors do not have convincing information about the soundness of their banks.

With deposit insurance, however, bank customers do not rush to withdraw deposits as long as they have faith in the solvency and commitment of the government. The insurance avoids the unnecessary collateral damage triggered by a bank run by eliminating the incentives for depositors to remove their deposits rapidly. Deposit insurance reduces the potential externalities generated by the information asymmetries that trigger bank runs.

But again, with perfect financial markets there is no need for these types of interventions. Depositors can assess on their own the quality of each bank's assets, so there is no contagion, which is when weakness in one bank causes depositors in other banks to withdraw funds, triggering the unwarranted failure of these other banks. If depositors are nervous about the quality of any single bank, they can simply hold their deposits in several banks, purchase deposit insurance in private markets, or choose to not hold their savings in banks that cannot confidently communicate the quality of their assets. Furthermore with perfect markets externalities do not exist: if one bank fails, this will not disrupt the allocation of capital to sound firms. Since other investors have the same information about the bank's client firms as the bank itself, other investors will immediately fund sound firms if that firm's bank fails. Thus sound firms will not fail, suppliers will get paid, and productive workers will continue working.

As a second example consider regulatory restrictions on bank investments, such as capital regulations that force banks to hold safe assets as a cushion against potentially adverse shocks to its more risky assets. Governments may fear that (1) a bank's failure would have large, adverse effects on the economy or (2) a bank's owners have so much more information about, and control over, the bank's investments relative to its debt holders that they will outmaneuver those debt holders and dramatically increase bank risk-taking, with potentially large, adverse effects on the economy. If the government believes that such market failures undermine the ability of debt holders to contain bank risk, the government could restrict bank risk.

Again, with perfect markets there is no need for government intervention. There are no externalities associated with a bank's failure, no economies of scale or scope encouraging financial institutions to become big or broad in the first place, and no informational asymmetries limiting the ability of debt holders to contain bank risk. With perfect markets well-informed debt holders and shareholders will negotiate the risk-taking behavior of the financial institution: full stop. If individual investors want to play the roulette wheel, so be it. If a group of investors want to pool their resources and play blackjack, so be it. If shareholders or debt holders do not want the assets of the financial institution used for those purposes, they will exert influence over the firm or invest their savings elsewhere. If people want their funds invested only in very safe assets, they will negotiate contracts with the financial institution to that effect. With perfect markets individuals know how institutions are investing, understand the risks, and write contracts accordingly. There are no ramifications to anyone beyond those choosing to take the risk.

From Classic to Extreme Laissez Faire

Assuming that markets and legal systems are perfect, or so close to perfect that this view is a useful approximation to the real world, the classic laissez faire policy recommendation is simple: government should not intervene in financial markets or institutions. There are many reasons to question the assumptions underlying laissez faire and hence its policy recommendations. But even when its two core assumptions hold, there is an operational limitation.

With perfect markets and legal systems, laissez faire adherents can make a logical case to eliminate *all* financial regulations, but the laissez faire approach provides no logical guidance on removing *some* regulations. When there are many regulations, laissez faire does not offer any insights on assessing the efficacy of removing one or two or a few regulations. Thus—and this is critical, even when markets and legal systems are perfect, the classic laissez faire approach to financial regulation does not support an *extreme* laissez faire policy recommendation, such as "the fewer regulations, the better."

Removing one regulation could upset the delicate checks and balances among shareholders, debt holders, and regulators, and trigger an explosion of risk. For example, in many countries (1) deposit insurance reduces the incentives of debt holders to constrain bank risk and (2) regulatory agencies constrain bank risk. Under these conditions, removing one regulation, such as any of the regulations constraining bank risk, can cause risk to explode even when there are no market imperfections because the remaining government intervention, deposit insurance, helps bankers to take ever greater risks with the funds provided by depositors. Even with perfect markets the extreme laissez faire view is logically flawed—unless the government is perfect too! The extreme laissez faire policy recommendation only holds if markets are perfect and government is so perfect that if one regulation is removed, it is able to adjust all of the other regulations to maintain sound incentives in the financial system.

To recap, the classic and extreme laissez faire regulatory recommendations are built on implausible assumptions. Market imperfections exist: Externalities, economies of scale and scope, and informational asymmetries all affect financial markets. Legal systems are not perfect either, certainly not costless, and unequal in finance—large banks (even small banks!) can afford more talented legal representation than the authors of this book. Government officials create an array of financial regulations, many of which will not be repealed for political and economic reasons. Thus the core assumptions underlying laissez faire hold only in the fairytale world of academic models and the temples of devout "free marketeers." In the real world, ignoring market failures and political constraints on removing some regulations is a recipe for a crisis.

We recognize that advocates of laissez faire frequently view their battle as a fight for individual liberty and against repressive, intrusive government. The government should not interfere with private choice in this view. If someone wants to purchase synthetic collateralized debt obligations that could very likely result in large losses, no government should interfere with that decision either. The government should "let us be."

But the drive for individual liberty does not necessitate or even commend an extreme laissez faire approach to financial regulation. When we criticize laissez faire, we are not arguing against individual freedom. We are not even arguing against the view that people should severely limit government's role in financial markets. Nor are we arguing against the possibility that under some conditions, small government interventions could metastasize into broader assaults on individual liberties. We are arguing what market economists, including Adam Smith as we describe below, have recognized for generations that (1) even with perfect markets, removing one or more regulations from a mix of many will not necessarily make financial markets function better and (2) with imperfect markets, government intervention is *necessary* for making markets work efficiently.

Public Interest Approach

The public interest approach to financial regulation argues that governments should use regulation to ameliorate the adverse effects of market and legal system imperfections. Besides presuming that governments are well intentioned, the public interest view assumes that governments are sufficiently knowledgeable and powerful to accomplish their socially beneficent objectives.

We now discuss several types of regulatory interventions and their public interest justifications. One goal is to show how market imperfections motivate a wide array of government interventions. A second goal is to illustrate the extent of actual government interventions into financial market activities.

Consider deposit insurance. We have already described how two market imperfections—information asymmetries and externalities—motivate deposit insurance and regulatory restrictions on bank risk. With information asymmetries banks runs could lead to the failure of healthy banks, with adverse ramifications on sound firms and productive workers. Deposit insurance represents a mechanism for reducing the likelihood of such an unwarranted and costly banking crisis.

However, deposit insurance also motivates additional government interventions because it reduces the incentives for depositors to constrain bank risk-taking, providing greater latitude for bank shareholders to increase risk. Advocates of the public interest view hold that governments should create deposit insurance to avoid costs to society of potential bank runs. Such advocates also believe that governments should impose other regulations to curtail excessive risk-taking, such as capital regulations to reduce the chance of bankruptcy and ensure that owners have more at risk, regulations that force banks to issue uninsured debt to create a group of private debt holders with powerful incentives to limit bank risk-taking, and more direct regulatory restrictions on bank behavior.

In the United States, the Federal Deposit Insurance Corporation (FDIC) both insures deposits and regulates banks. When banks do not have deposit insurance, depositors—especially those who are financially sophisticated—will tend to monitor the risks that banks are taking, and withdraw their money when a bank is getting too risky. These rapid withdrawals of money—bank runs—can cause bank failures. But they have beneficial effects too. When depositors monitor banks and threaten banks that become too risky with a bank run, this can help restrain banks from taking on too much risk; it can have a disciplining effect on bank risk-taking.[3] By providing deposit insurance, the FDIC reduces the incentives of depositors to monitor bank risk, so that the FDIC must regulate bank risk taking. But the FDIC did not effectively regulate banks. It did not prevent bank owners from increasing bank risk or force banks to hold adequate capital reserves. While there might be sound economic reasons for deposit insurance and regulatory restrictions on risk, governments and their agencies can still be ineffectual or even make matters worse by reducing the incentives of private investors to monitor the risk-taking of banks without developing effective official oversight.

The public interest view also provides a conceptual basis for both regulatory restrictions on financial institution investments and regulatory mandates regarding the maintenance of capital to support assets, even in the absence of deposit insurance. As described above, one motivation for regulation stems from a combination of (1) economies of scale and scope that encourage the formation of large, complex financial institutions and (2) externalities that imply extensive fallout from the failure of such a large, complex financial institution.

With these market imperfections, financial institutions will become too risky from a societal perspective because the institutions do not bear the full costs of their risk-taking. If the institution fails, people and firms beyond the financial institution will be hurt. Controlling shareholders and managers of financial institutions will look out for their own interests and not take the external costs that affect others into account when determining the riskiness of the firm's portfolios.

The decision makers at financial institutions—controlling shareholders and managers—would invest more prudently if they had to compensate those firms and individuals who are jeopardized or damaged by the financial institution's investments. When shareholders were exposed to unlimited liability in early centuries, they behaved differently because they could not walk away from losses and pass them on to depositors or taxpayers. Modern limited liability protects them—at the expense of exposing others to their risk-taking. It is not unlike the risk of reckless driving. A driver does not pay all the costs associated with driving recklessly; the driver not only engages in self-endangerment but also endangers others. The driver would drive more cautiously if it were necessary to compensate others for the risks posed.

Adherents of the public interest view argue that a beneficent, omniscient, omnipotent government can and should correct the adverse effects of these market imperfections. Financial regulators could impose taxes on risk to dissuade financial institutions from becoming too fragile, or impose other restrictions on their behavior to enhance their stability and reduce the potential for economywide damage from their failure.

Market imperfections plus the public interest view have given rise to the large black notebooks with thousands of pages of rules that fill the shelves of financial regulatory agencies around the world. The numerous and lengthy notebooks of regulations keep growing as externalities extend the focus from the fragility of a single financial institution to concerns about the fragility of the overall financial system. For example, while capital regulations are numbingly complex in practice, they are quite simple in principle: to maintain stability, capital regulations force financial institutions to hold more safe assets as the riskiness of their other assets increases per unit of capital. The complexity reflects the difficulties with measuring risk.

The list goes endlessly on. Regulators around the world engage in "fit and proper" assessments of potential owners and managers of financial institutions. The goal is to weed out those with a tendency toward excessive risk-taking or that might be more inclined toward fraudulent activities. If there are externalities associated with bank failures and if informational asymmetries limit the ability of debt holders to contain risk-taking by banks, then the public interest view holds that a more informed, well-intentioned government can help in selecting bank leaders. Regulators frequently limit competition in finance to boost profits. If regulators protect the bank so that it has monopolistic profits, then bank owners will have less of an inclination to increase fragility and lose that regulatory-induced stream of monopoly profits.

A trendy issue in financial regulatory circles is "macroprudential" regulation, which means regulating risk-taking of financial institutions by examining the collective impact of their behavior on overall financial system fragility. Rather than simply regulating the riskiness of a single institution, which is "microprudential" regulation, macroprudential regulation focuses on the systemic implications of each financial institution's behavior. Given the potential externalities, the public interest view motivates far-reaching government interventions in assessing and limiting risk.

Pushed to its logical conclusion, the combination of market imperfections and faith in the good intentions and capabilities of the government justifies massive government involvement in every aspect of finance, including in the direct allocation of credit and even in government ownership of financial institutions. With informational asymmetries, financial institutions might overestimate the risks of lending to lower income households and underestimate the social benefits of boosting homeownership among the poor. Such an argument formed the foundation of US policies to encourage financial institutions to increase their lending to nonprime borrowers. Around the world and throughout history, such arguments have been used to justify all sorts of government programs to boost lending to particular groups. Governments with better information encourage the flow of credit to socially productive ends. The government knows best, or so the argument goes.

Private Interest Approach
The private interest approach to financial regulation acknowledges that there are market and legal system failures but argues that government officials frequently lack the incentives and capabilities to ameliorate the damaging effects of those imperfections. In contrast to the laissez faire view, the private interest approach recognizes that information asymmetries, externalities, and economies of scale and scope characterize financial markets. In contrast to the laissez faire view, the private interest approach recognizes that a beneficent, omniscient, omnipotent government *could* use financial regulations to eliminate adverse repercussions of these market and legal system imperfections. In contrast to the public interest view, the private interest approach highlights government failures.

According to the private interest view, government officials do not necessarily work to promote social welfare; they work to maximize their own private interests, just as butchers, brewers, bakers, and bankers work for their self-interests. The private interest view is at odds with many economists, who schizophrenically assume that everyone behaves in a self-interested manner, except government officials—who are assumed to behave in an altruistic manner. The private interest view is much more egalitarian, assuming that self-interest affects everyone's behavior.

Social and personal welfare could coincide. Government officials might derive personal welfare from promoting the social good. The political system might impose sufficient constraints on government officials, so they are compelled to promote the public interest. For example, effective oversight of government officials could reduce corruption. Well-structured bureaucracies could incentivize officials to maximize social welfare. A well-functioning democracy, in which the public can effectively monitor the behavior of politicians and vote accordingly, could induce politicians to act in the public interest as an unintended by-product of their private interest objective: getting reelected.

But this is not necessarily so. The private interests of public officials might differ from those of the public and the public might be unable to compel its elected representatives and government bureaucrats to act in the public interest, regardless of their personal interests. As discussed, several factors might induce the private interests of politicians and government officials to deviate from the public interest. For instance, many have argued that the financial services industry shapes the interests of politicians and government officials through campaign contributions, the allure of postgovernment lucrative jobs, and other enticing pressures and rewards. Moreover even well-intentioned, incorruptible officials might be subject to the same human psychological factors that induce referees and umpires in sports to conform to the interests of the home crowd. As discussed in chapter 1, around the world, across all major sports, officials, referees, and umpires are systematically biased in favor of the home team. According to the behavioral view, the powerful psychological tendency to conform to and please the community in which one operates creates a home field advantage, in which officials subconsciously make choices that favor the home crowd. For politicians and regulators, the most vociferous "fans" are typically members of the financial services community; the financial services industry tends to enjoy a similar home field advantage with regard to the enactment and implementation of financial policies. In this variant of the private interest view, it is quite possible to believe in the probity of regulatory officials and yet not accept that they are always regulating in society's best interests. Just as sports referees might be trying to do their best, and yet still make calls in favor of the home team, Icelandic, Irish, UK, and US regulators could have had a clear conscience as they stood by in the run up to the recent crisis and allowed economic conditions to become far worse than would have occurred had they altered course and taken containment action earlier.

Regardless of why the private interests of government officials deviate from those of the public, the private interest view of financial regulation argues that governments are imperfect: political systems are unable to force politicians and bureaucrats to always act in the public interest. Since political systems, even the best political systems in the world, do not perfectly align the private interests of politicians and government officials with those of the public, politicians and officials can employ the coercive power of the state to enrich themselves, promote special interests of narrow elites that help them get reelected, or respond to the home field advantage enjoyed by the financial services industry to the detriment of society.

Besides questioning the motivations of public officials and the ability of the public to compel those officials to act in the public interest, the private interest view also holds that governments are neither omniscient nor omnipotent. Sometimes officials don't know what they are doing. Other times they might follow a false ideology. Frequently officials do not have the resources to design and implement effective policies. Even if well intentioned, governments might be ineffective at reducing the undesirable effects of market imperfections.

Empirical evidence overwhelmingly supports the private interest view. Individual country studies from all corners of the globe indicate that politicians and regulatory officials frequently use financial-sector policies to reward politically connected firms and individuals, not to ameliorate the effects of market imperfections. While theory suggests a potentially positive role for the helping hand of government, reality indicates that the grabbing hand of government often employs financial regulations to achieve the narrow, private ends of politicians and government officials.[4]

Cross-country comparisons also support the private interest view, as demonstrated in our earlier book, *Rethinking Bank Regulation: Till Angels Govern.*[5] In countries where the government plays a greater, direct role in shaping financial market performance, corruption in bank lending tends to be more severe. Theory suggests that powerful governments could improve the allocation of capital, but evidence indicates that they actually use that power in a manner that helps elites, not the public at large. While a very well-functioning democracy seems to mitigate the corrupting effect of a powerful regulator, the core findings remain. We should not presume that increasing financial regulatory power would improve the operation of financial markets.

The actions of US and foreign policy makers in the decade or so before the current crisis bolster the private interest view, as we will show. While the Guardians of Finance who oversaw these failures frequently claim that impotence and ignorance explain their performance, we argue that these are only part of the full story; focusing only on these parts is leading to partial, inadequate reforms. For now, we make a simpler point. Whether it was corruption, adherence to a flawed ideology, psychological bias, or too little power, the regulatory apparatus did not act with sufficient competence to eliminate market failures and promote social welfare. There were massive and costly government failures.

An Example from US Bank Deregulation

Another illustration of the weakness of the public interest view is the history of geographic restrictions on banking in the United States.[6] The Constitution prohibited states from taxing international trade and interstate commerce, so states needed to look elsewhere for revenues. They looked to the chartering of banks. In return for funding projects, paying taxes, and shelling out bribes, states granted banking charters. To maximize what entrepreneurs were willing to pay for a charter, states created local monopolies for chartered banks by restricting the branching of banks within a state. The state would not allow one chartered bank to open near another. Furthermore, since states received no charter fees from the entry of banks chartered in other states, they prohibited interstate banking. While these policies boosted fiscal revenues, they also impeded bank competition.

The geographic restrictions that protected local banking monopolies produced a powerful constituency for maintaining those restrictions even after the original fiscal motivations waned. That constituency lobbied both state governments and federal authorities to prohibit interstate banking and maintain limits on branching within states. Their lobbying efforts were extraordinarily successful.

These restrictions created a bizarre and highly inefficient banking system. The system was bizarre because the United States had over 30,000 banks by 1920, making it appear competitive, but the banking system was actually composed of thousands of small, local monopolies, making it very uncompetitive; all but about 700 were "unit" banks, with just one office and no branches. Such small banks regularly failed in downturns that affected the local areas around the banks, giving the United States a more crisis-prone system than any of the now high-income countries. This monopolistic system also was highly inefficient, as reflected in lower returns on savings, higher interest rates on loans, and slower rates of economic growth in states.

The public interest view would argue that governments should have abolished the regulatory imposed geographic restrictions that produced this situation once politicians learned of the social costs. As soon as it was clear that these regulations hurt wages, employment, and economic progress, state governments should have removed the geographic restrictions. But that is not what happened.

In reality, the private interest view of financial regulation provides a more accurate perspective on the repeal of geographic restrictions on bank branching. Technological innovations in the 1970s and 1980s diminished the economic and political power of banks benefiting from geographic restrictions. In particular, a series of technological innovations lowered the costs of accessing distant banks. The invention and far-reaching distribution of automatic teller machines weakened the geographic link between a bank and its clients. The creation of checkable money market accounts, which could be accessed through mail and telephone, also reduced the importance of the physical location of the bank. The increased sophistication of credit-scoring techniques, and improvements in information processing and telecommunications reduced the informational advantages of local bankers. All of these innovations reduced the monopoly power of local banks and weakened their ability and desire to lobby for the maintenance of geographic restrictions. Politicians switched their votes accordingly, and the geographic regulations were abolished.

Discussion: The Laissez Faire, Public Interest, and Private Interest Views
The discussion of the major approaches to financial regulation emphasizes the economic and political complexity of financial regulation. Yes, there are good economic reasons for financial regulations, such as consumer protection laws, minimum capital requirements, regulations that encourage market monitoring of financial institutions, micro- and macroprudential regulation of financial institution risk, rules to foster information disclosure and transparency, and other official interventions to address

market failures. Consequently an enormous body of work examines the technical details of designing regulations that ameliorate the adverse effects of market failures without triggering other problems.

But, financial regulation is not just a technical economic problem. Politics makes financial regulation much more challenging. As explained, government officials will not always use their interventions in the financial sector to achieve socially beneficial goals. The degree to which the Guardians of Finance will use financial regulations for socially beneficial purposes depends crucially on the political system and the full range of institutions associated with aligning the interest of public officials with those of the people.

Adam Smith and James Madison on Making the Guardians Work for Us

The "fathers" of economics and the US Constitution would have recognized the daunting economic and political challenges to creating and maintaining sound financial policies and offered guidance on how to make the Guardians work for us. In this section we use the insights from Adam Smith and James Madison to highlight key economic and political features of financial regulation.

Adam Smith: The Father of Economics

Adam Smith would have understood the complexity of financial regulation and rejected simplistic policy prescriptions. He would have agreed both that market failures motivate financial regulations and that government failures motivate wariness about empowering the Guardians. Some will find our interpretation of Smith surprising. Advocates of laissez faire frequently point to Adam Smith's *Wealth of Nations*, published in 1776, to support their approach to public policy. But Smith did not support laissez faire. Rather, Smith had a much more balanced view of the relationship between government and markets.

Adam Smith explained both the role of the *invisible* hand of the market in boosting living standards and the role of the *visible* hand of the government in making markets work.[7] Of the invisible hand, Smith argued that under certain circumstances, each individual contributes more to society by pursuing his or her selfish interests than by consciously working to promote the social good. There was no need for the guiding hand of the government to dictate socially beneficial activities. In fact no authority was sufficiently knowledgeable to coordinate complex economic systems effectively. Rather, the invisible hand of many individuals behaving in a self-interested manner would produce socially desirable outcomes. Smith separated intent from result: self-interest would trigger market exchanges that spur economic progress, raising living standards for everyone.[8]

On the visible hand, Adam Smith recognized the relevance of market failures and the beneficial role of the government in a market economy. He wrote about externalities and the tendency toward monopoly, collusion, and hence the adverse effects of imperfect—and unregulated—markets.[9] Smith also emphasized the positive role of government in reducing harmful effects of such market imperfections. For example, he stressed that education has considerable positive externalities for society. He emphasized that free markets would provide too little education, especially for lower income families.[10] To rectify this situation, Smith recommended the provision of *compulsory*, publicly funded education. Given the positive social externalities of education, Smith emphasized that the government should "facilitate . . . encourage, and . . . even impose upon almost the whole body of the people the necessity of acquiring those most essential parts of education."[11] This ain't laissez faire. Or, as more eloquently put by Professor Jerry Z. Muller of the Catholic University of America, [12]

The visible hand of the state might be required to rectify the potentially stultifying effects of the invisible hand of the market.

Most important, Adam Smith stressed that the market economy itself depends on key services that private markets will not properly supply. According to Smith, only the state can provide the system of property rights and market institutions necessary for people to participate in voluntary exchanges, namely to participate in a market economy. Private markets and individual freedom require the government to provide key services: "Liberty, reason, and the happiness of mankind" require the authority of civil government, the system of justice, the provision and maintenance of infrastructure, such as roads, canals, bridges, and harbors, and, more generally, on the "institutions for facilitating the commerce of society."[13] Financial regulation is, arguably, an example of intangible infrastructure that facilitates "the commerce of society."

But Smith was very wary of government too because he observed that when the government interfered in markets, they tended to favor the rich and politically connected:[14]

Whenever the legislature attempts to regulate the differences between masters and their workmen, its counselors are always the master.

Smith was worried about government intervention *not* primarily because markets are perfect but because governments are imperfect. He was suspicious of the motivations and capabilities of legislators and officials. [15]

James Madison: A Lead Architect of the US Constitution

James Madison would have had suggestions about creating institutions that both address Smith's call for the visible hand of the government to make markets work better and address Smith's suspicions about empowering government officials.

We believe that Madison would have argued that the major hurdle to getting the financial regulatory apparatus to "work for us" is developing proper checks and balances over the financial regulatory system. Building on our earlier book, *Rethinking Bank Regulation: Till Angels Govern*, we again stress the inextricable connections between designing a sound financial regulatory system and the operation of the political system. Madison argued in the *Federalist Papers*, Number 51:

But what is government itself, but the greatest of all reflections on human nature. If men were angels, no government would be necessary. If angels were to govern men, neither external nor internal controls would be necessary. In framing a government which is to be administered by men over men, the great difficulty lies in this: you must first enable the government to control the governed; and in the next place oblige it to control itself.

If men had only angelic intentions, and markets were perfect, there would be no need for government or financial regulation. But people are not angels and markets are not perfect, so there is a potentially positive role for government.

If angels were to govern men, then the public interest view would hold and we could rely on financial regulators to fix market imperfections and improve the functioning of markets. We would not have to worry about constraining the private interests of politicians and government officials, and we could presume that angels would not be subject to psychological biases that affect sports referees and all other humans. But angels do not govern, nor do they regulate financial institutions, so we must worry about obliging politicians and government officials to act in the public interest. We must worry about imposing checks and balances on financial regulators. We must worry as much, if not more, about the incentives of politicians and financial regulators, as we do about how financial market imperfections affect the incentives of financial market participants.

In building a financial regulatory apparatus that is to be administered by people over people, the great difficulty lies in enabling it to ameliorate market imperfections and improve the incentives of financial market participants while simultaneously providing it with incentives to behave in the public interest. Designing effective checks and balances to oblige government to control itself was Madison's strategy for dealing with a world without angels.

The fatal weaknesses of financial regulation around the world today follow directly from failures to recognize the insights of Adam Smith and James Madison. The Guardians of Finance too frequently ignore the nuance and sophistication of Adam Smith's analyses, which stress the potentially positive role of regulation in supporting the market while simultaneously warning of the potentially negative role of powerful regulators. Rather, current discussions too often begin with either an extreme laissez faire faith in markets or the misplaced belief that unmonitored and unaccountable financial regulators will strive to promote the public good. Today we also tend to ignore James Madison's urgings to find ways to limit the unchecked power of government officials and agencies. Current discussions about reforming financial regulation too often focuses on technical details and too infrequently consider ways to oblige the Guardians of Finance to work for us. We focus unrelentingly on showing that there are systemic institutional failures in how the financial regulatory system designs, implements, evaluates, and changes financial policies, that current reforms fail to address the core problems with the financial regulatory system, and that there are straightforward ways to create checks and balances on the regulatory apparatus that make the system work better.

Innovation and Financial Regulation

As if financial regulation were not complex enough, financial and economic innovations are constantly changing the activities, incentives, and risk exposures of financial markets and institutions so that financial regulation itself must adapt over time to maintain sound incentives among financial market participants. Besides the challenges of designing regulations that reduce the deleterious effects of market imperfections within the context of particular, potentially changing, political systems, regulation must also adapt to financial and economic innovations that alter the playing field in which financial market participants conduct business. Financial regulation is really hard to do right.

But limiting financial innovation in order to simplify financial regulation will have big, adverse consequences because sound financial innovation is crucial, perhaps indispensable, for long-run economic progress. Healthy financial innovation—the creation of new securities, markets, and institutions—improves the ability of the financial system to evaluate projects and firms, mobilize and allocate capital to promising endeavors, monitor the use of that capital to ensure that it is used appropriately, and facilitate risk management and transactions. Financial and technological innovations are inextricably linked. The very essence of economic growth involves increased specialization and the use of more sophisticated technologies. The increased complexity makes it more difficult for the existing financial system to acquire and assess information about new firms and technologies or manage their novel risks. Economic progress itself makes any existing financial system obsolete. Without a commensurate modernization of the financial system, the quality of financial services falls, slowing economic growth.

History provides many examples. Neither London's capital markets of the nineteenth century nor America's mid-twentieth-century financial system could have fueled the explosion of technological innovations in information processing, telecommunications, and medicine that we have experienced in the past thirty years. As nascent high-tech information and communication firms struggled to emerge, traditional commercial banks were reluctant to finance them because these new firms did not yet generate sufficient cash flows to cover loan payments and the salaries of scientists with no managerial experience who ran the firms. Conventional debt and equity markets were also wary of these developments because the technologies were too complex for investors to evaluate. There was a problem: potentially profitable high-tech firms could not raise sufficient capital because the existing financial system could not evaluate them.

So financiers innovated. Venture capital firms arose to evaluate and fund high-tech entrepreneurs. Staffed by "techies," venture capital firms screened potential enterprises and made large, longer term financial commitments to the most promising ones, which encouraged the blossoming of new technologies that have reshaped our lives.

The story of biotechnology in the twenty-first century provides a natural continuation of this virtuous cycle of financial innovation, technological change, and economic growth. The venture capital model of corporate finance did not work well for biotechnology. Venture capitalists could not effectively evaluate biotech firms because of the scientific breadth of biotechnologies, which frequently require input from biologists, geneticists, chemists, engineers, bioroboticists, and other scientists, enormous capital injections, and expertise with the myriad laws associated with bringing new medical products to market. It was infeasible to house all of this expertise in banks or even venture capital firms.

So again financiers innovated. They formed new financial and contractual partnerships with the one kind of organization that has the breadth of skills to screen biotech firms: large pharmaceutical companies. Through scientific know-how, legal expertise, and connections with product distribution networks, pharmaceutical companies identified promising biotech firms, helped them create valuable products, and attracted other investors.

While financial modernization was not the only cause of technological change, the adaptation of corporate financing techniques has greased the wheels of technological inventiveness. Put differently, without financial innovation, improvements in diagnostic and surgical procedures, prosthetic devices, parasite-resistant crops, and an array of other life-saving and life-improving inventions would be occurring at a far slower pace.

The connection between evolving financial arrangements and economic growth did not begin in the twentieth and twenty-first centuries.[16] When steam-powered railroads emerged in the nineteenth century, they too posed a challenge to financiers. While potentially profitable, railroads were technologically complex and spanned large geographic areas. These novel characteristics dissuaded the conventional sources of capital at the time—wealthy investors and banks. Financial innovation helped circumvent these obstacles. Specialized investment banks emerged to evaluate the profitability of railroad companies, stock and bond markets grew and expanded, and new accounting methods made it easier for investors to monitor railroad performance. While other forces also promoted railroads, financial modernization helped advance this crucial ingredient of the industrial revolution.

The synergistic connection between financial and economic development goes back even further in history. The creation of tradable debt contracts 6,000 years ago in Samaria lowered transactions costs, fostered specialization, and boosted productivity. Ancient Rome developed a stock exchange to ease the mobilization of capital for large mining projects. To finance oceanic explorations in the sixteenth through eighteenth centuries, financiers modified the corporate form from the *commenda*, to limited partnerships, and to the joint stock company.

These examples illustrate the essential role of financial innovation in fostering economic growth. The intrinsic nature of economic progress makes production more complex. This greater complexity makes the existing financial system less effective at evaluating new endeavors and managing their risks. Without corresponding innovations in finance therefore, the quality of financial services falls, slowing technological change.

The key policy implications are straightforward. First, financial regulations that impede *sound* financial innovation slow technological progress and economic growth. This policy implication is vitally important for current regulatory debates. Concerns about the recent financial crisis could motivate regulations that curtail innovation in the name of encouraging financial stability. While crises are costly, so are regulations that obstruct financial innovation and technological progress. The goals of financial regulation are not simply to limit risk and avoid crises but also to reduce the adverse effects of market imperfections, provide sound incentives to financial market participants, and to facilitate improvements in living standards. Thus financial regulation must also consider the impact of financial innovation on long-run economic growth.

Second, as economies change and financial systems innovate, the regulatory apparatus might have to adapt to maintain sound incentives among financial system participants. For example, while a regulatory system might work well before structured finance, credit default swaps, and venture capital funds, these innovations might require the modernization of the financial regulatory apparatus. Keeping a regulatory system static while the financial system innovates is just as negligent and reckless as enacting poorly designed regulations. As we show throughout this book, the global financial crisis that began in 2007 happened in part because of the fatal inconsistency between a dynamic economy and a regulatory system that failed to adapt appropriately.

Of course, not all financial innovations promote technological progress and economic prosperity. Financial innovations, like all innovation, can be abused. Newly engineered financial products are undeniably woven into the tapestry of this crisis and past ones as well. But the misuse of new products is not limited to finance. Information technology eases identity theft. Webcams facilitate child pornography. Drugs are dangerously abused. But just as we should not conclude that medical research does not promote human health because we observe drug abuse, or because disreputable people try to pretend that some drug is good for consumers when its chief real benefit is to the providers' bank accounts, we should not conclude that financial innovation does not promote economic growth because of the devastatingly costly crisis through which we are now suffering.

In finance, as in medical research, encouraging the healthy application of human creativity requires some regulatory guideposts and, most important, the ongoing adaptation of regulations so that regulations themselves do not *encourage* the abuse of financial projects and the development of harmful financial innovations. Regulations must adapt over time to maintain sound incentives in a dynamic economy.

International Financial Regulation: A Sisyphean Task

A multitude of challenges face financial regulators. The value of enacting or repealing just one regulation or a package of regulations depends on the effectiveness of the legal system in enforcing contracts, the efficiency with which markets allocate resources, and the existence of other regulations and policies. The appropriate design of financial regulation depends on the political system and the degree to which it induces the Guardians of Finance to act in the public interest. A dynamic, innovating economy implies that the regulatory apparatus must continuously adapt to maintain sound incentives.

Now consider the daunting challenge facing international financial institutions that are striving to develop uniform best practices for all countries! Three complicating factors emphasize the almost hopeless nature of their charge and provide some guidance on how they might approach their task.

Since legal systems, political regimes, regulatory systems, and the degree of economic dynamism and innovation differ across countries and over time, financial regulations must be tailored for each country and evolve with changing conditions. While basic principles apply everywhere, there are always unique political, legal, and economic characteristics that shape the appropriate design of financial policies.

Thus international institutions seeking to develop harmonized checklists of financial regulations will almost never get it right. How could they? Switzerland is different from Botswana. The United States is different from China—and China today is different from China twenty years ago and China twenty years from now. This does not imply that every country in every time period is completely unique. But it does mean that there are differences across countries and time, so designing a static, harmonized template of financial regulations is at best potentially counterproductive.

Second, just as there are good reasons to worry about the incentives and capabilities of domestic politicians and financial regulators, there are also good reasons to question the incentives and capabilities of international institutions. International institutions will not necessarily advance the public interest either.

As an example of how politics, rather than the public good, influences the decisions of international financial institutions, consider the International Monetary Fund and World Bank. As part of their broader objectives to support sustainable growth and reduce poverty, these institutions work to secure financial stability and the sound functioning of financial systems at both the national and international levels. Toward these ends, they started the Financial Sector Assessment Program (FSAP) in 1999. In the FSAP, a joint team of IMF and World Bank experts, working collaboratively with a country's national regulatory agencies, conduct an extensive assessment of a country's financial system, determining key sources of risk, areas needing improvement, and the types of technical advice and changes that would enhance the functioning of the financial system and simultaneously reduce systemic risk.

This effort began as a well-intentioned diagnostic effort: teams of financial professionals, including regulators, former private-sector financiers, and economists, would learn about the weaknesses and vulnerabilities of a particular financial system and work with national officials to design strategies for improving a country's financial system.

However, industrial country authorities, which dominate the governance of these international institutions, quickly decided that they knew best how to regulate finance. Through a variety of groups—such as the Basel Committee on Bank Supervision—industrial country authorities promulgated literally dozens of "best practice" standards. They also insisted that FSAP teams investigate whether countries complied with these standards, even though there was no testing of whether these best practices were any good at producing desirable outcomes. They were best practice because industrial country authorities said so.[17]

One consequence of this explosion of international standards (for banking, securities markets, accounting and auditing, etc.) was that FSAPs quickly became more like a checklist than a diagnostic. The greatest loss was that the teams of multi-disciplinary financial professionals had little time to work together to provide a comprehensive assessment of financial policies. Rather, they had to fill out the prescribed checklist forms for their different subdisciplines. Certainly there were some very good assessments when high-quality teams were assembled and given sufficient time, but unfortunately this outcome was not so common. This might explain why, for example, the 2006 FSAP of Ireland, which had one of the worst crises and was in the midst of one of the most pronounced real estate bubbles in history, earned a clean bill of health; even its score on bank supervision, which failed disastrously as we will see in chapter 5, earned top marks.[18]

Politics also led to one of the greatest omissions imaginable. Since the International Monetary Fund is charged with securing global financial security, one might logically expect that it would conduct an FSAP of the country with the largest financial system, the United States. But the US authorities, which through their veto power exert considerable influence on IMF decisions, successfully argued—until after the crisis—that it was obviously more important for the FSAP to focus on emerging markets and less advanced countries, and that the FSAP could not uncover any weaknesses in the United States because the US Guardians, or the financial markets, would have found them already. So the FSAP carried out evaluations of a diverse set of financial systems, including those in Albania,

Estonia, Gabon, and Madagascar, and even in tiny St. Vincent and the Grenadines. But they did not do an assessment of the most systemically important financial system—the US financial system.

Third, international institutions have frequently designed regulations that might be sound for one financial institution, or even one country, but that are destabilizing for other countries and the global financial system. For example, take the Basel Committee on Bank Supervision, which is a group of bank supervisors from the major economies that establishes bank supervisory and regulatory guidelines, including the standards on bank supervision (just mentioned) that are assessed in the FSAP. Decisions by the Basel Committee do not have the force of law but acquire influence when they are incorporated into national regulations. Most regulatory bodies have the discretionary power to adopt a large portion of the committee's recommendations without a vote by the country's legislature. Furthermore the Basel Committee's judgments influence the recommendations and loan conditions that the International Monetary Fund and World Bank make and impose on developing economies, which broadens the impact of the committee's recommendations.

For several years Basel placed the analytical spotlight on assessing the risk of one bank at a time, which had the perverse effects of increasing aggregate risk. Take, for example, securitization. With securitization, a bank bundles up some of its loans, such as mortgages, and sells the entire bundle to a firm that takes that bundle and issues securities backed by it. Instead of holding mortgages, which are promises by homeowners to pay the bank, the bank now holds cash after selling the mortgages. The bank can then use that cash to make loans. Securitization allows banks that have good lending opportunities, but not much cash, to sell existing loans, obtain cash, and realize those lending opportunities. It allows those with cash to purchase securities backed by a bundle of loans that they could not themselves make.

The Basel Committee's recommendations, however, distorted incentives and helped push banks to abuse securitization. The committee recommended that banks should be forced to hold safer assets (or more capital) when holding mortgages than when holding highly rated securitized bundles of mortgages (called mortgage-backed securities, or MBS). The reason for having lower capital requirements for securitized assets was that the securitized bundle is a (presumably) diversified portfolio of mortgages, and high ratings from credit rating organizations supposedly attested to the greater safety of the securities.

This makes some sense for an individual bank but makes less sense when viewed from a national or international perspective. Based on the Basel recommendations, banks around the world faced higher capital charges for originating and holding mortgages to borrowers that they knew well. They faced lower charges for selling those loans and buying a security backed by a bundle of mortgages composed of borrowers about whom the bank had extremely little information. So banks responded and the result was deterioration in the overall quality of lending. To avoid being forced to hold low-return, safe assets (or to avoid holding more capital), banks sold their loans to borrowers about whom they might have had lots of information and purchased bundles of loans linked to borrowers about whom they had little information. Moreover these developments diminished the incentives for banks to expend lots of resources acquiring sound information on borrowers in the first place: they were going to sell those loans anyway to avoid the capital charges. Basel helped disturb the balance associated with the decision that banks make between holding a diversified portfolio and focusing their attention, and hence their familiarity, with a less diversified set of loans. The Basel capital recommendations pushed the global banking system in one direction, and thus helped unhinge the global financial system. Certainly there were other forces encouraging securitization, but Basel became a key factor in its rapid expansion.

Similarly Basel endorsed allowing banks to set their capital charges by using their own models to assess risk. The danger here is that to the extent that bank supervisors bless one type of model—and they did, the so-called value-at-risk, or VAR, model—many banks will make decision based on this one model. Then all these banks will be encouraged to make similar asset allocation decisions, which is bad for the safety of the overall banking system. Sure enough, in the words of Avinash Persuad, chairman of Intelligence Capital Ltd., in his 2000 prize winning essay (and note that this was seven years in advance of the crisis), the VAR approach helped send the herd (of banks) over the cliff together.[19]

The important points here are that designing a uniform set of financial regulations is a daunting challenge, and that the types of rules that emerge from international committees largely reflect political comprises rather than a sound assessment of global financial regulation. Well-intentioned policies that seem appropriate at the bank, or even at the national level, might induce banks around the world to march in lockstep, which can increase, not decrease, risk—as popularly illustrated by the collapse of the Broughton Bridge in 1831 due to the synchronized marching of a British rifle corps.[20]

The complications associated with international financial regulation do not mean abandoning the effort, but rather suggest modifying the objectives and strategy. We believe the international financial institutions have an invaluable role to play in promoting improvements in financial regulation. The lessons learned from cross-country comparisons can inform regulatory choices around the world. International institutions might also provide a "Madisonian" check on domestic financial regulators by identifying weaknesses in regulatory systems. Along these lines, international institutions might push national Guardians of Finance to act more in the public interest and constrain them from using their power to promote narrow interests. And as economies evolve, international institutions can help, and perhaps force, domestic regulators to adapt regulations and maintain sound incentives among financial market participants. But one must be wary of the tendency of international institutions to standardize policies into templates that might not be appropriate for any single country (let alone the entire world) and appease major constituents.

Complex but Not Hopeless

This chapter has emphasized the inherent complexity of financial regulation. Although there are sound economic reasons for financial regulation, regulations cannot be evaluated in isolation. The impact of adopting, repealing, or weakening any regulation depends on the other regulations, policies, and institutions affecting the incentives of financial market participants. Adding to the complexity, governments are imperfect. Just because financial regulation *could* in theory improve financial markets does not mean that governments *will* in practice use their power for this end. Thus the degree to which the political system induces the Guardians of Finance to act in the public's best interests shapes the appropriate degree of wariness about empowering the Guardians. But regulation is even trickier. Everything is changing: financial and technological innovations alter the rules and risks of the economic game, while political realignments, lobbying, and elections alter political system effectiveness. To maintain sound incentives therefore, the regulatory system must adapt to changing conditions, which adds to the complexity of getting financial regulation right.

The great and enduring financial regulatory challenge calls for the creation of an agile regulatory structure that reflects the public interest and adapts to maintain sound incentives among financial market participants in a vibrant, growing economy. This challenge will not be satisfactorily met by giving simple, bright-line, and easily verifiable rules to the Guardians. The problem is too intricate and dynamic for simple, fixed marching orders. Simple orders (e.g., banning the payment of interest) have a long history of being easily evaded in finance and, worse yet, having unintended, harmful consequences. In emphasizing the complexity of financial regulation and its value, this chapter motivates the design of better institutions for selecting, implementing, assessing, and revising financial regulations, which we describe later in the book.

But this chapter has also offered guidance on coping with that complexity. We are not the "dementors" of financial regulation, seeking to instill despair about financial reform.[21] By highlighting the complexity of financial regulation, we seek instead to disparage simplistic approaches and highlight more nuanced and more efficacious regulatory strategies.

The first lesson is, don't ignore the complexity. Using a simplistic dogma in a complex world is likely to distort incentives and trigger the type of severe pain through which we have been suffering from 2007 to 2010. Neither laissez faire nor the public interest approach will produce the type of financial system that will promote competitive markets, economic growth, and improvements in human welfare. As emphasized above, societies need effective financial regulation, not simplistic dogmas or theories.

Second, the examples in this book repeatedly stress incentives: the incentives of financial market participants and of politicians and regulators. Simple dogmas fail because they do not appreciate the complexity of influences on financial markets, politicians, and regulators. The focus on incentives provides a strategy, but not a checklist. It provides coherence in addressing intricate and consequential policy decisions, but it puts great demands on the Guardians of Finance, which means creating an adequate system of checks and balances to make them work for us.

3

Incentives Run Amok

If you are running a bank and have some people working for you and making money, watch them. If they are making good money, watch them closely; if they are making great money, watch them closer still; and if they are making fantastic profits, fire them!

—Anonymous bank CEO adage

Why did senior managers at so many financial institutions around the world take actions that resulted in the failure or the bailout of their institutions? Why didn't shareholders—and especially directors of banks' boards—step in to prevent this disaster? If a crisis was inevitable, why didn't it happen during the turbulence that buffeted industrial country financial systems in the 1990s? Why did the "big one" happen in the early twenty-first century, after supposedly dramatic advances in the "science" of risk management and all the knowledge gained from earlier crises?

In this chapter we explain that a confluence of factors in the 1990s and early 2000s weakened the ability of shareholders to govern their financial institutions and motivated the executives of financial institutions to take on ever-greater risks. Several developments within financial institutions fueled the increase in risk-taking, including changes in ownership structure, mergers and acquisitions, competition from nonbank financial institutions such as hedge funds (private investment partnerships that are open to a limited number of wealthy investors and that typically undertake high-risk complex investment strategies), the increased complexity of financial products, and new executive compensation schemes. These developments changed the incentives guiding the decisions of financial institution executives and help account for the fundamental differences between the financial system of the early 2000s and that of earlier decades. We also examine the role played by ratings agencies, which facilitated excessive risk-taking by financial institutions and were also affected by the changing incentive system. Finally, this chapter discusses models that were used by banks and ratings agencies. Rather than assist in managing risk, they at best gave many a false sense of confidence and at worst may have been used to obfuscate excessive risk-taking by financial institutions. Perhaps most important, official supervisory and regulatory policies underlie many of these destabilizing developments, but we save that discussion for later chapters.

By stressing how changes in governance mechanisms affected the risk-taking incentives of financial institution executives, we give little weight to two popular explanations of what went wrong in the early 2000s: (1) experienced professionals were incredibly myopic, stupid, and/or caught up in what Warren Buffett called a "mass delusion";[1] and (2) financiers became greedier and increased their risk-taking in search of higher returns. Perhaps there is some truth to these explanations. But we don't see much evidence of human gullibility and greed changing appreciably over time. Considerable evidence shows, however, that changes in the governance of financial institutions and changes in compensation dramatically perverted the incentives of those making decisions within financial conglomerates. It is these destabilizing developments, along with the financial regulatory and supervisory decisions underlying them, that form the core of our assessment of what triggered to explosion of risk-taking in the 2000s.

Why Shareholders Don't Rule

Shareholders are rarely the decision makers in financial institutions. In a number of high-income economies—Australia, Canada, France, Ireland, Japan, Norway, Taiwan, United Kingdom, and the United States—many major institutions, including banks, investment banks, and insurance companies, are widely held, meaning no owner has a particularly large fraction of outstanding shares. In most of these institutions no shareholder owns more than 10 percent of the voting rights. Consequently no controlling owner directly exerts a powerful influence over the decisions made by the institution's executives.

In theory, of course, shareholders still "rule" by electing a board of directors to act as their agents in overseeing the management of a financial institution. The board is charged with monitoring the actions of the institution's executives and ensuring that they act in the best interests of the shareholders. If the executives perform poorly, the board fires them and hires a new management team that more effectively promotes shareholder interests. This way a dedicated group of board members keeps the executives focused on advancing the long-term value of the financial institution and prevents them from abusing their positions by favoring private interests to the detriment of other stakeholders. That is the theory.

In practice, executives sometimes deviate from this ideal. Executives can, and sometimes do, use the resources of their financial institutions in ways that are very profitable for them but at a cost to shareholders. These "private benefits" come in many forms, including excessive compensation and perquisites, such as lavish bonuses and expense accounts, club memberships, private jets, and large loans at generous terms. These private benefits also involve the ability of the executives to make decisions about asset allocations that benefit them, and related parties, again at the expense of the shareholders. The opaqueness of financial institutions makes it difficult for their directors to oversee the executives and contain the extraction of these private benefits.

Furthermore executives sometimes exert a profound influence over the board of directors. While legally bound to act in the best interests of the shareholders, board members are often financially bound to the executives who selected them for those lucrative board seats. Consequently executives tend to choose loyal individuals as directors, some of whom are not necessarily sufficiently skilled in accounting and financial matters, and those directors may want to keep their positions by keeping the executives happy. Board members typically have neither the ability nor the incentive to confront executives on all important issues. This classic corporate governance problem gives executives great latitude in running financial institutions, and shareholders have difficulty compelling directors and executives to maximize shareholder value.

Executives also frequently seek to enlarge their conglomerates to promote their own objectives, not necessarily the goals of shareholders. Besides the drive to generate greater income through sheer expansion, the size of the institution is one metric by which executives compete with each other. Bigger is frequently better in the game between executives. Some research in the financial sector, however, indicates that shareholders do not benefit by the formation of conglomerates and would generally be better off if some large, complex financial institutions were dismantled and the pieces sold as smaller, more specialized entities.[2] However, this approach would not be in the best interests of those actually making decisions for financial institutions, the executives, as we suggest below.

These governance problems are particularly severe in financial institutions because of the comparative difficulty in ascertaining the exact nature and quality of financial institution assets. In contrast, although the health of Apple Inc. depends on many factors, anyone can purchase an Apple product and judge its effectiveness. Anyone can find sales data or go online to read consumer reviews about its products. By extension, anyone can judge Apple executives through company sales, profits, and customer reviews, though of course the opinions of experienced analysts might be more valuable than those of the casual iPod user. But in the financial industry, such straightforward indicators of performance in finance are not easy to find. Consider the practice of issuing mortgages or selling insurance. If shareholders were to judge executive performance by sales volume alone and to compensate executives accordingly, this would spur executives to motivate their employees to make lots of loans and sell lots of insurance, even if those actions exposed the institution to potentially fatal risks. In the case of financial institutions, sales volume and current income are poor indicators of performance, customer reviews are unhelpful, and risk is extraordinarily difficult to quantify, which explains why firms such as Bear Stearns, Lehman, Countrywide, and Merrill Lynch were so widely admired—almost up to the moment of their failure or disappearance as independent entities due to financial problems. These same information problems also make it difficult for minority shareholders to sue managers or board members of a bank, as differences in the interpretations of ambiguous information creates a high legal hurdle for would-be plaintiffs.[3]

Difficulty in governing financial institutions is not new. Since the late Middle Ages, at least, bank owners have understood that they are exposed to risks taken by bank managers. In fourteenth-century Italy, where modern banking is said to have taken form, banks flourished in part because innovations in bookkeeping and accounting helped protect against employee risk-taking and embezzlement. So it has been long realized that banks were exposed to the risks their employees take. These risks may be hard to assess, and not just by shareholders and boards of directors but also by executives running the banks. Thus the rogue trader Nick Leeson brought down Barings Bank in the 1990s because his managers in London were unable to monitor the risks he was taking with the bank's capital from his trading desk in Singapore. Those managers made an elementary mistake: they let someone taking risks with the bank's money also run the "backroom" that reported on those risks. As with CEOs of banks in the most recent crisis, it is hard to know whether Barings' senior management did not know better or whether their better judgment was clouded by the enormous profits that Leeson supposedly was generating. Clearly, they did not recall the adage at the beginning of the chapter that colorfully illustrates the correlation of high returns with high risk.

Just because corporate governance is imperfect doesn't mean banks are always teetering on the edge of failure. Shareholders purchase stock in widely held financial institutions because they believe problems of corporate governance can be ameliorated to a sufficient degree so that the investment is worthwhile. Well-designed compensation contracts can help align the interests of shareholders with executives. For example, tying executive compensation to stock prices is a popular device for linking the interests of shareholders and corporate decision makers, although here too ample room exists for abuse. If executives can manipulate short-term performance to boost stock prices and trigger a big payoff to themselves, they might do this even if it hurts the long-term performance of the financial institution. Corporate governance problems are ongoing and changing over time.

In the remainder of this chapter, we focus on factors that altered incentives within many financial institutions, causing a breakdown in governance that helped induce the financial system to go haywire with such devastating results.

Compensation and Incentives

Some maintain that eye-popping levels of financial-sector compensation in the years leading up to the crisis were just an incidental sideshow. One such pundit, a *New York Times* columnist, made this claim, backing up his assertion with a study by two distinguished scholars, René Stulz and

Rudiger Fahlenbrach, who found that bank CEOs suffered such large personal losses that it was not plausible to suggest that they deliberately risked the health of their institutions.[4] If bank CEOs were not deliberately taking outrageous risks, he concluded, then they were just wrong and didn't understand the "perfect storm" that was about to hit.

We disagree. Theory, evidence, and sworn testimonies suggest that several developments over the past two to three decades (1) made it more difficult for shareholders to govern financial institutions and (2) fostered changes in executive compensation packages that encouraged much greater risk-taking. All of these brought about dramatic changes in the incentives of financial institution decision makers. Among those developments:

• several major financial institutions changed ownership structure, from partnerships to limited liability corporations;

• mergers and acquisitions created larger and more opaque financial conglomerates and fostered a "go-for-growth" mentality among bankers; and

• financial products grew increasingly complex, and information about the true risk position of financial firms became increasingly hard to assess.

Consider the change in ownership structure. Several major investment banks moved from partnerships to limited liability corporations in the past two to three decades, which helped create a foundation for greater risk-taking. When banks were partnerships, partners had a strong incentive to monitor risks because much of their lifetime remuneration was tied up in the partnership; their long-term welfare was permanently linked to the bank. In a limited liability, publicly owned corporation, however, once executives collect their bonuses and cash out their options, their long-term financial well-being is de-linked from the firm's subsequent performance. Thus partners who extract private benefits are hurting themselves and their fellow partners, whereas the executives in a corporation who do the same are primarily lowering the returns for others and profiting themselves. Moreover, since the partners' long-term financial well-being is closely connected to the firm's profitability, partners tend to monitor one another as well as the entire firm's activities more closely compared with the monitoring performed by the directors of a widely held corporation.

The sound incentive characteristics of partnerships—relative to those of limited liability corporations—have been understood for a long time. The Medici Bank in the fifteenth century established a series of partnerships in order to create a "global" bank, while limiting incentives of distant executives to expropriate bank resources as a result of their ownership stake in the firm. More recently several US investment banks, including Bear Stearns, Lehman Brothers, Morgan Stanley, and Goldman Sachs, which had thrived for decades as partnerships, went public (in 1985, 1986, 1994, and 1999, respectively). This change in ownership form encouraged greater risk-taking. Managers were risking their own money when the firms were operated as a partnership, but later were risking the money of many unrelated shareholders once the firms became publicly owned.

Mergers and acquisitions increased the size and complexity of financial institutions, making it increasingly difficult for shareholders and boards of directors to monitor and constrain the activities of executives. To illustrate the dramatic changes in American banking, think about what the banks listed below have in common:

Bank One	Dime Bank
Bank United	HF Ahmanson & Co.
First Commerce Corp.	First Chicago NBD
First USA	Great Western Financial
Chase Manhattan	Chemical Bank
NBD	JP Morgan
Deerbank	Valley National Bank of Arizona
Manufacturers Hanover	INB Bank
Summcorp	Texas Commerce
Lincoln First Bank	Security National
Bensonhurst Bank of Brooklyn	First National Bank of Mount Vernon
Bank of Rockville Centre Trust	Hanover Bank
Guaranty Trust	New York Trust
Clinton Trust	Staten Island National Bank and Trust
Bank of Manhattan	Chase National Bank
Corn Exchange Bank and Trust	National Safety Bank and Trust
Continental Bank and Trust	Interstate Trust
Equitable Trust	

Adding two more banks, Bear Stearns and Washington Mutual, to the institutions above, gives away the answer: the list of thirty-seven banks represents the consolidation drive that produced JP Morgan Chase, one of the largest US banks today with more than 220,000 employees and about $2 trillion in assets as of early 2011. A longer list could have been assembled by looking at Bank of America, which is the combination of more than fifty entities.

Rather than being solely aimed at maximizing shareholder value, mergers and acquisitions seem to have been also driven by the prospect of maximizing CEO power and wealth. For example, James "Jamie" Dimon, who went from being the CEO of Bank One to COO and then CEO at Morgan Chase after Bank One's acquisition by the former, has enjoyed a total compensation from Morgan of about $130 million over the period of July 2004 to 2010 (or $1.67 million per month), far greater than the $32 million (a "paltry" $762,000 on a monthly basis) earned during his years (2001–July 2004) as CEO of Bank One.

Mergers and takeovers in banking were also driven by factors other than CEO income and "empire building," including deregulation and economies of scale. For most of the last two centuries, the US financial system had a large number of exceedingly small banks due to legal restrictions on acquisitions and branching across state lines or, in many cases, even within the states themselves. These small, geographically undiversified banks tended to fail in large numbers during regional cyclical downturns. The number and severity of banking crises through the early twentieth century accounted for the founding of the Federal Reserve System, despite long-standing opposition to a central bank in the United States. After the failure of about 15,000 banks in the 1920s and 1930s, the number of banks remained fairly constant (at roughly 15,000) until the late 1970s, when legal barriers to interstate acquisitions and branching were systematically lowered and then even more so with respect to branching in 1995, and then with respect to acquisitions in 2010. The deregulation that encouraged some of the more recent US mergers came in the form of the 1999 Gramm–Leach–Bliley Act, also known as the act that repealed the Glass–Steagall Act that separated commercial and investment banking. The 1999 legislation put investment and commercial banks in more direct competition with one another, a move that had begun in the 1980s as selected commercial banks were allowed to conduct some limited investment banking activities. We are not arguing that the Gramm–Leach–Bliley Act played an important role in triggering the crisis. Indeed, there was no Gramm–Leach–Bliley, or its equivalent, in other crisis countries (e.g., Iceland, Ireland, and the United Kingdom, as discussed in chapter 5), as they never had a Glass–Steagall Act to repeal. We are simply noting that the Gramm–Leach–Bliley Act facilitated the construction of larger financial conglomerates, but the trend to consolidation in the US financial sector was well underway before this Act, and also was in process in Europe.

Furthermore, recent evidence indicates that there can be real efficiency gains from running a larger bank relative to a smaller one.[5] These gains are plausible: once one sets up a department and a system to manage credit cards, to engage in risk management, or to serve as a "back office," then it is possible for that department and system to take on extra business at very little added cost.

Nevertheless, even with these potential efficiency gains from mergers and acquisitions, larger, more diversified banks are more difficult for shareholders to monitor, resulting in some cases in an actual drop in the stock market valuation of some bigger financial conglomerates. The corporate governance problems within banks are quite real. Even after accounting for economies of scale, the governance problems from mergers and acquisitions in some cases can hurt shareholder value while boosting the benefits for executives.[6]

In Europe, where mergers were somewhat fewer but larger, the complexity of financial institutions increased too. European consolidation was stimulated by the 1993 push to a "single market in banking" and was furthered in 1999 with the adoption of the euro by some countries. Not surprisingly, from the early 1990s to the period 1997 to 2002, mergers increased significantly, by five- to sevenfold in terms of assets. These mergers included some very large institutions: Union Bank of Switzerland (formed from UBS and Swiss Bank—which already included Dillon Reed and SG Warburg, some of the elite names in the history of finance—merged in 1997, and two years later bought Paine Webber); when Banque Nationale de Paris and Paribas merged in 1998, BNP became not only the largest bank in France, but in 2009 was the top bank in the world, in terms of assets; Hypobank and Bayerische Vereinsbank merged in the same year in Germany; Banco Santander and Banco Central Hispano merged (becoming the largest bank in Spain in 1999); and Bank Austria merged with Creditanstalt Bankverein (becoming the largest bank in Austria in 1999).[7] The banking transition process taking place during the 1990s also led to attempts by Western European banks to dominate the market in eastern European countries.

Competition in finance also began to intensify from a relatively new source: hedge funds (and, to a much lesser extent, private equity).[8] Hedge funds specialized in higher return strategies, including the shorting of stocks, for wealthy individuals and institutions willing to devote a fraction of their funds in an attempt to increase their overall returns. Greater accumulated wealth in the hands of the few—including those from emerging markets, such as China and India—and the rising importance of pension funds partly account for this change. But the "Great Moderation"—the period from the late 1980s to the 2007 crisis, which was characterized by historically low macroeconomic volatility (of national output and employment) and of low inflation—also likely encouraged those with high net worth to assume greater risk. Other factors contributing to the greater prominence of hedge funds and the rise of trading activities included increased volatility of asset prices from the 1970s onward, reflecting among other factors the end of the Bretton Woods System of fixed exchange rates; greater gyrations in oil prices; more than 2.5 billion new capitalists from transition economies; and more open international capital markets.[9] Hedge fund assets jumped tenfold over the 1998 to 2008 period, peaking at about $2.5 trillion.[10]

Banks responded by trying to mimic the investment and compensation strategies of hedge funds in some of their own activities. Competition to attract and retain talented workers spurred this response, as skilled staff began to migrate, particularly in the 1990s, over to hedge funds. Compensation was a key issue: hedge fund managers typically were paid a small percentage (1–2 percent) of assets under management plus an incentive, or performance bonus, of some percentage of returns or of returns above some benchmark, without being required to share in any losses.

Such a reward system encourages greater risk-taking: when fund managers get paid more for producing higher returns and still more for increasing the funds under their management, which typically follows from higher returns, and the managers are not penalized for taking on more risk, this tends to spur them to take greater and greater risk. Thus even one year of very high returns could lead to a gigantic bonus. True, this strategy could lead to horrible returns in subsequent years, but so what? With the promise of a seven- or eight-figure bonus from boosting the assets of the fund today, why worry about problems in a couple of years?

Under these incentives it would have been surprising if many traders and fund managers had not adopted riskier strategies.

This "volume-based" compensation model, which depended most importantly on the volume of assets under management (and the short-run returns on those assets), changed incentives remarkably. It spurred some executives to compete for control of more assets with higher promised returns, while reducing their concern about risk since any downside loss was not their problem; only the prospect of a positive return mattered for their compensation. This model tended to spread throughout the financial services industry in a number of high-income countries as many investment banks moved rapidly away from "white-shoe," or relationship-based, banking to trading activities for their clients and then with their own capital—similar in some respects to hedge funds.

Some of the bigger commercial banks followed the compensation model of the investment banks and also pushed trading to the forefront, a trend that clearly predated the repeal of Glass–Steagall in 1999, but which was no doubt encouraged by it. Banks such as Morgan (before its merger with Chase) and Bankers Trust increased their trading activities in the 1980s, with Morgan appointing Sir Dennis Weatherstone, a former foreign exchange trader, as its CEO in 1990. The riskiness of trading, and especially of banks' trading on their own proprietary income, rather than merely executing trades for clients, became clear in 1998 with the failure of the prominent hedge fund, Long-Term Capital Management (LTCM). Not only had major banks invested in LTCM, but a number of them were discovered—within a couple of weeks of Fed Chairman Alan Greenspan's testimony to the US House Banking Committee that hedge funds "were strongly regulated by those who lend them money"—to have imitated LTCM's trading strategy.[11] Although the Fed could claim that hedge funds were outside its purview, the fact that some of the commercial banks it was charged with overseeing were making the same bets as the hedge funds was an oversight that was eerily repeated in the current crisis, as noted in the next chapter.

Although this volume-based compensation system did not spread everywhere, it did have wide-ranging effects. It did not spread to smaller US and European banks that continued to serve local and/or niche markets. It also did not seem to occur in Canada and Australia, where among other differences, competition in banking was more limited, or in Japan, where the banking system continued to be affected by the 1990s crisis and foreign entry remained more limited. However, the growth of salaries and rewards for return-boosting strategies did extend to many financial institutions in the United Kingdom, Ireland, and elsewhere in Europe. Dutch and Swiss banks, formerly considered paragons of conservative banking, were also paying outsized rewards and, in the case of Fortis (Dutch) and UBS (Swiss), required large injections of taxpayer funds and ultimately mergers with sounder banks.

Even formerly conservative banks were transformed into much riskier institutions by increased competition, alterations in compensation schemes across the industry landscape, and the drive for growth. The merger in 1998 of Union Bank of Switzerland, founded in 1912, with Swiss Bank, which was discussed previously, was a forced marriage as the original UBS was taking on some of the same financial positions that led to the failure of LTCM. As the US securitization movement was growing more rapidly in the early 2000s, UBS management appeared determined to make their investment bank a dominant player. Unfortunately, that market imploded, and so too did UBS, requiring substantial government support to survive. In an April 2008 report by UBS management, it was acknowledged that the motivating factor was the drive for growth. "Essentially, bonuses were measured against gross revenue after personnel costs, with no formal account taken of the quality or sustainability of those earnings,"[12] the report stated. In other words, UBS rewarded current revenues with little or no attention to future risk, and this formula produced large bonuses as long as luck held out. UBS was so keen on achieving rapid growth that it not only helped package many of the complex securities that were later downgraded to below investment grade, it also bought or held on to them for their higher returns. Unfortunately, UBS wasn't the only bank to be infected by the "toxic waste" that it helped generate, all for the sake of growth.[13]

Going for Growth in Mortgage Lending

As compensation became increasingly connected to volume and short-run returns, many fund managers lined up to buy highly rated mortgage securities. The riskier, higher return paper helped secure larger bonuses for those who were buying them and whose pay was based on how their short-run performance (the return earned) compared to that of others. The larger demand for these riskier securities also fueled greater supply. The push toward volume also explains why banks in countries like Switzerland or Germany, with no housing bubbles of their own, wound up needing government support to survive: even though many assets of dubious quality were originated in the United States (and of course in Ireland, Iceland, and the United Kingdom, among others), less than half of the total of US mortgages were held domestically, with a large portion being held in Europe, where fund managers were also being paid using the "volume-based" compensation model. Managers restricted to buying only AAA-rated securities had a powerful incentive, in the form of a larger bonus, to find the AAA-rated securities with the very highest returns. As in the case of UBS, risk was often overlooked or forgotten in the process.

AAA-rated mortgage securities were known by those in the industry to be riskier than their rating suggested, yet they were in great demand. Even a first-semester business school student might venture that if highly rated mortgage instruments were paying a greater return than comparably rated corporate securities, as was the case, then the former must be riskier. (After all, if there were low-risk, high-return investments available, people would be rushing to buy them, raising their price and lowering the return). Moreover there was ample evidence cited in bank publications dating back to the 1998 to 2003 period that ratings for mortgage products were not consistent over time, and that they were biased in an optimistic direction by rosy assumptions (e.g., that the prices of the underlying securities were not correlated with one another).[14] Any financial professional protesting that they purchased AAA-rated mortgage securities because they were convinced that they were safe instruments either was disingenuous or not paying attention, arguably because they were blinded by the high pay they received in exchange for not questioning the ratings.

Besides the drive for income and growth, regulatory avoidance shaped this seemingly bizarre behavior. European (and American) banks were busy trying to avoid the higher capital charges of the Basel capital requirements. As discussed in chapter 2, AAA-rated securities, composed largely of mortgages bundled together, incurred a lower capital charge, compared with originating and holding on to mortgages. Banks were quick to respond to this particular incentive and reward employees who contributed to this distorted bottom line—distorted in that the incentive was to hold a bundle of supposedly diversified mortgages about which banks had relatively little information, instead of holding onto the loans that they originated, and about which they should have had relatively good information.

The same volume-based compensation model was operating in the institutions supplying mortgages. Mortgage brokers with no advanced training were earning mid-six-figure salaries (or higher) by originating as many mortgages as possible. New Century Financial, one of the large California-based originators of subprime mortgages, "made little if any effort to see if the broker had information about the applicant's circumstances that would justify a high LTV (loan-to-value) ratio," noted its bankruptcy examiner.[15] It also adopted the increasingly popular system of buying mortgages that were originated by thousands of independent brokers, who bore little or no responsibility for mortgages that went bad. This system functioned well with the proper safeguards by the institutions that were purchasing the mortgages. New Century had some reasonable policies in place for judging which mortgages to buy, but it purchased a large percentage of risky loans in violation of its own criteria on "an exceptions" basis, in the rush to feed the firms that were assembling more mortgage-backed securities, and of course to reward staff with larger bonuses for their great productivity.

Were there penalties—other than New Century's failure—for managers who took on excessive risk? No, not really. Bonuses bore little, if any, relationship to risk.[16] *The New York Times* reported that Dow Kim, co-president of fixed income at Merrill Lynch (and therefore the team that was packaging mortgage securities), received a salary of $350,000 in 2006 . . . plus a bonus of $35 million; that "a 20-something analyst with a base salary of $130,000 collected a bonus of $250,000. And a 30-something trader with a salary of $180,000 got $5 million," this in a year when Merrill paid out a total $5 billion to $6 billion in bonuses.[17] The same article noted what college professors have observed, namely that in contrast to a generation earlier, when weaker students were choosing careers in finance, now it was the academic stars who headed to Wall Street. "In college dorms, tales of 30-year-olds pulling down $5 million a year were legion."[18] When smart people get lavishly rewarded for generating volume regardless of risk, they tend to produce lots of volume—with lots of risk. Merrill Lynch's risk-taking ended with its forced sale to Bank of

America, and although the sale was at a premium relative to the market price in September 2008 when it was hastily arranged, it was at a huge discount compared to its price a year earlier.

The mortgage securitization process added jet fuel to the volume-based compensation schemes propelling growth and risk. At every stage in the process, from the origination of mortgages to their packaging as MBSs and to their re-packaging into still other securities, and to rating by ratings organizations, to their sales by investment and commercial banks, to the purchase by a variety of entities, commissions were paid along the way. Since executive bonuses increased with the flow of MBSs, the securitization business exploded. This created incentives for executives to grow the business and keep it moving as quickly as possible for as long as possible. If and when the entire system eventually collapsed, they would have already collected their millions, if not their tens of millions. The bulk of the losses would be borne by others. Thus the mortgage payments from borrowers were structured into new financial instruments and sold to pension funds, insurance companies, endowments, and a wide array of financial institutions around the world. More securities meant a bigger volume, which in turn translated into a bigger bonus.

One early and sensible motivation underlying structured finance was the desire of financial institutions to create financial instruments that were tailored to the risk appetites of specific purchasers. For example, pension funds, mutual funds, and insurance companies (as a group, institutional investors) normally do not have the large credit departments that would be found in banks, and so did not make loans. However, when a large number of loans were packaged together as securities and their quality was verified by SEC-approved rating agencies, institutional investors and others could with a seemingly high degree of safety buy these securities. Some institutional investors might want lower risk and correspondingly lower expected returns, while other investors might want greater returns with correspondingly greater risk. So this securitization process in theory could match the riskiness of assets with the risk preferences of the investors, at the same time making a larger supply of funding available for mortgage finance. Lower cost mortgage financing was a result. And, importantly, those carving the loans into securities could earn fees.

Beyond merely bundling loans together, financial institutions structured the cash flows from a bundle of securities, such as mortgages, in a manner that would appeal to a wider array of purchasers than the underlying securities themselves. In particular, with "structured" finance, the financial institutions created a new batch of securities that were paid first. That is, income from all of the underlying assets (e.g., the bundle of mortgages) was pooled together and the first payments went to cover the returns promised to the holders of these safest securities. This first tranche, or slice of the deal, comprised the safest and highest rated (AAA) portion of the new securities. Then there would be a second tranche. Payments next would be sent to the holders of this second tranche, which was riskier but offered a correspondingly higher expected rate of return. So the structure of the financial instruments was packaged, from the safest to the riskiest, with the lower rated (BBB or unrated), most risky securities paid last, to accommodate investors with different appetites for risk. Finally, at the bottom, lay the equity tranche, the unrated "toxic waste," whose investors were to be paid last with the payments from the mortgage holders.

This securitization and structuring process created a whole new array of securities, allowing financial institutions to collect fees for creating and selling them and credit-rating agencies to collect fees for rating them. There was no end to this packaging and re-packaging of mortgages, and since fees were available every time securities were created, this encouraged a dramatic increase in their supply. The explosion of compensation was a critical part of the process. Collateralized debt obligations (CDOs), were based on taking mostly the lower and riskier tranches of MBSs (already hundreds or thousands of mortgages), bundling them with other securities as well, and repeating the tranching process. The alchemy of this process allowed one to take lowly rated—and so, really risky!—securities and re-carve them (with a collaborating rating agency) into AAA-rated and lower rated tranches, and so on, until nearly everything became rated as investment grade. This meant that there were even CDOs of other CDOs (dubbed CDO-squareds, etc.).

Although securitization and structuring allowed for the customization of financial instruments for particular purchasers of securities, the process became perverted by the enormous bonuses available to financial institutions and rating agency executives from moving securities through the securitization, structuring, and ratings pipeline as fast as possible. Indeed buyers could even purchase exceedingly low-priced insurance (a credit default swap, or CDS) that would promise to compensate them in the event that a household defaulted on its mortgage payment and they, in turn, suffered a loss on their securities. AIG, the American Insurance Group, was a large seller of CDSs. How did they pay their employees in the group that was selling this insurance? Yes, with huge bonuses based on the volume of sales.

If a life insurance company paid its sales staff purely on the basis of the sales volume, those employees would be crowding hospital intensive care units, trying to insure every living person. But insurance companies have underwriting standards and departments to protect against such behavior. So why didn't they protect themselves against the overzealous selling of credit default swaps for mortgage-backed products in the years leading up to the crisis? Apparently their executives were too busy enjoying the vast revenue stream and correspondingly enormous bonuses to worry about the even larger amounts of money their insurance companies soon would have to pay out. It is plausible that many did not understand the risks they were taking on, but it is not believable that everyone in the companies that were selling CDSs was unaware of the earlier noted research on the problems with the ratings of mortgage securities.

Even conservative banks got sucked into this frenzy. Although Morgan Chase had largely stayed out of the structured finance mess, in mid-2006 it joined forces with Magnetar, a firm alleged to have been assembling structured financial products that were likely to fail so that Magnetar could bet against them. Morgan sold these products to institutional investors, such as pension funds, around the world. Yet within a few months of the closing of the sales, the value of those structured financial products plummeted to a fraction of its original value.[19]

Harder Evidence

The stories, testimonies, and reports that compensation and incentives in finance had changed fundamentally in the late 1990s and early 2000s are convincing, but there is even harder evidence of how these altered from earlier experience. Several studies document the undeniable role of compensation in the crisis and suggest a role in the regulation of finance. Most important is research by Thomas Phillipon and Ariell Reshef that shows that from the mid-1990s to 2006, as was the case in the run-up to the Great Depression, those working in the financial sector were earning an excess wage, compared to that in other sectors, well above what could be explained by factors such as education, the complexity of tasks in different industries, and the risk of the loss of one's job in that sector.[20] That is, the authors argue that while part of the rise in finance pay was justified by these factors—about a 20 percent increase in relative wages in finance relative to the remainder of the economy—a much larger part was not, as relative wages rose by roughly 65 percent. Unexplained or excess compensation in finance by the time of the crisis exceeded the heights that this figure attained in the late 1920s and early 1930s. Interestingly, this sea change was not a focus of regulators (except perhaps of those who moved from regulation into banking), even though the change was remarkable compared with historical norms and it was visible to anyone acquainted with the sector.

Evidence also shows that executives benefited so much from the boom in volume that the eventual collapse of their firms just didn't matter much. In the wake of the failure of Bear Stearns and Lehman, it became popular to argue that compensation was not a primary factor in the crisis because the senior executives at these firms owned a great deal of stock and stock options in their companies and suffered great personal financial losses.[21] It was this perspective that was put forth by the *New York Times* columnist mentioned earlier in this chapter. That these executives lost so much suggests that the crisis must have been a great surprise, so either it came as a "perfect storm" or these executives made terrible mistakes, or both.

However, Lucien Bebchuk, Alma Cohen, and Holger Spamann show that a very small group of senior executives (the top five) at these two firms were paid about $1.4 billion (at Bear Stearns) and $1 billion (at Lehman) in the period 2000 to 2008.[22] Whether some in this group might have made still more money had their firms survived and prospered is moot. For example, Bebchuk et al. document that the CEOs at these two firms each "lost" over $900 million due to the collapse in stock prices from their peak. While each might have preferred that their firms survived and that the stock prices continue to rise, in effect, a pumped up stock price was the instrument through which they were able to extract hundreds of millions of dollars in bonuses. These managers adopted high-risk strategies that paid off in the short run, allowing them to attract funds and leverage their bets, pumping up their returns even more. In the process they were paid handsomely—money they do not have to pay back as long as no fraud was involved. As Bebchuk put it, "Compensation was flawed top to bottom. . . . The whole organization was responding to distorted incentives."[23]

Nowhere was compensation more flawed than at Countrywide Financial, which became the largest originator of mortgages, only to be forced to submit to a takeover by Bank of America. Angelo Mozillo, the CEO, oversaw a boom in lending, in particular a jump in Countrywide's use of option-ARMs, according to which the borrower has the option in the initial years of paying less than the amount owed, with the difference between the amount owed and that paid added onto the principal of the mortgage. Thus borrowers who might have put little if any of their own money down could then borrow more than the original value of the house. Adjustable rates were used to make it easier for borrowers to take out a larger mortgage due to the lower initial interest rates. Mozillo's email record testifies to his concerns: "Since over 70 percent have opted to make the lower payment it appears that it is a matter of time that we will be faced with much higher resets [i.e., an automatic increase in the interest rate on the loan] and therefore much higher delinquencies."[24]

But Mozillo was still able to walk away with almost half a billion dollars while Countryside collapsed. What later became clear is that Mozillo was selling his shares of Countrywide stock. Subsequently he was charged with fraud by the SEC and settled without admitting guilt in the amount of $67.5 million. However, not only was Mozillo paid $521.5 million by Countrywide during the 2000 to 2008 period, but Bank of America covered $20 million of the fine. In other words, by rapidly growing Countrywide and running up its stock price Mozillo was able to pay himself a huge reward, and walk away with about $480 million and no criminal penalties. In contrast to the fines and criminal prosecutions of the saving and loan crisis, many are outraged that executives in the 2007 to 2009 crisis so far are escaping with fortunes and without jail time despite the losses suffered by shareholders.

In sum, many factors triggered a change in incentives confronting decision makers of large financial institutions, and those incentives in turn triggered a huge increase in risk-taking. The change in incentives, ignorance of which renders the crisis incomprehensible, was one of the most important characteristics of finance from the mid-1990s until the crisis.

Competitive forces and the drive to dominate a sector infected banks in many countries, and outright looting may have been at work.

It is remarkable that even commercial banks (at least the largest ones) were able to join in this frenzy, given that they are among the most regulated institutions in any economy. Never before in history have there been so many pages of bank regulations and resources devoted to supervising banks. The fact that supervisors failed to act when they saw the explosion of compensation is an issue to which we will return. As noted earlier, the pay phenomenon was known in college dorms, and as a number of staff from regulatory agencies were moving to the financial sector, the regulators had to know what was happening.[25] Yet with all of the astonishing rewards being paid, regulators did not seem to ask where the risks were that had to accompany those high promised returns. Although the data are not so detailed on compensation in other countries, anecdotal information suggests that booming pay characterized finance in Iceland, Ireland, the United Kingdom, and a number of continental European banks, among them UBS. For example, Thorvaldur Gylfason notes that in Icelandic banks "loan officers were rewarded according to the volume of loans they made and other transactions with emphasis on short-term profits."[26] He suggests that this encouraged them to offer foreign currency loans to clients who did not understand the risks that they were taking, much as large bonuses encouraged US mortgage brokers to make available risky loans, some clearly too risky for unsophisticated borrowers, and all such loans too risky if they could only be repaid if homes prices continued rising rapidly forever.

The Special Role of Ratings Organizations

No story of how the governance of financial institutions came to emphasize growth at almost any cost is complete without a discussion of ratings agencies. How were institutions that were supposed to be well regulated and concerned with risk management able to buy and sell such low-grade securities? As explained in the next chapter, a critical part of regulation was outsourced to the ratings industry, which took on a crucial role in converting low-quality securities to highly rated paper, thereby helping many to earn enormous rewards. But the ratings industry's poor performance was instrumental in the damage to the world economy. In this section we contend that the ratings industry was infected by the same virus that perverted the incentives of the financial system—the rating agencies made it easier for some, including rating agency executives, to profit at the expense of minority shareholders, creditors, and taxpayers. Basically some agency executives undoubtedly also went after rapid increases in volume, and the immediate outsized bonuses; when things ultimately fell apart, the executives would be rich and retired.

In recent testimony before congressional committees and the Financial Crisis Inquiry Committee (FCIC) from former executives and employees, a picture of a perverted incentive system emerges. According to a former senior vice president of Moody's, the agency's culture prior to the late 1990s was quite conservative, accuracy in ratings was prized, and the firm had a somewhat antagonistic relationship with bankers, who needed to have their products rated in order to sell them. But from Mark Froeba, a lawyer who rose to senior vice president at Moody's and who left the firm in 2007, managers there began receiving compensation in the form of stock and stock options in 2000, as the firm became a separately traded entity. As he described what happened with this change to the Commission:

Under the guise of making Moody's more business friendly, making it more responsive to clients . . . Moody's senior managers set in motion a radical change in Moody's analytical culture that not only changed the rating process but also profoundly affected Moody's ratings. . . . When I joined Moody's in late 1997, an analyst's worst fear was that he would contribute to the assignment of a rating that was wrong, damage Moody's reputation for getting the answer right, and lose his job as a result. When I left Moody's, an analyst's worst fear was that he would do something that would allow him to be singled out for jeopardizing Moody's market share, for impairing Moody's revenue, or for damaging Moody's relationships with its clients and lose his job as a result. . . . In the latter case, the fear was real, not rare, and not at all healthy. You began to hear of analysts, even whole groups of analysts, at Moody's who had lost their jobs because they were doing their jobs, identifying risks and describing them accurately.[27]

In congressional testimony, the former managing director of Moody's, Eric Kolchinsky, emphasizes that changes in the compensation system perverted the rating of securities:

In my opinion the cause of the financial crisis lies primarily with the mis-aligned incentives in the financial system. Individuals across the financial food chain, from the mortgage broker to the CDO banker, were compensated based on quantity rather than quality. The situation was no different at the rating agencies. It is my firm belief that the vast majority of the analysts at Moody's are honest individuals who try hard to do their jobs. However, the incentives in the market for rating agency services favored, and still favor, short-term profits over credit quality and quantity vs. quality. At Moody's, the source of this conflict was the quest for market share. Managers of rating groups were expected by their supervisors and ultimately the board of directors of Moody's to build, or at least maintain, market share. It was an unspoken understanding that loss of market share would cause a manager to lose his or her job. . . . Prior to the crisis, it may have been reasonable to believe that the pursuit of market share could be unrelated to credit quality. People would say, "we are credit specialists—it is our job to be able to analyze anything we are asked to." After the crisis, it became clear that the drive for market share was the main cause of the deterioration in credit standards in the ratings of structured finance. . . . Senior management would periodically distribute emails detailing their departments' market share. . . . Even if the market share dropped by a few percentage points, managers would be expected to justify "missing" the deals which were not rated. Colleagues have described enormous pressure from their superiors when their market share dipped.[28]

Kolchinsky himself was moved to a lower position (and later asked to leave) as a result of calling attention to the fact that his unit was being pressured to assign high ratings to securities that another part of the company was about to downgrade. His and others' testimony asserts that Moody's senior management allowed banks putting together securities for rating assignments to request the removal of uncooperative Moody's staff (those not willing to assign high ratings without supportive data) from work on their "deals." The "carrot" of stock and stock options for generating more business, and the "stick" of being moved off deals or fired for upholding credit standards, were effective tools for changing the ratings industry from the protector of credit standards to an instrument to undermine the financial system.

Standard and Poor's (S&P), another ratings organization, was also using models that churned out optimistic grades. Suppose, for example, that university professors were paid by the number of students in their classes. Although this might encourage more exciting classes, it would also lead many teachers to give out A-pluses to all students; those not playing along would lose out on "market share" and suffer in terms of pay. Similarly the easiest way for ratings' employees to participate in the securitization money machine was to give as many AAA ratings as possible; those trying to get securities rated would bring their business to those giving out high ratings quickly. And no surprise, the revenues of the ratings organizations boomed. Many of their employees were widely reported to be trying regularly to obtain jobs at the banks giving them securities to rate, where pay was even better, and a few employees of ratings agencies ended up with attractive salaries at banks.[29]

Thus a conflict of interest encouraged overly generous ratings of securities, whose supply was critical to the seemingly perpetual money machine in the sector. The promise of high returns on allegedly safe securities attracted more money from around the world, "justifying" the record bonuses. All this behavior was taking place in the regulated market, but the regulators were sadly silent.

Risk Managers and Risk Models: Where Were They?

Even if every other actor was being highly paid to play along with the mortgage machine process, why didn't banks' risk managers intervene to stop the madness? Did they not realize that many of the securities the banks were moving off their balance sheets might come back to them when the inevitable defaults occurred? Where were the vaunted risk models, those products of a supposed revolutionary advance in the quantification of risk? Throughout the 1980s and 1990s, risk management became an important and quantitatively sophisticated endeavor in financial institutions, consulting firms, and business schools. So what happened in the 2000s? Weren't the risks obvious to managers and their models?

After all, what was occurring in several countries was an unprecedented housing boom, with sharp rises in household debt-to-GDP ratios, at historically low interest rates. Loans were going out the door—to borrowers who could only qualify with artificially low "teaser" rates, to borrowers whose salaries were never verified and could not possibly be accurate (a six-figure income for a graffiti artist?), and to borrowers taking out second mortgages and thus with potentially little if any equity in their houses. In the United States, many were using their homes as ATM cards; "prime" borrowers and others, having seen their property values jump, refinanced their homes, taking out larger mortgages and extracting some of the increased value to use for a variety of purposes, from paying college tuition to buying flat-screen TVs and taking nice vacations. Raghu Rajan does a nice job in *Fault Lines* in explaining how flat real wages and growing income inequality played into this new trend.[30] In some countries, such as Iceland and a number of eastern European countries, people were borrowing in foreign exchange because those interest rates were lower than the rates in their own currency, a practice that has ended badly innumerable times in history; borrowers seemed only to understand the low initial interest rate they would enjoy from a foreign currency loan, and not its risk.

Where were the risk managers, and why weren't they pointing out the dangers of these practices? In some banks, risk management did in fact seem to induce more cautious behavior. Banks such as Morgan Chase and Goldman Sachs avoided the worst of the crisis (and even prospered) and seemed to have paid more attention to their risk management staff, though, as mentioned in the last section, even at Morgan, some risky behavior took place toward the end of the bubble.[31] At other banks, risk management was simply pushed aside. At Lehman, in the years immediately preceding its failure, according to Andrew Ross Sorkin's account, the risk manager was actually asked to leave the room when risks were under discussion in executive committee meetings, and she was dropped from that committee in 2007.[32] When Michael Gelband, the head of fixed-income trading, in 2006 tried to warn the CEO, Richard Fuld, about the risks Lehman was taking and the need to retrench, he was told that he needed to take more risk so as to not miss any deals. To his credit, Gelband resigned rather than fire employees who were being blamed for "going slow" on real estate deals.[33]

Lehman's behavior proved to be a typical pattern. Whether the goal was to grow in order to survive or drive up profits in the short term so that senior staff could enjoy nice bonuses, managers that were determined to take more risk typically ran roughshod on their risk management staff. The "stars" winning the biggest compensation packages in these banks appear to have been those who played along, just as in the ratings agencies, and not those who warned of problems. Given the record level of compensation being paid in the financial sector, it is not surprising that risk managers were ineffective in trying to highlight risks. Simply put, when people are being rewarded so highly in the present, they tend to ignore or discount risks in the future. The fact that it had been a long time since a serious downturn in the US real estate market reinforced this tendency. It is a behavior seen in other crises; for example, when oil prices boomed in the 1970s, many bankers began to base their decisions on projections of continued increases of oil prices. While some are sufficiently naïve to believe such forecasts, others merely want to believe them as they serve as a tool that can be used to pay out high rewards in the present. Unfortunately, if the reward is sufficiently high, there will be no shortage of staff who will respond to incentives. To be sure, many working in rating agencies, AIG, Bear Stearns, Lehman, and UBS, to name a few, were not even aware of the risks being run, much less did they partake of the "gambling," and they suffered from the impact of the crisis on their firms. However, an evident lesson from crises throughout history is that it only takes a few "gamblers" using the capital or reputation of a firm to destroy both completely.

If risk managers were ineffective, what about the vaunted risk models? Three problems plagued these models.

First, they were based on very little data and inaccurate assumptions. The Basel Committee on Bank Supervision required only five years of data to estimate the risk models of commercial bank portfolios. But events within any five-year period will cause predictions to vary. If, as was the case, the five years are characterized by an economic boom (in this case, a housing bubble), then the models will underestimate future risks. The models also assumed that new borrowers would behave as borrowers had in the recent past, but the US housing market was opening to more buyers, many of whom had never had a mortgage before, and downpayments were being reduced. The models further assumed that mortgages were unchanged, but they had become riskier, with NINJA loans (loans requiring no documentation of income, jobs, or assets) or option-ARMs (adjustable rate mortgages, which in the initial years allow the borrower to pay less than the monthly payment owed, with the difference added on to the balance of the loan and therefore requiring much bigger payments in the future), products that had been rare or unavailable previously. These innovations were designed to get around banks' own standards, as they allowed borrowers who were not qualified to obtain mortgage financing, often with little of their own money at risk. Some borrowers might have taken out these loans knowing that they could not afford to pay unless housing prices continued rising, while others simply did not know what they had signed. According to the documentary *American Casino*, real estate closings took place in parking lots, on the hoods of cars, with buyers merely trusting those providing the financing to look out for their interests.[34] We now know that some mortgage brokers were fraudulently altering the loan documents—by getting borrowers to sign a large stack of papers, with only the top ones pertaining to the loan that the borrower wanted and the rest for a loan that would yield increased fees for the broker.

There is no right answer to the question of how many years of data (when they are accurate) are needed to make reliance on risk models sensible. A few years of data, particularly when that period does not include a recession, will produce rosy forecasts. A hundred plus years of data are of no use because a good part of the data will no longer apply; the horse-and-buggy industry is no more. Risk management is part art and part science because industries and economies are constantly evolving. In another respect, however, the world is remarkably repetitive: sharp operators come along to offer the promise of enormous returns, whether they're selling miracle health cures or miracle investment securities. While regulators have enjoyed a fair degree of success banning dangerous drugs, financial regulators actually blessed the risk management models used by banks and ratings organizations.

A second problem associated with risk models involved their misuse: managers could manipulate the models into justifying any line of business that would produce large bonuses. Some firms, such as Morgan, understood that the data really did not exist to estimate the risk models properly, which is what helped restrain that bank's role in the securitization process.[35] Goldman Sachs was among the first to notice that prices of some securities were behaving oddly and cut back its exposure, later turning to shorting the mortgage market, that is positioning itself to benefit when mortgage defaults rose and the value of mortgage securities declined.

But in many other banks the models were there to justify risks being taken. It was well known, since at least 2000, that the so-called value-at-risk models—the models that banks and ratings agencies used to estimate the risks being faced—underestimated the likelihood of rare events, especially when they were estimated using data from very recent years, which happened to be characterized by rapidly rising housing prices and low interest rates. Modelers applied certain statistical assumptions (that risks were normally distributed), even though it was long recognized that this assumption was driven more by convenience than accuracy. In the summer of 2007 many banks and hedge funds that were experiencing losses defended themselves by pointing to their models and claiming that the losses were only due to an incredibly rare event. The problem with this explanation is that according to some of the models used at the time, the history of the universe could have been run and re-run dozens of times and that still would not have been sufficient time to make the decline seen in the value of securities likely to occur—in other words, their models' assumptions implied the such events essentially would never happen. Of course, the alternative interpretation, that their models were based on incorrect assumptions, was in fact the more accurate explanation!

As employees of ratings organizations testified, the models assumed continued house price appreciation. Even a leveling off of prices would have raised default rates above those being forecast. In reality, prices leveled off and then fell—and fell some more. Holders of the securities whose values were plummeting discovered that the higher returns they had been earning was compensation for the risk that prices might actually decline; a few years of high returns in most cases were not high enough to compensate fully for losses.[36]

In another example of misuse, the models assumed that the components of the securities were not correlated. But many of the prime and subprime loans had been taken out at a time of record or near-record low interest rates. In some loans with "teaser" interest rates, where the initial rate typically was set at very low levels for the first three or five years to help the borrower qualify for the mortgage (a lower interest rate resulting in an initially lower monthly payment), the models ignored the fact that it was written into the contract that the rate would rise, regardless of what happened to market interest rates. So more or less simultaneous increases in rates, which spurred defaults, affected many supposedly AAA-rated securities.

A third problem with the risk models was that the models ignored the impact of, well, the models. The use of similar risk models across the banking industry—and similar approaches were encouraged by regulators, whose approval was required—was a change in the way the world worked. As seen in the LTCM crisis in 1998, if banks have similar risk exposures and similar models, they tend to move together. Those models assumed that when a firm wanted to sell off its assets, it could do so with ease. However, when other firms had taken the same position, the impact was similar to that in a crowded theater during a fire: everyone's simultaneous rush for the exit ensures that many cannot get out. Moreover, by virtue of the fact that many investors in the years leading up to the crisis were so confident in this more scientific approach to risk management, more liquidity flowed into asset markets, pushing up prices and making the models look correct (the theater became more crowded with the same small number of doors). Thus the models were just another manifestation of "new era" thinking seen in every bubble, the rationalization that thanks to new opportunities, new markets, new inventions, we are in a new world in which the old concerns about risk do not apply.[37]

Until, that is, they do again.

4

How US Regulators Encouraged the Financial Crisis

Popular government moves slowly . . . and this is especially true when its financial authorities and thinkers are governed by faddism and special interests . . .
—H. Parker Willis, "The Banking Act of 1933—An Appraisal," *American Economic Review*, 1934

Senior US financial policy makers and regulators repeatedly designed, implemented, and maintained policies that increased the fragility of the global financial system in the ten to fifteen years before the crisis that shook the world in 2008. Those policies encouraged financial institutions to engage in imprudent activities that generated enormous short-term profits while increasing long-term fragility. These policies were not simply mistakes or accidents. They do not primarily reflect unforeseeable and unstoppable events. Time after time, regulators recklessly endangered the economy by selecting and, most important, by maintaining destabilizing policies. Even though regulatory agencies learned that their policies were undermining the safety and soundness of the financial system and even though they had the power to alter their policies, they frequently chose not to adapt to changing and deteriorating conditions.

The main purpose of this chapter is not to assign blame, but to diagnose what went wrong in order to fix a broken system. The reason that we pull no punches in critiquing the accident view of the crisis is because it deflects attention from the prominent role of policy makers and regulators in causing the crisis, from the systemic institutional flaws in the regulatory apparatus, and from steps that must be taken to build and maintain a well-functioning financial system. Only by candidly examining the constellation of factors that caused the crisis—including systemic institutional weaknesses in how the system designs, evaluates, and reforms regulations—can countries develop comprehensive, meaningful, and lasting reforms.

Six important policies increased the fragility of the US financial system:

1. Federal Reserve policies that allowed banks to reduce owner-contributed equity capital cushions through the use of credit default swaps, which are over-the-counter (OTC) derivatives;

2. Federal Reserve and SEC policies concerning OTC derivatives in general;

3. SEC policies toward the consolidated supervision of major investment banks;

4. SEC and other regulatory agency policies toward credit rating agencies;

5. FDIC policies toward banks; and

6. congressional and the Office of Federal Housing Enterprise Oversight policies toward Fannie Mae and Freddie Mac.

We focus on how these policies affected the operation of the financial system between 1996 and 2006 and how officials responded or didn't respond to the changes. We evaluate the period before the onset of the crisis—before policy makers shifted into "crisis response" mode. We examine a relatively calm period in which officials observed and learned about the effects of their policies and had ample time to reform those policies without the intense pressures of being in the midst of a crisis.

We also ask a number of questions, the answers to which are crucial to designing a better financial regulatory system. Why did the Fed choose to maintain its policies, even though, as we make clear below, it possessed detailed information that its policies had to be inducing banks to take on excessive risk, and even though it had the power to alter those incentives to curtail such risk? Why did the SEC become willfully and woefully blind to the systemically important risks taken on by gigantic investment banks? Why didn't the FDIC take prompt corrective action against banks that it identified as engaging in excessively risky behavior, since it was mandated by Congress to act promptly to stop such risks? Answering these questions is essential to achieving the goal of creating an institutional structure that reduces the likelihood and magnitude of the next crisis while fostering economic growth and expanding economic opportunities.

Greenspan's Fed

The Federal Reserve is unique and uniquely powerful. It makes money by creating money. When the Fed purchases Treasury securities from banks, it pays for the securities by creating and giving reserves to the banks, which the banks can turn into money by making loans or other investments. Then the Fed receives a stream of interest payments, and ultimately a principal payment, from the US Treasury on those Treasury securities. It's as if you could magically create money to purchase a car for transportation. It is good to be the Fed.

The Fed uses this power in an attempt to achieve several goals. To promote sustainable economic growth while containing inflation, the Fed alters the amount of securities that it purchases in order to influence national interest rates and credit conditions. To stimulate sluggish investment and economic growth, it purchases securities, pushing down interest rates. When it perceives that the economy is overheating, it tightens credit conditions by selling securities.

The Fed is one of the foremost Guardians of Finance, the principal financial supervisor and regulator in the United States. Besides having authority over the biggest banking institutions, it is charged with maintaining the stability of the entire financial system. During the recent crisis the Fed put its money-creating powers to work to keep those financial institutions it viewed as systemically important, or "too big to fail," from total collapse: it used its discretionary powers to purchase an unprecedented quantity and variety of securities, not just US Treasury securities as had been its practice, almost $1.5 trillion worth as of the end of 2010 from a wide range of struggling financial institutions.

The Fed's formal financial policy duties are as follows:[1] (1) supervising and regulating banking and financial institutions to ensure the safety and soundness of the nation's banking and financial system and protect the credit rights of consumers, and (2) maintaining the stability of the financial system and containing systemic risks that may arise in financial markets.

The Fed states that it conducts an on-site inspection of each bank (financial) holding company with more than $1 billion in assets at least once a year and continuously monitors them through off-site supervision, which involves the collection and processing of numerous data. It assesses (1) the riskiness of bank holding company assets and determines whether the institution is holding enough safe assets to cover potential losses on its risky assets, and whether it has borrowed too much money, given the riskiness of its assets and potential disruptions to the financial system at large; (2) the management team of each bank holding company to determine whether it has the skills and organizational structure to run the financial institution safely and soundly; (3) the earnings and profits of the bank holding company and subsidiaries to determine whether the flow, and likely future flow, of income and expenses threaten the banking institution's viability; and (4) the maturity, structure, and liquidity of the institution's assets and liabilities to make sure that likely withdrawals of deposits and other liabilities can be easily satisfied through the sale of liquid assets.

The US banking system is heavily supervised and regulated. The Fed, with an operating budget of $4 billion, employed about 22,000 people at the start of 2010. The FDIC has a budget of $4 billion and employs 6,000 people for the purposes of ensuring the safety and soundness of the nation's banks. The OCC contributes another $1 billion and 4,000 employees toward overseeing nationally chartered banks.[2] And these are just the federal bank regulators; there are also state supervisors of state-chartered banks in all the states.

While it is perfectly reasonable to argue that supervision and regulation failed to work for us, it is demonstrably wrong to contend that banks were unsupervised and unregulated. This is important because popular accounts of the crisis erroneously argue that the free-markets approach to regulation failed. This is not true because we did not have free markets; there are extensive regulations in commercial banking. It is more correct to argue that the particular mixture of extensive regulations and enforcement actions (or lack thereof) that existed in the United States and in a number of other countries from 1996 through 2006 failed—not that free markets or capitalism failed to work for us.

The Fed is financially independent. By using its money-creating powers to purchase income-generating assets, such as Treasury securities, it produces enough income to pay its operating expenses and still distribute about a whopping 90 percent of its income back to the US Treasury. The Fed is also designed to be politically independent. The seven members of the Federal Reserve Board are appointed by the president and confirmed by the Senate. They serve staggered terms; that is, one member's fourteen-year term expires on January 31 of each even-numbered year. This is meant to partially insulate the Fed from short-term political influence or manipulation.

The Federal Reserve System is not independent of private banks; it has a network of twelve Federal Reserve Banks that, among other things, have some responsibility in supervising member banks within their districts.[3] The Reserve Banks have their own boards of nine directors, six of which are elected by commercial banks in the district (though the new Dodd–Frank Act of 2010 reduces the influence of the directors elected by the commercial banks in selecting the Reserve Bank's president).[4] Thus private banks are intimately intertwined with those charged with regulating the nation's major banks. For example, the current president of the New York Federal Reserve, William Dudley, is a former Goldman Sachs partner. Fed employees, at both high and low levels, can and often do depart for "greener pastures" in the private financial sector. After leaving public office, every past president of the New York Federal Reserve went to work for a financial institution, except its first president, Benjamin Strong, formerly president of Bankers Trust, who died while in office. Gerald Corrigan, who was president of the New York Federal Reserve Bank from 1985 to 1993, is now a senior executive at Goldman Sachs. David Mullins resigned as a member of the Board of Governors of the Federal Reserve System to become a partner in the now-infamous Long-Term Capital Management, which failed spectacularly in the 1990s. The revolving door spins often and rapidly.[5]

It is difficult to exaggerate the power of the Fed, although people try. Professor Brad DeLong from the University of California, Berkeley, called the United States the "Republic of the Central Banker." David Wessel of *The Wall Street Journal* has described it as the "fourth branch of government."[6] The 1989 best-selling book about the Federal Reserve by William Greider is grandly titled *Secrets of the Temple: How the Federal Reserve Runs the Country*. While not a "secret temple," the Federal Reserve clearly is an exceptionally powerful institution, and does keep much information to itself.

It is also difficult to exaggerate the influence of Alan Greenspan, the chairman of the Federal Reserve from 1987 to 2006, although people try to do that too. Robert Woodward titled his 2000 book on Greenspan, *Maestro*. L. Ray Canterberry's 2006 book on Greenspan's years at the Fed was subtitled *The Oracle behind the Curtain*. David Wessel, author of *In Fed We Trust*, noted that Greenspan is frequently referred to as "The Wizard," as in the great and powerful man behind the curtain in *The Wizard of Oz*. None other than President George W. Bush remarked that Alan Greenspan had achieved "rock-star status."[7] Greenspan was "The Man," and his views profoundly shaped public policy.

As a disciple of philosopher and novelist Ayn Rand, Alan Greenspan is a proponent of laissez faire capitalism, arguing for reducing regulatory restrictions on private financial institutions and for the self-correcting virtues of free markets. Ayn Rand argued,

I am for an absolute laissez-faire, free, unregulated economy. Let me put it briefly. I am for the separation of state and economics.[8]

Greenspan embraced this view, noting in his autobiography,

It hadn't taken long for us to have a meeting of the minds, mostly my mind meeting hers [Ayn Rand].[9]

Greenspan decided to implement his Ayn Rand, free-market view as a Washington insider, not as a philosopher-novelist, as he expressed in his autobiography

I had long since decided to engage in efforts to advance free-market capitalism as an insider, rather than as a critical pamphleteer.[10]

Greenspan successfully pushed to reduce regulatory impediments on, and supervisory oversight of, financial institutions and markets and also repelled the efforts of some to add new financial regulations and transparency requirements.[11] Many policy makers and regulators in the United States and around the world embraced Greenspan's perspectives on the regulation of financial markets.

Although we also emphasize that evidence strongly supports an approach to financial policy that takes a wary view of government intrusions into the activities of private financial markets and that stresses the central, beneficial role of competitive private markets in allocating capital, the free-markets approach took a dangerous turn in the ten or so years before the crisis started in 2007.[12] The Guardians of Finance focused too little on the incentive effects of removing one regulation at a time or in deciding not to adjust the supervisory environment in response to emerging financial innovations. As noted in chapter 2, there definitely is a case for some regulation in finance. And just because one regulation is unappealing, removing it could have adverse ramifications depending on the existence of other policies. Similarly financial innovations can change the impact of existing regulation on the incentives of financial firms. Thus, to maintain prudent incentives, policies need to adapt to changing conditions on an ongoing basis.

The excessive focus on deregulation without a complementary focus on incentives facing private financial firms helps explain why US policy makers systematically selected and maintained policies that incentivized many financial institutions to engage in destabilizing activities.

The Fed, Credit Default Swaps, and Bank Capital

Much has been written about the role of complex over-the-counter (OTC) derivative contracts (i.e., those not traded on formal exchanges, including credit default swaps) in the failure of AIG and the fragility of major banks around the world. A credit default swap (CDS) is an insurance-like contract written on the performance of a security or bundle of securities. For example, a purchaser, bank A, buys a credit default swap from issuer B on security C. If security C later has a predefined "credit-related event," such as a missed interest payment, a credit downgrade, or a bankruptcy filing, then issuer B must purchase security C from purchaser A at face value to compensate for the loss in value.

Although possessing insurance-like qualities, a credit default swap is not a formal insurance contract, and it is not regulated like an insurance contract. Neither the purchaser nor the issuer of the CDS needs to own the security (C). In other words, buying a CDS is like buying fire insurance on your neighbor's house. Furthermore issuer B, who is also the counterparty to the CDS contract with the bank, can trade its "insurance" obligation to a new counterparty, purchaser D. Because a CDS is not an insurance contract, it is not regulated like insurance products. The CDS is a financial derivative that, so far, has been transacted in unregulated, over-the-counter markets.

In principle, banks can use credit default swaps to reduce both their exposure to credit risk and the amount of capital they must hold against potential losses. For example, if a bank purchases a credit default swap on a loan, this can reduce its credit risk: if the loan defaults, the counterparty will compensate the bank for the loss. If the bank's regulator concludes that the counterparty to the CDS will actually pay the bank if the loan defaults, then the regulator typically allows the bank to reallocate its capital to assets with higher risk and greater expected returns.

Following the creation of CDS in 1994 by JP Morgan, the Fed made a momentous decision in 1996: it permitted banks to use credit default swaps to reduce their owner-contributed equity capital.[13] Regulators treated the securities guaranteed by an issuer of the credit default swap as having the same risk level as the issuer (or, more accurately, the counterparty) of the credit default swap. Thus a bank that purchased credit default swap protection from AIG on collateralized debt obligations (CDOs) linked to subprime loans would have those CDOs treated as AAA securities, for capital regulatory purposes, because AIG had an AAA rating from a Nationally Recognized Statistical Rating Organization, namely from an SEC-approved ("blessed") credit-rating agency.

Banks used credit default swaps to reduce their capital cushion, which simultaneously enabled them to invest ever more in lucrative, albeit more risky assets. A bank with a typical portfolio of $10 billion of commercial loans, for example, could reduce its owner-contributed capital against these assets from about $800 million to under $200 million by purchasing credit default swaps for a small fee.[14] The CDS market boomed following the Fed's decision to allow such behavior. By 2007 the largest US commercial banks had purchased $7.9 trillion in credit default swap protection, and the overall CDS market reached a notional value of $62 trillion.[15]

But there were serious problems associated with allowing banks to reduce their capital via credit default swaps. Given extraordinarily active trading of the swaps, it was sometimes difficult to discern the exact identity and ordering of the actual counterparties responsible for compensating a bank if an "insured" security failed. Plus some bank counterparties developed massive exposures to CDS risk. For example, AIG had a notional exposure of about $500 billion to credit default swaps (and related derivatives) in 2007, while having a capital base of only about $100 billion to cover all its traditional insurance activities, as well as its newer financial derivatives business. The growing exposure of AIG and other issuers of CDSs should have—and did—raise concerns about their ability to satisfy their obligations in times of economic stress.

The Fed was well aware of the growing danger to the safety and soundness of the banking system from derivatives. There is a long history of such awareness. As early as 1992 the president of the New York Federal

Reserve Bank, Gerry Corrigan, expressed grave concerns that derivatives threatened the stability of banks and threatened to impose tighter regulations on banks.[16] But Fed chairman Alan Greenspan rejected those concerns and successfully convinced Congress in 1994 to keep derivatives largely unregulated.

Even so, the growing size of the derivatives market continued to instill fear among some Fed officials. Gillian Tett in *Fool's Gold* recounts how Timothy Geithner, then president of the New York Federal Reserve Bank, became concerned in 2004 about the lack of information on credit default swaps and the growing counterparty risk that banks were facing. He called on Gerald Corrigan, then a partner at Goldman Sachs, to head a task force to examine the opacity and risk of credit default swaps. While Corrigan in one sense was a logical choice, both as former president of the New York Federal Reserve and because he had repeatedly expressed concerns about derivatives, he was also an odd choice since Goldman was making a fortune designing and marketing customized credit default swaps.

Internal documents at the Federal Reserve in Washington, DC, also indicate that the Fed knew by 2004 of the growing problems associated with subprime mortgage-related assets. Indeed the FBI was issuing public warnings in 2004 of an epidemic of fraud in subprime lending. Many credit default swaps had been written on those subprime mortgage-related assets, and detailed accounts illustrate the Fed's awareness by 2006 of AIG's growing fragility and the corresponding exposure of commercial banks to credit default swap counterparty risk.[17]

Yet policy makers now frequently claim that the CDS-caused demise of AIG in September 2008 was a surprise. But it was not a surprise to the Fed or to *Time* magazine, which ran an article on March 17, 2008, under the headline "Credit Default Swaps: The Next Crisis." The article reported that AIG had recently taken an $11 billion write-down on its CDS holdings and that losses on CDS holdings had severely damaged Swiss Reinsurance Co. and other entities that sold CDSs, such as MBIA and AMBAC Financial Group Inc. The article noted explicitly that these developments could be devastating for financial institutions that had purchased credit protection from these insurers. Yet on March 16, 2008, Treasury Secretary Paulson noted in a CNN interview, "I have great, great confidence in our capital markets and in our financial institutions. Our financial institutions, banks and investment banks, are strong."

The authorities did not prepare for the potential failure of AIG or other major sellers of credit default swaps in the spring of 2008. As of the fall of 2010, US taxpayers had handed over about $180 billion to AIG.

Yet even more momentous than the original decision allowing banks to reduce their capital through the use of credit default swaps, the Fed neglected to adjust its policies once it learned that the mushrooming use of increasingly suspect credit default swaps was undermining the financial strength of the entire banking system.

Why didn't the Fed revise its capital regulations? Bank purchases of credit default swaps boomed immediately after the 1996 regulatory decision allowing a reduction in bank capital from the purchase of CDSs. Why didn't the Fed respond by demanding greater transparency before granting capital relief? Why didn't the Fed conduct its own assessment of the counterparty risks facing the systemically important banks under its supervision? Why didn't the Fed adjust in 2004, as it learned of the opaque nature of the CDS market and as the FBI warned of the fraudulent practices associated with the issuance of the subprime mortgages underlying many CDS securities; or in 2006, as information became available about the fragility of AIG; or in 2007, when hedge funds warned the Fed, the Treasury, and G8 delegates about the growing fragility of commercial banks?[18] Why didn't the Fed prohibit banks from reducing regulatory capital through the purchase of credit default swaps until the Fed had confidence in the financial viability of those selling CDSs to banks?

The Fed's decision to maintain its regulatory stance toward credit default swaps was not a failure of inadequate or unavailable information or a shortage of regulatory power. The Fed's top officials might not have appreciated the severity of the growing problems, but their subordinates certainly brought requisite information about the condition of financial markets to their attention. Fed staff fully understood and appreciated the growing fragility of the financial system in the decade before the crisis.[19] Even in 2004 the Fed issued Interpretive Letter #998 that reiterated its capital regulatory policy with respect to credit default swaps.

The Fed could have modified its capital regulations to reduce the likelihood of future problems based on two simple and prudent premises—one pertaining to its mission, the other to its capability. First, the Fed is responsible for the safety and soundness of the financial system, for which it is important that the largest banks hold capital commensurate with their risks. Second, the Fed did not have reliable methods for assessing the credit risk of those selling credit default swaps to banks, nor should it have relied on the credit rating agencies to assess that counterparty risk, as we explain below. Based on these principles, the Fed could have prohibited banks from reducing their regulatory capital through the purchase of credit default swaps until the Fed had confidence in the financial viability of those firms selling CDSs to the banks.

The Fed did not have regulatory authority over credit default swaps, the credit-rating agencies, AIG, or many other sellers of CDSs, so it could not have directly taken action to improve the counterparty risk associated with CDSs. But the Fed was, and is, responsible for overseeing the safety and soundness of the major banks and the financial system as a whole. If it had refused to allow banks to reduce their capital, or to increase their assets relative to the capital they held, through the purchase of CDSs, the Fed could have enhanced the stability of the major banks and indirectly created incentives for improvements in the credit default swap market.

The Fed could have acted to improve things, but it chose not to. It was a conscious choice; it was a failure of regulatory governance and an abdication of the Fed's responsibilities.

We are not suggesting that the Fed's decision to allow banks to reduce their regulatory capital through the purchase of CDSs was the most important cause of the global financial crisis. It is quite difficult to quantify the degree to which this policy increased risk-taking at any individual bank or the fragility of the financial system as a whole, but CDSs did seem to fuel the demand for risky securities, and thereby contributed to a willingness by banks to take on greater risk.

What we are suggesting is that the Fed's approach to bank capital and the CDS market illustrates three key features of the financial crisis that are frequently ignored in current discussions of regulatory reform. First, the Fed knew many years before the crisis that its policies were increasing the fragility of the financial system. The problems with credit default swaps and bank capital was not a surprise in 2008; there was ample warning that things were going awry years before then. The Fed recklessly endangered the global financial system by not fulfilling the main purpose for its very existence.

Second, the Fed had the power to reform policies that were increasing the fragility of the system. Nonetheless, it maintained those policies over many years, even as the Fed learned about the ramifications of its policies. This was not simply an accident, a lack of discretionary power, or a regulatory gap. This was a deplorable and destructive choice that was made year in and year out for over a decade.

Third, the dominance of the laissez faire ideology over a prudent assessment of incentive effects facing financial market participants helps explain why policy makers did not adjust their policies. The innovation of the credit default swap, which allowed banks to circumvent, or at least ameliorate, their capital regulations, boosted bank profits but severely weakened the capital foundation that safeguards bank stability against adverse shocks. The innovation transformed a sound supervisory system into an unsound one. But an ideological predisposition against any change that might be seen as strengthening regulation apparently impeded appropriate regulatory reform in response to emerging problems. We cannot deny that referee bias, as described in chapter 1, might well have played a role in the behavior of Fed staff, who might or might not have agreed with The Maestro.

Born versus Greenspan, Rubin, and Levitt: Guess Who Won? Guess Who Lost?

There were warnings. In 1994, Orange Country in California went bankrupt because of its exposure to over-the-counter derivative contracts, many of which are custom-designed contracts, including credit default swaps, in which the parties to the contract may "bet" on the price of another asset, such as a bond, a stock, or currency. The Orange County treasurer had borrowed $14 billion and invested the funds in OTC derivative contracts based on the paid advice of Merrill Lynch. This earned Merrill more than $100 million between 1991 and 1994. Without admitting wrongdoing for its role in advising, or some might even say enticing, a county treasurer to invest in complex, interest-sensitive derivatives, Merrill paid $30 million to settle a criminal investigation. In 1996, Bankers Trust forgave about $160 million owed by Procter & Gamble—essentially a "payment" to settle a lawsuit. P&G had accused Bankers Trust of manipulating it into purchasing OTC derivative contracts while obfuscating the true risks of those contracts. Indeed Bankers Trust had charged off (which translates in plain English to "paid") about $300 million to settle disputes concerning derivatives with an assortment of unsophisticated clients. These problems suggest that numerous problems plagued the OTC derivatives market—and Frank Partnoy has so marvelously documented many of them.[20]

Brooksley Born, who was appointed chair of the Commodity Futures Trading Commission (CFTC) in 1996, recognized the warning signs of risk associated with this "dark market," which was huge and growing exponentially. In 1996, it was a $25 trillion market, and it grew about twentyfold over the next decade. A market that big and growing so fast posed a clear potential risk to the entire financial system and hence to the economy at large. But it was difficult to evaluate the systemic importance of the OTC derivatives market because officials simply didn't have the requisite data. They didn't know the exposure of systemically important financial institutions to OTC derivatives. And they had no way to find out. Although the CFTC was responsible for exchange-traded derivatives and collected information on those contracts, neither it nor the other regulatory agencies had clear authority to oversee the large and booming market.

"We didn't truly know the dangers in the market because it was a dark market," Born recalled in 2006. "There was no transparency." In a 1998 speech, she noted that the absence of basic information allowed traders "to take positions that may threaten our regulated markets or, indeed our economy, without the knowledge of any federal regulatory authority."[21]

Born's CFTC trumpeted a loud warning in 1998, suggesting that regulators shine a bright, clarifying light on the large, opaque OTC derivatives market. Her call to arms, and the stunning response by the rest of the Guardians of Finance, has been documented in a PBS Frontline program, *The Warning*. In short, the CFTC issued a report in May 1998, calling for greater transparency of OTC derivatives.[22] The commission sought greater disclosure, improvements in record keeping, and controls on fraud. It did not call for draconian controls on the market, just improved transparency.

The response was swift, ruthless, and coordinated. Fed chairman Alan Greenspan, Treasury Secretary Robert Rubin, Rubin's assistant Larry Summers, and SEC chairman Arthur Levitt immediately went on the attack. As noted by Timothy O'Brien, Sunday business editor for *The New York Times*, "They were all part of a very concerted effort to shut her up and to shut her down. And they did, in fact, shut her up and shut her down."[23] Indeed, he added, "Bob Rubin and Alan Greenspan were very much in lockstep. They had very similar views on Wall Street. It boiled down to the less regulation, the better."[24] According to Michael Greenberger, Greenspan even questioned whether there was a need to have rules against fraud. The market would root out problems and get rid of those companies that developed poor reputations.[25] In terms of OTC derivatives, Greenspan—The Maestro, Oracle, Wizard—vehemently rejected CFTC's push toward transparency. "Regulation of derivatives transactions that are privately negotiated by professionals," he said, "is unnecessary."[26] Greenspan, Rubin, and Levitt cited "grave concerns" about shedding light on the OTC derivatives market in an unusual joint statement.[27]

Larry Summers took a different tack. According to several accounts, he told Born in a phone call that he had thirteen bankers in his office arguing that her proposal would cause the worst financial crisis since World War II. According to *The Washington Post* and other accounts, Summers argued that Born's proposal would cast "a shadow of regulatory uncertainty over an otherwise thriving market." He was not simply miming the Greenspan–Rubin–Levitt argument that less regulation of the OTC derivatives markets would be better. He was making a different point, in effect, arguing that the OTC derivatives market was already so big and so systemically important that simply recognizing the extreme opacity of the market could cause a catastrophe. At some level, he was saying, if you pile unstable dynamite near a population center and then tell people in the area to stop playing with matches, this is dangerous. It is dangerous because it will signal that the pile of dynamite is potentially unstable, which could start a panicked evacuation that might itself trigger a dynamite explosion. In essence, Summers was arguing that it was better to allow the pile of OTC derivatives to keep expanding—which it did, from about $25 trillion in 1996 to over $500 trillion in 2006—because publicly acknowledging the opacity of the market risked introducing fears that might disrupt the growth, and hence the stability, of the market.

The lines were drawn: Born wanted improved regulatory-enforced transparency of the over-the-counter derivatives market, while Greenspan, Rubin, Levitt, and Summers did not.

In 1998, the huge hedge fund Long-Term Capital Management (LTCM) blew up, in part because of its highly levered exposure to OTC derivatives. John Merriwether, who had been a bond trader at Salomon Brothers, and two finance-gurus, Myron Scholes and Robert C. Merton, who would both win Nobel Prizes in 1997, had founded LTCM in 1994. David Mullins had resigned as a governor of the Federal Reserve to join LTCM as a partner. The hedge fund had phenomenal success for several years, even though investors had little idea what it was doing. "LTCM did business with 15 of Wall Street's biggest banks, leveraging $5 billion into more than $1 trillion in derivatives."[28] LTCM was huge, it was connected, and it was failing by 1998. But nobody, including the Federal Reserve, had an accurate picture of which financial institutions were exposed to LTCM. The Treasury, Fed, SEC, and CFTC simply could not compute the ramifications of an LTCM bankruptcy for the financial system and the overall economy. "Born warned the House Banking Committee: 'This episode should serve as a wake-up call about the unknown risks that the over-the-counter derivatives market may pose to the US economy and to financial stability around the world.'"[29]

When ideology confronted the reality of a systemic meltdown, the Fed put ideology on hold. On September 22 and 23, 1998, the Fed encouraged fourteen private banks to contribute almost $4 billion to rescue LTCM. The banks yielded. It has hard for them to say no to the chief Guardian of Finance, the creator of money, and the ultimate systemic risk overseer who might decide the fate of their financial institutions in some future crisis. The LTCM affair strengthened the communal bonds and informal, mutual obligations between the Fed and the major banks; interestingly, only Bear Stearns refused to participate in the LTCM rescue, and it was one of two investment banks allowed to fail ten years later.

With the LTCM crisis solved, the Guardians again embraced ideology and pushed Brooksley Born aside. Rubin, Greenspan, Levitt, and Summers convinced Congress that regulating the OTC derivatives market would be counterproductive. Born left her position at the CFTC.[30] A year or so later, in 2000, Congress passed the Commodity Futures Modernization Act, which exempted the OTC derivatives market, and hence the CDS market, from government oversight.

Senior regulators and policy makers lobbied hard to keep the markets opaque for credit default swaps and other derivatives. This policy was not an accident; it was a choice, a hard-won choice. The Fed, Treasury, and SEC waged a vicious fight to keep the market dark. The Guardians won, and the public lost. Arthur Levitt is the only member of the group to have admitted that Born was right.

The SEC: See Nothing, Know Nothing, Do Nothing[31]

We have a good deal of comfort about the capital cushions at these firms at the moment.
—Christopher Cox, SEC chairman, March 11, 2008.[32]

On March 14, 2008, only three days after the chairman of the Securities and Exchange Commission—the chief regulator of securities markets, including investment banks, brokers and dealers, and mutual funds—expressed confidence in the financial soundness of the major investment banks, the New York Federal Reserve provided an emergency $25 billion loan to Bear Stearns in a vain attempt to avert its collapse. A few days later, with additional financial assistance from the Fed, a failed Bear Stearns merged with the commercial bank JP Morgan Chase. Within six months, Lehman Brothers had gone bankrupt, and a few months later, Merrill Lynch, on the brink of insolvency, merged with Bank of America. Also in the fall of 2008, the Federal Reserve allowed and according to some encouraged Goldman Sachs and Morgan Stanley into becoming bank holding companies, arguably rescuing them from failure through an assortment of public assistance programs, including access to the Fed's lending window for commercial banks.

The SEC's fingerprints are indelibly imprinted on this debacle. Four years earlier, the SEC had essentially exempted the broker-dealer subsidiaries of the five largest investment banks from using the traditional method for computing capital to satisfy the net capital rule, which was a 1975 rule for determining the minimum capital standards at broker-dealers. As SEC commissioners debated the exemption policy in 2004, they noted that it could lead to a "potential catastrophe" and questioned whether "we really will have investor protection." Yet they ultimately voted for it, with one commissioner noting, he would keep his fingers crossed.[33] As a result of the exemption, investment banks were permitted to use their own mathematical models of asset and portfolio risk to compute appropriate capital levels. They responded, naturally by issuing more debt to purchase more risky securities without putting commensurately more of their own capital at risk. Leverage ratios soared from previous levels as the banks' own models indicated that they had sufficient capital cushions to expand assets. Higher leverage allowed the investment banks to earn larger profits in the short-run, justifying large bonuses.[34]

In its defense, the SEC has correctly argued that the new capital rule never applied to the holding company, but rather only to the broker-dealer affiliate of the investment bank. But this argument, while apparently legally accurate, misses the broader context in which the net capital rule was reinterpreted. The SEC implemented a combination of policies in 2004 that dramatically increased financial system fragility.

In a second and much more important policy change in 2004, the SEC implemented reforms that induced the five major investment banks to become "consolidated supervised entities" (CSEs), meaning that the SEC would oversee the entire financial firm. Specifically, the SEC now had responsibility for supervising the holding company, the broker-dealer affiliates, and all other affiliates on a consolidated basis.[35] These other affiliates included other regulated entities, such as foreign-registered broker-dealers and banks, as well as unregulated entities, such as derivatives dealers. The SEC was charged with evaluating the models employed by the broker-dealers in computing appropriate capital levels and assessing the overall stability of the consolidated investment bank. Given the size and complexity of these financial conglomerates, overseeing the CSEs was a systemically important and yet difficult responsibility.

The SEC created the consolidated supervised entity program because the investment banks requested it. The major US investment banks had lobbied the commission to create the program because they didn't want to be regulated and supervised by the European Union. The EU Conglomerate Directive required that affiliates of US registered broker-dealers, in order to do business in the European Union, demonstrate that they were subject to consolidated supervision by a US regulator. If they couldn't, they would be forced to operate under EU regulatory and supervisory guidelines. To accommodate the investment banks and not lose supervisory authority over these globally important financial institutions, the SEC created the CSE program and made its capital and supervisory requirements less onerous than those of the European option.[36]

Third, and most important, the SEC eviscerated its ability to conduct consolidated supervision of the major investment banks at just the wrong moment. After the effective dismantling of the net capital rule and the added complexity of consolidated supervision, the SEC needed to increase its ability to assess the riskiness of investment banking activities. Indeed Annette L. Nazareth, the head of market regulation, reassured the commission that under the new rules, the companies for the first time could be restricted by the commission from excessively risky activity.[37] But the SEC never developed the capacity to do so. The commission had in fact only seven people available to examine the parent companies of the investment banks, which controlled over $4 trillion in assets.[38]

Under Christopher Cox, who became chairman in 2005, the SEC weakened its ability to assess the risk of investment banks and enforce its own rules and regulations. The SEC eliminated its risk management office and did not undertake a single inspection of a major investment bank in the year and a half before the collapse of those banks.[39] Cox also weakened the Enforcement Division's freedom to impose fines on financial firms under its jurisdiction. "Former senior enforcement officials say Cox has used his control over the commission's calendar to delay major cases and water down others," noted one critic.[40] Inspectors grew discouraged. "The perceived absence of support for major investigations has alienated many staff members and prompted some of the enforcement division's senior officials to quit."[41] As summarized in congressional testimony from the Government Accounting Office, "According to many investigative attorneys, the penalty policies contributed to an adversarial relationship between Enforcement and the Commission, where some investigative attorneys came to see the Commission less as an ally and instead more as a barrier to bringing enforcement actions."[42] The SEC under Cox reduced the fines it collected from $1.5 billion in 2005 to about $500 million in 2007.[43]

A report from the SEC's own Office of Inspector General noted in 2008 that even when the commission found problems, it did not act.[44] For example, the inspector general found that that the Division of Trading and Markets "became aware of numerous potential red flags prior to Bear Stearns' collapse, regarding its concentration of mortgage securities, high leverage, shortcomings of risk management in mortgage-backed securities and lack of compliance consistent with the spirit of certain Basel II standards, but did not take action to limit these risk factors."[45] Continuing, the report emphasized that the Trading and Markets Division in 2006 "identified precisely the types of risks that evolved into the subprime crisis in the U.S."[46] Yet the SEC did not use its power over the investment banks to induce them to reduce these systemic risks. Furthermore the court-appointed investigator of the causes of the Lehman Brothers bankruptcy reached a similarly harsh conclusion: The report, from Anton Valukas, noted that (1) Lehman regularly exceeded its own risk limits, and (2) the SEC knew about these excesses and yet did nothing.[47]

Perhaps even more important than ignoring excessive risk-taking, the SEC publicly argued that it was doing an effective job of supervising the large investment banks (or, as they were by then known, the consolidated supervised entities). In stunning testimony before the US House of Representatives Financial Services Committee on April 25, 2007, the SEC's deputy director claimed that the SEC was successfully supervising the major investment banks and there was consequently no need to pass new laws to help in this regard:

The bill as introduced would subject the CSEs that already are highly regulated under the Commission's consolidated supervision program to an additional layer of duplicative and burdensome holding company oversight. The bill should be amended to recognize the unique ability of the Commission to comprehensively supervise the consolidated groups . . .. Because the Commission has established a successful consolidated supervision program based on its unique expertise.

The SEC's public assertion that it was doing an exemplary job of supervising the major investment banks was particularly dangerous because it reduced the incentives of private investors to scrutinize those investment banks before purchasing their securities. By informing private markets that (1) the SEC was overseeing investment banks and (2) the investment banks were sound, the SEC effectively gave its approval to purchase the banks' securities. This also made it much easier for investment banks to sell debt instruments to private investors and become even more leveraged, and thus more fragile. The SEC's stamp of approval also boosted the stock prices of investment banks, adding to the bonuses and wealth of their executives. The reliance on SEC's policies reduced market monitoring of the investment banks, which helps explain why investors allowed, and indeed fueled, the banks' increasingly risky investments and fragile balance sheets.

A short eighteen months after the SEC argued that it was successfully supervising the five major investment banks, every single one of them had either gone bankrupt, failed and merged with other firms, or was forced to convert to a bank holding company, with billions of taxpayer dollars spent on facilitating these arrangements.

While the SEC used its discretionary power to eliminate supervisory guardrails, it simultaneously told the markets that it was effectively overseeing the major investment banks. That is, while the SEC reduced the incentives of private markets to monitor the major banks by assuring markets and Congress that it was overseeing the banks, the SEC actually decided not to supervise them adequately. This extraordinarily reckless, indeed negligent, behavior weakened both private and official monitoring of the investment banks. The death of major investment banks was no "accident," by any reasonable definition of the term. The SEC created an environment in which excessive risk taking was the natural result. The Guardians of Finance were supposed to work for the public and failed in this task.

The SEC's performance during the years before the crisis begs caricature. Under Cox, the commission seemed to see nothing and know nothing. If it stumbled upon something that should have been viewed as troublesome, it made sure to do nothing. All the while, it was sending out staff to tell elected officials that it was effectively supervising the major investment banks. Even though it acted without malice, the SEC helped push the financial system to the edge of, and then over, the precipice.

Why did the SEC choose to not supervise the consolidated supervised entities effectively? Why did it choose not to enforce the law? Why did it not respond to growing signs of fragility among securities firms?

One view is that Cox and the SEC behaved incompetently. In his book *In Fed We Trust*, David Wessel describes a telephone call in which decisions were being made about the future of Bear Stearns[48]:

The SEC was legally Bear Stearns's chief regulator, but Cox, its chairman, wasn't on the call. Apparently, he wasn't missed. Top officials at both the Fed and the Treasury had decided the SEC and its chairman weren't up to the job of coping with the collapse of an investment bank. Cox was largely a bystander.

In another example, Andrew Ross Sorkin in *Too Big to Fail* explains that private financiers also showed little respect for Cox during meetings at the New York Federal Reserve Bank regarding the meltdown of Lehman Brothers.

Christopher Cox, as impeccably dressed and coifed as ever, made a brief statement, telling everyone in the room that they were "great Americans" and impressing upon them "the patriotic duty they were undertaking." Most of the bankers in the room rolled their eyes at the sentiment, as they regarded Cox as a lightweight and would later describe him as "cryogenically frozen."

We doubt that mere incompetence explains why the SEC deliberately dismantled its ability to monitor complex investment banks. Incompetence does not explain satisfactorily why the SEC disrupted the ability of its enforcement division to identify violations and penalize violators. We do not believe that incompetence explains why the SEC did not respond when it uncovered evidence that the investment banks were taking excessive risks that threatened the stability of the financial system.

Although many factors might have been at play, it seems likely that Cox competently implemented a flawed ideology. Like Greenspan at the Fed, Cox was a follower of Ayn Rand.[49] Like Greenspan, Cox too often pushed for deregulation at the SEC without fully appreciating the complex incentive effects associated with changing regulations: (1) that removing one regulation in the presence of many will not necessarily improve the effectiveness of markets, (2) that financial institutions with little owner-contributed equity capital will respond powerfully to policies that induce them to take excessive risk, and (3) that financial institutions and markets will reduce their monitoring of investment banks if the SEC publicly asserts that it is monitoring them, and adds that they are in good financial shape.

The SEC's current chair, Mary Schapiro, agrees:

I think everybody a few years ago got caught up in the idea that the markets are self-correcting and self-disciplined, and that the people in Wall Street will do a better job protecting the financial system than the regulators would. We do think the SEC got diverted by that philosophy.[50]

While it is encouraging that Schapiro has identified the key ideological failures of her predecessor, this is not enough. To create a more robust and effective financial regulatory system, we need to reform the institutional environment so that it is possible to challenge the prevailing ideology—while decisions are being made, not after suffering a global financial crisis with enduring detrimental effects on human welfare. We need to create an institution that can assess financial regulatory policies more objectively than the regulatory agencies that are involved in the day-to-day supervisory processes. We need an institution in which the revolving door between regulated, regulator, and lobbyist spins less often and less rapidly.

The Credit-Rating Agencies: The SEC, Congress, and Everyone Else

These errors make us look either incompetent at credit analysis or like we sold our soul to the devil for revenue, or a little bit of both.
—A Moody's managing director responding anonymously to an internal management survey, September 2007.[51]

But it didn't require any sort of genius to see the fortune to be had from the laundering of triple-B-rated bonds into triple-A-rated bonds.
—Michael Lewis in *The Big Short*

Credit-rating agencies played an indispensable role in the crisis. If structured finance could be seen as a long canal, running from issuer to purchaser, then the ratings agencies oversaw the system of locks through which all the crazy securities flowed so easily and profitably—for bankers and raters alike.

To appreciate the role of the rating agencies, consider the following sequence of transactions underlying the vast misallocation of global credit: Mortgage companies routinely provided loans to borrowers who had little ability to repay those debts because (1) the mortgage companies earned fees for each loan and (2) they could sell those loans to investment banks and other financial institutions. The investment banks and other financial institutions gobbled up those mortgages because (1) they earned fees for packaging the mortgages into new securities and (2) they could sell those new mortgage-backed securities (MBSs) around the world to other financial institutions, including other banks, insurance companies, and pension funds. These other financial institutions bought the MBSs in part because credit-rating agencies said the securities were safe and the managers of these other financial institutions were being paid high bonuses for buying high-return securities as long as the credit-rating agencies said the securities were safe, regardless of their actual risk. By fueling the demand for MBSs and related securities, credit-rating agencies encouraged a broad array of financial institutions to make the poor investments that ultimately helped topple the global financial system. Thus an informed postmortem of the financial system requires a dissection of how financial institutions relied unquestioningly on the assessments of credit-rating agencies.

How did these agencies become so pivotal? Until the 1970s credit-rating agencies were comparatively insignificant, moribund institutions that sold their assessments of credit risk to subscribers. Given their poor predictive performance, the demand for their services was limited for much of the twentieth century.

Once again, the answer lies with the Guardians of Finance, especially the SEC, which created a climate in which it is virtually impossible for a firm to issue a security without first purchasing a rating.[52] In 1975 the SEC created the Nationally Recognized Statistical Rating Organization (NRSRO) designation, which it granted to the largest credit-rating agencies. The SEC then relied on the NRSROs to assess credit risk and thereby to help establish capital requirements on SEC-regulated financial institutions.

In creating and relying on the NRSROs, without any effective oversight of the ratings process, the SEC and a cascade of regulatory decisions increased the demand for credit ratings. Bank regulators, insurance regulators, federal, state, and local agencies (as well as foundations, endowments, and numerous entities around the world) either started, or intensified, their use of credit-rating agencies to establish capital adequacy and portfolio requirements.[53] Virtually all the Guardians of Finance from all corners of the globe now rely on NRSROs in assessing the risk of financial securities. The Basel Committee on Bank Supervision, which sets standards for the "advanced" countries' approach to regulation, allowed banks to hold less capital against highly rated securities, which helped stimulate the market demand for highly rated securities—and the ratings agencies helped make sure that there was an ample supply to meet this demand.

Private endowments, foundations, and mutual funds used NRSRO ratings in setting asset allocation guidelines for their investment managers. NRSRO ratings shaped investment opportunities and capital requirements, and hence the profits of insurance companies, pension funds, and a dizzying array of other financial institutions. If the NRSRO ratings were good enough for the SEC and the Fed, they were good enough for banks, pension funds, insurance companies, endowments, and foundations. The NRSROs became gatekeepers, and their pivotal (and profitable) positions were created and protected by official regulators.

So we shouldn't be surprised to learn that NRSROs shifted from selling credit ratings to their subscribers to selling ratings to the issuers of securities. Since regulators, official agencies, and private institutions typically required NRSRO ratings, virtually every issuer of securities was compelled to purchase one, and under the SEC licensing procedures and market conditions, an oligopoly emerged. Three agencies—Moody's, Standard & Poor's, and Fitch—controlled about 90 to 95 percent of the world market for rating securities.

Frank Partnoy, a professor at the University of San Diego School of Law, has characterized the NRSROs as organizations that essentially sell licenses (their ratings) to firms to issue bonds, equities, asset-backed securities, and other financial products; they do not primarily provide valuable assessments of credit risk.

Clear conflicts of interest are associated with the sale of NRSRO ratings to the issuers of securities: the issuers have an interest in paying more for better ratings, since those ratings influence the demand for (and pricing of) their securities. And NRSROs can promote repeat business by providing higher ratings. In this context it is interesting to note a 1957 statement by one of Moody's vice presidents. "We obviously cannot ask payment for rating a bond," he said. "To do so would attach a price to the process, and we could not escape the charge, which would undoubtedly come, that our ratings are for sale."[54]

Nevertheless, credit-rating agencies convinced their regulator, the SEC, that their own reputational capital—their standing in the financial community—would reduce the incentive to sell ratings. If an agency failed to provide sound, objective assessments, it would eventually suffer. The "burned" purchasers would stop relying on the agency's ratings, and issuers would turn to another agency for more accurate rating services. Reputational capital will reduce conflicts of interest—but only under particular conditions. The demand for securities must respond sufficiently to poor agency performance in order to constrain the agency from issuing bloated ratings.

But these conditions didn't hold, for two reasons. First, regulations weakened the degree to which a decline in a NRSROs reputation reduced the demand for its services. Regulations maintained instead a strong demand for NRSRO ratings, regardless of NRSRO performance. Second, and crucial to this discussion, there was a financial innovation in the early 1970s—securitization—which eventually exploded in terms of size, growth, and profitability and dramatically changed incentives for executives in the rating agencies. Selling bloated ratings might damage an agency's long-term reputation, but in the short term the money coming in, in the form of profits and bonuses, could seemingly make inflating the ratings a no-brainer. Securitized and structured financial products, worth trillions of dollars, were packaged and rated, and enormous fees associated with these processes flowed to banks and NRSROs. Impediments, such as the issuance of too many low credit ratings on the securities, could gum up the system, reducing agency profits and executive bonuses. We saw in the last chapter how ratings agencies used incentive pay and the threat of removal to induce their employees to produce a large supply of highly rated securities.

The NRSROs began in fact to offer ancillary consulting services to the banks to facilitate the processing of their securitized instruments, increasing NRSRO incentives to exaggerate ratings on structured products. The banks were now paying twice: first for guidance on how best to package their securities to obtain higher ratings, and then for the higher ratings themselves.

In an extensive article in *The New York Times Magazine*, Roger Lowenstein described the rating of a mortgage-backed security by Moody's.[55] The article demonstrates the speed with which complex products had to be rated, the poor assumptions on which those ratings were based, and the profits generated by rating structured products. Other information indicated that if, for example, the agency issued a lower rating than Countrywide (a major purchaser of NRSRO ratings) wanted, a few phone calls would solve the problem.[56] Internal emails indicate that NRSROs lowered their rating standards to expand their business and boost revenues. A Standard & Poor's employee noted in 2004:[57]

We are meeting with your group this week to discuss adjusting criteria for rating C.D.O.s of real estate assets this week because of the ongoing threat of losing deals. Lose the C.D.O. and lose the base business—a self-reinforcing loop.

A collection of documents released by the US Senate in April 2010 also demonstrates that NRSROs consciously adjusted their ratings to maintain clients and attract new ones (see chapter 3 for some testimonial evidence).[58] The short-term profits from these activities were mind-bogglingly large. The operating margin, which is a measure of firm profits on each dollar of sales, at Moody's averaged 53 percent between 2000 and 2007. This compares to operating margins of 36 and 30 percent at Microsoft and Google, or 17 percent at Exxon.

The NRSROs faced little market discipline, had no significant regulatory oversight, were protected from competition by regulators, and enjoyed a burgeoning market for their services, as long as they kept the ratings of structured products high—as long as they kept the locks open along the securitization canal and the securities moved rapidly through. In *The Big Short*, Michael Lewis observes:[59]

To judge from their behavior, all the rating agencies worried about was maximizing the number of deals they rated for Wall Street investment banks, and the fees they collected from them. Moody's, once a private company, had gone public in 2000. Since then its revenues had boomed, from $800 million in 2001 to $2.03 billion in 2006. Some huge percentage of the increase . . . flowed from the arcane end of the home finance sector, known as structured finance.

Where was the SEC? It had been charged with licensing and overseeing the NRSROs. Indeed the 2006 Credit Rating Agency Reform Act specifically charged the SEC with guarding against conflicts of interest at the NRSROs. The SEC had enjoyed broad supervisory powers long before the 2006 Act.

But it is not only the SEC's fault. Other regulatory agencies, in the United States and around the world, were complicit in allowing the same incentives percolating in the NRSROs to infect the global financial system. They too could see the incentives facing the rating agencies, the ballooning profits, and the academic literature that started warning in 1999 about the combustible mixture of the conflicts of interest and the growth of securitized and structured products.

The regulatory agencies knew about the deteriorating incentives driving the NRSROs but did not adapt to take corrective action.[60] The SEC, which had been discussing the conflicts associated with issuers paying for ratings in the mid-1990s, brought up the topic again in the early 2000s. The SEC publicly documented the intensification of conflicts of interest associated with the NRSRO's selling of ancillary consulting services in the early 2000s. Law professor Frank Partnoy, in a famous 1999 article that came to be known as "Partnoy's Complaint" in financial regulatory circles, explained that the conflicts of interest would become particularly destructive as securitization and structured products boomed, and that the bad incentives in NRSROs would facilitate the unhealthy growth of these products.[61]

There was an uncomfortable similarity between the rise in conflicts of interest through the sales of ancillary consulting services among the NRSROs and the rise in conflicts of interests when accounting firms began to sell consulting work to the companies they were auditing. The corporate scandals that emerged from that crisis, less than a decade ago, motivated the Sarbanes–Oxley Act of 2002.[62] Yet no alarms went off for regulators, who didn't respond as the rating agencies pursued increasingly profitable lines of business. Again, the problem was not a lack of timely information. The problem was one of decision-making among policy makers.

It is impossible to imagine the current crisis without the activities of the NRSROs; and it is impossible to imagine the behavior of the NRSROs without the Guardians of Finance, who permitted and, through their discretionary actions, encouraged those activities. The conflicts of interest within the NRSROs have been known for decades and the further perversion of incentives due to securitization was predicted for years before the crisis. The decision makers at NRSROs made enormous amounts of money. What they did was logical, rational, and presumably legal. As noted in an internal email by an S&P employee, "Let's hope we are all wealthy and retired by the time this house of cards falters."[63]

The FDIC: People Are People

The Federal Deposit Insurance Corporation (FDIC) is a prominent member of the Guardians of Finance. The Glass–Steagall Act of 1933 created the FDIC in the wake of roughly 10,000 bank failures and millions of families losing their savings. The FDIC's mandate is to insure deposits in banks and to ensure the safety of those banks through supervision and regulation. The agency in 2011 was overseeing almost 8,000 banks that together were holding more than $13 trillion in assets. The FDIC is the primary supervisor of almost 5,000 financial institutions and the backup supervisor for about 3,000 more, in which the Fed or the Office of the Comptroller of the Currency (OCC) is the primary federal supervisor.[64] This way the FDIC directly or indirectly assesses the viability of all entities with insured deposits.

The FDIC has the authority to take corrective action against banks that do not satisfy its guidelines. It can penalize and even take away their insurance, and can maneuver several regulatory levers to persuade the banks to adjust their risk-taking. For example, it can force riskier banks to pay higher premiums for their deposit insurance, and if the risk premiums are priced correctly, this should (in theory) discourage excessive risk-taking. The FDIC can also raise a bank's capital requirements, which cushion against potential losses, and force it to either purchase additional safe securities or reduce the amount of borrowed funds it uses to make risky investments.

Not only does the FDIC have the power to take corrective action, it must by law do so when it discovers problems with the banks it insures. The 1991 FDIC Improvement Act was created to eliminate too much lenience being extended toward troubled, poorly capitalized institutions. It is natural for regulators to engage in regulatory forbearance: they are reluctant to close banks. But regulatory forbearance with banks has a disastrous history, including experiences from the US Savings and Loan Crisis of the 1980s, Japan's banking crisis of the 1990s, and other crises around the world. In each case, regulatory forbearance dramatically magnified the costs of the system's ultimate failure, and for well-understood reasons: undercapitalized banks have enormous incentives to gamble for resurrection. Their owners have little to lose since the bank is close to bankruptcy, if not already insolvent. So the best remaining option of the owners is to roll the dice with the bank's assets. If the gamble wins, the owners win; and if the gamble fails, the bank's owners lose no more than their capital, which may have already been nearly or completely lost anyway. Consequently the 1991 act mandates that the FDIC respond with increasingly stringent and prompt corrective action whenever a bank's capital falls below a series of predetermined levels or if the bank exhibits other traits that pose a significant risk of failure.

Yet the FDIC still failed to protect the nation's banking system from systemic failure, as documented in its own self-assessments, which are conducted, by law, whenever the agency has to pay depositors (directly or indirectly) because of a bank failure.[65] These Material Loss Reviews (MLRs) tell us when the FDIC actually saw growing risks in the banking industry and whether the FDIC now believes it responded appropriately to its own inspections.[66]

In the years before the crisis of 2007 to 2009, the FDIC was extremely good at identifying fragile banks. In 79 percent of the commercial banks that failed and that were included in the MLRs on the FDIC's website, agency inspectors had identified their excessive exposure to the real estate sector years before they actually failed.

A major issue raised in these reports is a lack of action. Although the MLRs discuss shortcomings with some FDIC inspections, more than 95 percent of them discuss shortcomings with FDIC supervision or note actions that FDIC officials could have or should have taken following their inspections. The FDIC consistently chose not to act, even after identifying problems in a bank. Typical comments in the reports note that examiners "did not always follow up on red flags during examinations" or that "certain management practices should have heightened examiner attention" or that "[f]or the most part, examiners identified the management deficiencies and brought their concerns to bank management," but "many of the deficient management practices continued until the bank's failure."[67] Again, and again, the MLRs indicate that the FDIC knew its member banks were issuing short-term, volatile securities to make long-term real estate loans. Again and again, the MLRs indicate that FDIC inspectors correctly recognized these risks but took no action. "Its often we'll see in our reports that the FDIC detected problems in the bank in a timely fashion," said the FDIC's inspector general in 2010, "but in some cases forceful corrective action wasn't required by the FDIC to be taken quickly enough."[68]

The MLRs also provide some glimpses into why the FDIC did not respond. There is no evidence of corruption or regulatory capture. There is no evidence of technical incompetence or political interference. Although there were occasional shortcomings in its inspections, the FDIC typically identified the major problems in banks years before they failed. In contrast to Federal Reserve and SEC decisions, ideology does not seem to have played much of a role at the FDIC. It is certainly possible that the general free-market approach biased FDIC officials toward allowing banks greater latitude in selecting more concentrated portfolios of real estate assets and more nontraditional forms of liabilities. But an extreme form of laissez faire regulation does not seem to have dominated FDIC decision-making.

Rather, the FDIC's failure seems to reflect a basic human reluctance to break cultural norms and rile communal ties. Furthermore ample evidence from psychology and behavioral economics indicates that humans judge errors of commission much more harshly than errors of omission. Thus FDIC regulators might have chosen to do nothing except write down their observations, rather than make an error of commission. The same is true in sports, as explained in *Scorecasting* by Tobias Moskowitz and

Jon Wertheim (see chapter 1). Referees are reluctant to decide the game by calling a penalty, so they would rather commit a potential error of omission and ignore a penalty at a key moment, especially if the oversight would help the home team. Indeed the MLRs frequently highlight precedent as an explanation for failing to act. The FDIC discovered new risks, but there was no precedent for taking action against them. In a changing, uncertain world many of us might have chosen not to act to correct emerging problems in a timely manner—especially if we were not accountable for the results.

To get a feel for how interpersonal relationships might have shaped the FDIC's response, imagine that you are an FDIC inspector. Following your examination, you determine that the bank has a dangerously high concentration of loans for commercial real estate purchases and for construction and development projects. Moreover you recognize that the bank is funding this asset mix less and less with household deposits, which have very predictable, stable withdrawal patterns, and more and more with commercial paper and other liabilities, which have less predictable and more volatile withdrawal patterns. You haven't seen these types of risks before, and neither has the FDIC. Yet you've watched this situation develop over many years and become increasingly convinced that the bank's stability is at serious risk.

As you sit down to talk with the bank's senior management team, you decide that now is the time for corrective action. Yes, the bank has grown spectacularly, generating healthy profits. True, the bank has helped fund the economic development of the community. Admittedly, the bank has received the FDIC stamp of approval each year, even as the riskiness of its balance sheet has grown. But your concern is the growing fragility of the bank and your inspection report reflects that concern. This time you have to make the case to the bank's management and impose compulsory actions to reduce the bank's risk of failure.

Your presentation ignites a firestorm of protest. The bankers correctly argue that the FDIC has never taken corrective action for these issues before; this is unprecedented. They want to know how you can take extraordinarily invasive actions when the bank is so profitable. They note that you and other regulators have witnessed the prospering of these particular lines of business over many years, and that all of you never objected. They correctly explain that curtailing these activities now will disrupt the flow of capital, reduce investment, and slow economic growth, and—critically—it will make the bank more fragile, not more stable, by slashing its profits. The bankers complain, with enough veracity to make you uncomfortable, that you and the FDIC are making up new rules and stymieing economic progress, and that you have never actually run a business or managed a bank.

This barrage of arguments would lead most of us to question our decision. It might lead us both to remain true to our analyses by detailing our concerns in the inspection report and to refrain from imposing compulsory actions or sanctions on the bank. This quintessentially human compromise—maintaining personal integrity by the drafting of a sound report while hoping to maintain communal harmony by not antagonizing professional counterparts—is understandable. Besides, there is no real penalty imposed on regulators for going along or engaging in forbearance. This situation also means that we must build a financial regulatory apparatus that recognizes these human frailties and strives to reduce their adverse effects on financial policy. It means building better institutions that work for us.

Failures at the FDIC relate to the accident narrative. A dynamic, innovating financial system and a static, un-adapting regulatory regime created an environment in which the old supervisory rules no longer maintained a safe and sound banking system. While financial institutions developed new products and exposed themselves to new risks, the regulatory regime was unwilling to adapt to these changing conditions to maintain a secure, well-functioning financial sector. The FDIC did not adapt, even though it correctly identified problems and even though it had the power and obligation to respond. The Guardians of Finance effectively stood by and watched as the system steadily headed into collapse.

Fannie Mae and Freddie Mac

Background

The government, through the Federal Housing Finance Agency, placed into conservatorship both the Federal National Mortgage Association (Fannie Mae) and the Federal Home Loan Mortgage Corporation (Freddie Mac) on September 7, 2008. Together, these two regulated housing-finance giants owned or guaranteed almost $7 trillion worth of mortgages. Fannie

Mae and Freddie Mac are congressionally chartered, stockholder-owned corporations.

These government-sponsored entities (GSEs) were designed to facilitate housing finance. They purchase mortgages from banks and mortgage companies that lend directly to homeowners, package the mortgages into mortgage-backed securities (MBSs), guarantee timely payment of interest and principal, and sell the MBSs to investors around the world. Besides this core securitization activity, the GSEs also buy and hold mortgages and MBSs. By increasing the demand for, and hence the price of, mortgages in the secondary market, the GSEs can reduce the interest rates that homebuyers pay on mortgages in the primary market, thereby fostering greater homeownership.

While facilitating housing finance is a raison d'être, the GSEs also use their privileged positions to earn substantial profits. Specifically, the GSEs borrow cheaply: the debt issued by these two financial institutions enjoyed an implicit federal government guarantee, which was made explicit when their regulator placed them into conservatorship in September 2008. Thus the GSEs could borrow at low interest rates and buy mortgages with higher interest rates. Over time the GSEs increased the degree to which they bought and held mortgages relative to their securitization role, by which they bought, packaged, guaranteed, and sold MBSs. As long as there were not too many mortgage defaults, the GSEs made enormous profits. Indeed profits were limited primarily by the size of the mortgage market and threatened by any regulatory intervention that might curtail growth of the GSEs, with a concomitant lowering of GSE profits. Fortunately for the GSEs, Congress and other policy makers helped expand the mortgage market and kept regulatory interventions limiting growth through high leverage to a minimum.

Policy Changes, the GSEs, and the Effects

Two policies combined to expand the mortgage market for GSEs: the expansion of the affordable housing mission of GSEs and the Community Reinvestment Act (CRA) as discussed in Barth et al. (2009), Joint Center for Housing Studies (2008), and Wallison and Calomiris (2008). Enacted in 1977, the CRA was designed to boost lending to disadvantaged areas by prohibiting discrimination. In the mid-1990s, under the CRA, regulators started using quantitative guidelines to induce greater lending to low- and moderate-income (LMI) areas and borrowers. The Department of Housing and Urban Development (HUD) in the mid-1990s put corresponding pressure on the GSEs to adjust their financing standards to facilitate the flow of credit to LMI borrowers, thereby encouraging the GSEs to finance lower quality mortgages. Furthermore Congress also added an affordable housing mission to the GSEs. In 1991, Fannie Mae announced a $1 trillion affordable housing initiative, and in 1994, Fannie Mae and Freddie Mac initiated an additional $2 trillion program for LMI borrowers.

These policies permitted and encouraged the GSEs to accept lower quality mortgages and hence spurred primary market lenders to lend more to more suspect borrowers. For example, by 2001, the GSEs were purchasing mortgages that had no down payment; between 2005 and 2007, they bought approximately $1 trillion of mortgages with subprime characteristics, which accounted for about 40 percent of their mortgage purchases.[69] By signaling to mortgage lenders that they would purchase mortgages with subprime characteristics—such as mortgages with low FICO credit scores, high loan-to-value ratios, negative amortization, low documentation—Fannie and Freddie triggered a massive movement into the issuance of lower quality mortgages. Mortgage companies were more willing to accept the fees for making loans to questionable borrowers if they knew that the GSEs would purchase the loans later.

The push into lower quality mortgages created a complex "mutual dependency" between Congress and the GSEs, fueling their increasingly risky investments (Wallison and Calomiris 2008). Congress relied on the GSEs to both promote housing policies and to provide campaign donations. The GSEs relied on Congress to protect their profitable privileges and help contain regulatory interventions. Each party satisfied its side of the bargain. The GSEs provided generous campaign contributions and greatly expanded their funding of LMI borrowers. Profits and bonuses soared. In turn policy makers limited regulatory oversight of the GSEs. Even after the House Banking Subcommittee and the GSE's regulator (the Office of Federal Housing Enterprise Oversight, or OFHEO, at the time) accused them of accounting deficiencies in 2000, 2003, and 2004 and even as evidence emerged of their financial fragility, Congress did not pass a proposed bill that would have strengthened supervision of the GSEs and prohibited the GSEs from buying and holding MBSs. Such a policy shift would have limited GSE exposure to the low-quality mortgages that ultimately led to their conservatorship. However, OFHEO did increase the capital requirements modestly for the GSEs in 2004 and subsequently imposed growth restrictions, but only for on-balance sheet assets, on them in 2006. As the housing meltdown worsened, OFEHO allowed the GSEs greater flexibility to manage their portfolios so as to help some subprime borrowers avoid foreclosure in 2007. It then removed the growth restrictions entirely in March 2008 as the downward spiral in housing continued. The flip-flop in regulatory actions demonstrates the problem with creating institutions that are designed both to earn profits and to support affordable housing.

A Postmortem of the GSEs

Deterioration in the financial condition of the GSEs was not a surprise. *The New York Times* warned in 1999 that Fannie Mae was taking on so much risk that an economic downturn could trigger a "rescue similar to that of the savings and loan industry in the 1980s," and again emphasized this point in 2003.[70] From 2003 through 2007 the GSE's regulator warned of excessive risk-taking, the Treasury acknowledged ineffective oversight of the GSEs, Congress discussed the fragility of GSEs and their illusory profits, Alan Greenspan testified before the Senate Banking Committee in 2004 that the increasingly large and risky GSE portfolios could have enormously adverse ramifications, and Taleb (2007) warned that the GSEs "seem to be sitting on a barrel of dynamite, vulnerable to the slightest hiccup."[71]

Congress did not respond to warnings, including warnings from the Guardians of Finance, and instead allowed increasingly fragile GSEs to endanger the entire financial system. It is difficult to discern exactly why. Some elected officials did not want to jeopardize their role in supporting more affordable housing for a broader segment of the population. Some received generous campaign contributions from the GSEs. Rather than reflecting a failure of the major regulatory authorities, the long history of the GSEs highlights failures with the legislative process, which did not respond to take corrective action as the GSEs became ever more systemically fragile.

Some Final Remarks

This chapter has a simple message: Senior US policy makers and regulators endangered the stability of the US economy in the decade before the crisis of 2007 to 2009. Some of the major policy and regulatory decisions that helped cause the financial crisis were not only the result of ignorance or impotence. They were not simply the result of complex financial innovations. Rather, systemic institutional failures caused the repeated selection and maintenance of bad policies over time.

Treating the crisis as reflecting only a series of unfortunate, unforeseeable, and unstoppable events misses essential elements of the crisis. Such a narrow focus also prevents a thorough assessment of what went wrong, which thwarts the development plan for fixing the system for selecting, evaluating, and modifying financial sector policies and regulations on an ongoing basis.

This chapter also suggests some of the problems with the US regulatory system. It is impossible for the public and its elected officials to obtain on a timely basis an informed, expert assessment of financial policies and regulation, which means the public and its representatives are unable to shape financial policies in the best interest of the people. If the public does not know what is going on in terms of financial regulation, they cannot pressure their representatives about what to do. If the public and its representatives cannot assess the impact of regulations and supervisory policies, then they cannot have an intelligent debate about changing those regulations and policies. As things stand now, the Federal Reserve in particular but also the SEC, FDIC, and other regulatory agencies have too great a control over information and expertise as well as control over what is released to the public and when the information is released. No authoritative entity acting purely on behalf of the public had the information and expertise to challenge the Federal Reserve on its policies that allowed banks to reduce their capital through the use of credit default swaps. No such entity had the information and expertise to challenge the SEC's claim that it was effectively monitoring the major investment banks while simultaneously reducing its ability to do so. No such entity had the information and expertise to challenge the FDIC's decision not to implement its own rules with respect to acting promptly to correct weaknesses in the banks it was inspecting. While many were suspicious about the financial health of Fannie Mae and Freddie Mac, the Secretary of the Treasury kept informing the public that they were sound. No public entity had the information and expertise to challenge these pronouncements. No private entity can effectively challenge the decisions of the Guardians of Finance because the Guardians have control over financial and regulatory information and expertise. No person or entity can meaningfully question their decisions and actions. Giving such discretionary regulatory power to unelected and unaccountable officials is both undemocratic and economically dangerous. Even in professional US football, coaches have the opportunity to question a referee's actions or lack of actions through replay. This provides a check and balance on the actions of referees. But no such checks and balances currently exist for our far more important financial referees.

5

American Crisis? Ain't Necessarily So

It ain't necessarily so
It ain't necessarily so
De things dat yo' liable to read in de Bible
It ain't necessarily so
—George and Ira Gershwin, *Porgy and Bess*

The predominant view of the global financial crisis that began in 2007 is that it originated in the United States, and that financial innovation and an array of complex financial products had a leading role in the drama. US monetary policy, the housing bubble, US subprime mortgages, complex financial securities, regulatory loopholes, the handling of the failure of Lehman Brothers, and the strong belief of a few regulators in the power of markets are all blamed for what became a crisis that spread globally and led to large-scale government interventions in numerous countries. This narrative is particularly convenient for regulators outside the US because it largely absolves them of blame for what happened in their own countries. Who, after all, could have predicted this perfect storm caused by all of these factors occurring at the same time? Who would have known that even the average price of US homes would fall when many said that this had never occurred (disregarding the fact that real housing prices declined in 40 percent of the past 130 years)? Who could have clearly seen through the complex array of financial products to realize that the financial system was heading over a cliff? Who would have thought that US regulators would not have taken sufficient action to prevent such a severe crisis? This version of events suggests that regulatory reform is the solution to preventing future problems: introduce some tougher modifications in capital regulation, perhaps add some more stringent liquidity requirements, tighten up on mortgage lending, avoid the blatant mistakes of US regulation, above all keep financial products simple, and all will be well in the years ahead.

A good story, but it "ain't necessarily so." First, this crisis was not only "made in the USA." As already seen in chapter 3, the perversion of incentives was not limited to the US financial system; incentives clearly changed dramatically in a number of European countries as well, which helps explain not only which countries experienced a crisis but also why so many US securities found their way into European portfolios. As we will see below, the crises that affected so many countries were largely or entirely homegrown. Second, complex financial products were mostly absent or played a minor role in a number of crises around the world. And several countries with crises did not feature multiple regulators with banks innovating to take advantage of gaps in oversight between the different agencies, as argued by some to have been important in the US crisis.

In this chapter we review in some detail the crises in three countries, Ireland, the United Kingdom, and Iceland, which have in common that their crises' fiscal costs are estimated to be *well above* those in the US case. Most important, investigations into the events in these countries have revealed information that is often ignored in discussions of regulatory reform, critical information that suggests that regulators had ample warnings to take action but did not. We also comment briefly on the crises in Spain and eastern European countries, where the weaknesses that led to their severe difficulties were every bit as easy to spot early on as those in the other countries that we examine in more detail. What all of these crises had in common with that in the United States is that a number of banks started "going for asset growth" at almost any cost, and, most of all, regulators ignored warning signs that are not just evident in retrospect but that any student with a passing grade in Banking 101 would have been able to spot in the years leading up to the crisis.

This chapter is important because it undercuts some influential views of the causes of the crises. Novel financial instruments—and the American crisis itself—do not explain the crises in other countries. According to official reports in each country, they would have occurred without the US crisis. The common factor in each of the crises was instead regulatory inaction. This means that any proposed solution must confront the crucial and central issue: how to get regulators to act in societies' best interest. To return to the sports analogy of chapter 1, how can one ensure that officials are working for us and not biased by the home crowd, the bankers? Some might also regard regulatory failure in so many different countries as evidence that regulation is an impossible task, and therefore that dramatic restrictions need to be imposed on banks. As we show, where crises resulted from astronomical growth of banks' balance sheets, it does not take a rocket scientist, or even the most experienced bank supervisor, to realize that risks must also be rising rapidly and should therefore be capped. Moreover not all countries that experienced a slowing in their growth rate or even a recession suffered a financial crisis; most countries did not. Canada and Australia survived the crisis quite well. Thus we conclude this chapter by discussing the characteristics of some of the financial regulatory systems that weathered the most recent storm successfully.

The Luck of the Irish

Ireland has had a sad history—occupation by the British for over 300 years after hundreds of years of invasions by the Vikings and others, the Potato Famine of the 1840s that decimated its population by death and emigration, and continuing emigration of its youth in search of better opportunities abroad. Its population in 2010 is barely over two-thirds of the peak of 8.2 million attained in the 1840s. Thus many misunderstand the phrase "the luck of the Irish." More often it is intended to be ironic, given the astounding misfortunes of that country.

This tragic history makes the zeal with which its people embraced the Irish Economic Miracle of the 1980s and 1990s more understandable. Economic growth boomed (6 percent per year gains on average in real GDP from the late 1980s until 2007) and unemployment plummeted (from 16 percent in 1994 to 4 percent by 2000).[1] At last, some of the country's talented sons and daughters returned to the booming economy quickly dubbed the Celtic Tiger. Rising incomes meant increased demand for more and better housing. Then as membership in the European Monetary Union and the 1999 adoption of the euro approached, Irish interest rates converged to the much lower levels of France and Germany. As every homebuyer knows, lower interest rates translate either into a decrease in the monthly mortgage payment or an opportunity for the purchaser to pay more for a house. From the late 1995 to 2006 Irish housing prices in real terms soared by over 250 percent, compared with an 86 percent increase in US prices over roughly the same period. And Ireland saw a larger relative increase in the supply of housing than in any other country in Europe.

Although many believed that the wave of prosperity was permanent, a basic characteristic of all bubbles is that people seem to forget that prices of any asset cannot continue rising rapidly in perpetuity, or in other words, that "trees do not grow to the sky."[2] Even the head of a major Irish bank admitted to having advised his children to get into real estate before they would be unable to afford a house. This was in 2007, after the market, as we now know, had already turned downward. So in many respects the Irish crisis showed signs consistent with the suicide/accident view noted in chapter 1: greedy buyers, with a desire to get into the housing market to get rich, and greedy real estate developers and bankers with a desire to pay themselves great sums, came together to produce a bubble and in effect went off the cliff together.

Inevitably the massive boom did end, and both the property bubble and the banks that made real estate loans collapsed, along with the rest of the economy. Of the twenty-three countries classified in an IMF paper as having suffered a systemic or borderline financial crisis in 2007 to 2009, Ireland placed second, based on both the decline in real GDP (21 percent from the fourth quarter of 2007 to the third quarter of 2010) and in the increase in public debt to pay for the crisis (roughly three and four times, respectively, the corresponding measures of the crisis in the United States).[3] The jump in the official unemployment rate to over 14 percent by the fall of 2010, the tripling of youth unemployment, and the surge in emigration all paint a picture of economic despair. Due to the steep fiscal costs of the crisis, with sharp declines in tax revenue and increased unemployment compensation, in addition to the costs of covering the losses of banks, public-sector workers took 6 to 23 percent pay cuts in late 2009, yet the deficit still reached 32 percent of GDP in 2010 (from a position of small surpluses prior to the crisis). Further austerity measures are expected as this book goes to print.

When the crisis first hit in the fall of 2008, the Irish government argued that this dire situation was an accident. According to this view, the Irish were the unlucky victims of the mishandling of the US crisis, the accompanying jump in interest rates, and the vanishing of liquidity in international financial markets in the summer and fall of 2007, as rising defaults on US mortgages awoke international investors to the reality that the AAA ratings were wildly inaccurate. Then, when the investment bank Lehman Brothers was allowed to fail in the fall of 2008, financial markets around the world froze up and interest rates to all but the safest governments soared. It seemed to many that the American crisis spread via contagion to affect "innocent" bystanders, including the Irish financial system.

Nothing could be further from the truth: Not one, but two reports commissioned by Irish Finance Minister Brian Lenihan conclude that the Irish crisis was *entirely* homegrown, and while events in the United States and elsewhere might have influenced the timing, the blame for the crisis lies overwhelming in Ireland. Property developers and buyers on a run-away binge, bankers determined to grow their institutions at all costs, and regulators not doing their job were the essential parts of the Irish catastrophe.[4]

What is interesting about the Irish crisis is that financial innovation, securitization, and complicated financial products were absent, which should have made it easy for regulators to identify the growing fragility of the system. This crisis was in fact more akin to the US savings and loan disaster of the 1980s, in which the banks that originated many home loans continued to hold them on their balance sheets.

It was difficult *not* to see the crisis coming. First, the magnitude of the increase in home prices was breathtaking: by late 2006 buyers were paying on average 10 times their incomes nationwide, and 17 times income in Dublin, this compared with about 4 times earnings in the period up to the mid-1990s.[5] Second was the daunting pace of growth by the leading Irish banks. Anglo Irish Bank began in the late 1990s as the smallest of the top four banks (which accounted for over 90 percent of the assets of the banking system), then pushed the growth of its balance sheet at all costs, averaging close to a 40 percent *real* rate of expansion over the 1999 to 2007 period, leaving its assets at the end of the period approximately 20 times their size at the start. Allied Irish and the Bank of Ireland, the top two banks, saw a tenfold expansion in their size over this relatively short period.

A bank growing at 20 percent per year is doubling in size roughly every three and a half years; 40 percent growth means that the balance sheet is doubling in less than two years. None of the authors of this volume have seen a bank manage a 20 percent per year growth rate for very long without failing, let alone the rate seen by Anglo Irish Bank. Banks growing that rapidly are essentially shoveling money out the door as quickly as possible and, invariably, rewarding those staff shoveling the fastest.

Rogue banks, bent on expansion at all costs, usually signal their intentions. Before Crédit Lyonnais, France's largest bank, went bust in 1993, its advertising slogan was "Crédit Lyonnais: the power to say yes." In other words, its management wanted borrowers to know that no matter how poor their credit record, they could obtain a loan. Similarly, in the savings and loan crisis, one bank advertised that it had applied for a license to be the first bank on the moon. This strange claim was meant to convey that the bank was really pro-growth and "modern." In the case of Anglo Irish Bank, its advertisement was its rapid growth itself, and it led an expansion of the banking system, with Allied Irish Bank and the Bank of Ireland quick to follow.

A popular story is that management at these latter two banks felt that they had to respond to the boom in lending at Anglo Irish, which effectively was a "rogue" bank. The managers of these banks saw a way to reward themselves with bonuses based on growth, so the volume-oriented compensation system appears to have been in operation again. If Allied Irish and the Bank of Ireland were only responding defensively to Anglo Irish, they should have set aside much of their earnings for future losses, but instead their officers enjoyed record pay. The expansion of Irish banks' balance sheets translated into a generous supply of credit: whereas previously banks had limited borrowing to a multiple of two to three times income, in the boom it became acceptable for home buyers to take out mortgages at five to ten times their incomes, with 100 percent loan-to-value mortgages, or no down payment. And overall credit to households and nonfinancial firms soared from about 60 percent of GDP in 1997 (compared with a eurozone average of 80 percent) to over 200 percent by 2008 (vs. 100 percent in Europe).[6]

Ireland did not have the housing finance institutions of the United States (there were no government-sponsored enterprises (GSEs) like Fannie Mae and Freddie Mac) to guarantee mortgage debt, though excessive borrowing was encouraged by fiscal policy (e.g., tax breaks for property investment), nor were there the subprime loans that marked the US experience.[7] But the impact of the credit expansion in Ireland was substantial:

private credit soared and housing supply jumped, leaving Ireland with a serious debt and housing overhang.

There was no shortage of warnings, both by academics and by the highly respected Economic and Social Research Institute, that the Irish housing market was greatly overvalued.[8] For example, consider this measured view, by the then Professor (and future governor of the Central Bank of Ireland) Patrick Honohan:

All we can hope to do is identify whether a country is within or outside a "zone of vulnerability" where a crisis could arise if confidence were to falter. So is Ireland in such a zone? I think that the answer must be yes. Certainly the rate of credit expansion—the classic indicator that is one of the many to have been employed in the past—is waving a red flag at present.[9]

What is interesting about this comment is that it was made in 2004, when housing prices were on their way up with significantly more increases still to come. In 2007 another well-known Irish expert, Morgan Kelly, warned of a possible 50 percent fall in Irish housing prices, but the Central Bank dismissed the warnings rather than investigate what might happen to the banking system if such a decline occurred.

Despite the clear nature of the sector's problems, the Irish regulator did little to check the reckless expansion in the Irish banking system that was taking place right before its eyes. During the fall of 2009 it became public knowledge that Irish banks had been using the oldest trick in the books (sic)—moving some loans off their balance sheets a few days before the end of the quarter or fiscal year, by selling the loans, but with the promise to buy them back. With the loans off their books at the end of a period when supervisors are known to be checking the banks' accounts, this ploy helps them hide the risks that they are taking; banks that are rapidly growing their real estate lending instead would look like banks with fewer such loans. Insurance companies or offshore entities were eager purchasers to pick up a high return, even if for a short period. The Irish banks were willing to pay such a high return for this service because it allowed them to fool the regulators and the public. By masking their risks, the Irish banks were allowed to hold less capital; as explained in chapter 2, higher leverage (lower capital) helped them show higher returns on equity, justifying nice bonuses, while of course exposing the banks to greater risk of insolvency, especially as a good part of the loans being concealed were loans to bank directors—often a danger signal. When the regulator checked their quarterly reports, the banks looked less worrisome than they would have a few days before or would again a few days later. Given that computers permit millisecond-by-millisecond monitoring of a bank's books, it is not clear how bank supervisors fell for this maneuver, in particular when the housing stock and prices were expanding so rapidly. Someone must have been lending funds to support this bubble, and with just four banks accounting for over 90 percent of bank assets, it should not take a Sherlock Holmes to deduce the sources. It strains credulity to think that regulators could have been unaware of the dangers of this excessive credit growth, especially in a small financial community in which many of the players and regulators know each other well. Yet the Financial Stability Reports put out by the Central Bank of Ireland played down any concern.

Governor Patrick Honohan, who took over that post in September 2009 after the Irish crisis was well underway, concluded in a recent report that:

[T]he root causes appear to have been threefold:

i) a regulatory approach which was and was perceived to be excessively deferential and accommodating; insufficiently challenging and not persistent enough. This meant not moving decisively and effectively enough against banks with governance issues. It also meant that corrective regulatory intervention for the system as a whole was delayed and timid. This was in an environment that placed undue emphasis on fears of upsetting the competitive position of domestic banks and on encouraging the Irish financial services industry even at the expense of prudential considerations.

ii) an under-resourced approach to bank supervision that, by relying on good governance and risk-management procedures, neglected quantitative assessment and the need to ensure sufficient capital to absorb the growing property-related risks.

iii) an unwillingness by the CBFSAI (the combined Central Bank & Financial Services Authority of Ireland) to take on board sufficiently the real risk of a looming problem and act with sufficient decision and force to head it off in time. "Rocking the boat" and swimming against the tide of public opinion would have required a particularly strong sense of the independent role of a central bank in being prepared to "spoil the party" and withstand possible strong adverse public reaction.[10]

The Honohan report, as it is now called, details specific instances in which the Financial Regulator underperformed.[11] For example, in the spring of 2007 (Irish property prices had peaked in late 2006), an inspection of one bank found that 28 percent of its credits required exceptions to the bank's own policies. Yet the inspectors issued no "high-priority" findings, which in their system is a call for action by bank management. By contrast, in an inspection of that same bank two years earlier, there were "high- and "medium-priority" findings issued, including the "lack of an overall defined credit policy . . . the large and imprecise appetite for risk . . . insufficient Board oversight . . . the lack of a provisioning policy . . . no procedures for identifying and dealing with problem credits . . . and the lack of independence of the credit risk unit review."[12] Individually, and especially collectively, these findings regularly are cited as grave warning signs of mismanagement in banking and supervisory courses.

Unbelievably, even though the earlier problems (those identified in 2005) should have led to immediate limits on the bank's lending, at least until the troubling matters were resolved, possibly including the removal of management, nothing was done! The Honohan report furnishes numerous examples in which regulators went beyond a "deferential and accommodating" approach and effectively abdicated their responsibility.

It is difficult to explain the seemingly willful blindness of regulators. It is difficult to believe that regulators could have been so committed to the "light touch" approach to regulation as to maintain that course notwithstanding the clear dangers in the Irish financial system. It is possible that regulations were not enforced either because of relationships between regulators and the banks or because regulators understood that their future employment prospects would be dimmed by vigorous enforcement actions. In terms of the sports analogy of chapter 1, Irish regulators, like referees, may have been influenced by the "fans," and those paying closest attention were the bankers and the developers. Whatever the explanation, Irish regulators had little oversight and any accountability was too late. Irish taxpayers will pay the cost for decades to come.

As a result of the crisis, financial regulation was moved back into the Central Bank (though it is not at all clear that the location of the regulator played any role in its failure); and from that post the Irish Financial Regulator has announced tough new procedures and policies.[13] The problem with this unsurprising announcement is that it is not clear why Irish taxpayers should be convinced that better regulation in fact is and will be taking place. Indeed a recent 80-plus-page report on new supervisory policies in the wake of the crisis does not mention how the supervisor will be held accountable. The Honohan report noted the tendency of supervisors to avoid "rocking the boat" or "spoiling the party" but it did not look at the ways in which regulators are captured by the industry that it regulated, a tendency we noted in chapter 2. While the new Irish Financial Regulator should be sufficiently chastised by the crisis to implement a tougher policy, how long will this last? If cognitive or even outright regulatory capture is endemic to financial regulation, the answer is, not long enough.

In sum, Ireland's crisis seems to have been different from that in the United States in a number of respects. There was only a single regulator, so regulatory gaps, or choosing one's regulator, was not an issue. There was no significant financial innovation, and banks were growing at an amazing pace, so it is hard to argue that the crisis was impossible for any to see, and although US interest rates can affect those in other countries, as a member of the eurozone it seems a stretch to blame the Irish crisis on low US interest rates.

However, the great similarity between Ireland and the United States is that those charged with enforcing regulation too often turned a blind eye to incredible risks and allowed banks to ramp up growth to a pace never sustained anywhere. Ireland, like the United States, had significant capital inflows, and the warning signs of an unsustainable bubble were evident for any to see. The responsibility of the regulators could not be more apparent.

The Run on the Rock

In September 2007 there was a run on the British bank Northern Rock, the first run on a British bank since 1866, initiating the start of a costly financial crisis. According to an IMF study, of the twenty-three countries suffering a financial crisis in the period 2007 to 2009, the United Kingdom ranked third in total fiscal costs, right behind Ireland. As happened in Ireland, British real estate prices had exploded, rising anywhere from 122 to 146 percent, depending on the index used, in nominal terms over the period 1999 to 2007. This was a significantly larger increase than the roughly 86 percent rise in the United States. Unlike Ireland, but like the United States, the United Kingdom did experience some financial innovation. Securitization rose in importance but ultimately only accounted for 18 percent of mortgage debt at the start of the crisis. UK bank leverage ratios expanded (from about 20 in 2000 to close to 30 by 2008), as mortgage debt rose from 50 to 80 percent of GDP. Part of this increase in debt—almost 40 percent—was in the form of home equity loans, allowing households to increase spending beyond their incomes. Another 25 percent of the mortgage loans by 2007 were for investment purposes ("buy-to-let," or purchasing with the idea of renting out while waiting for prices to rise). The Turner Review, a report by Lord Adair Turner (head of the UK regulatory agency, the Financial Services Authority [FSA]) in response to a request from the Chancellor of the Exchequer and from which these data were taken, also reported that the run-up to the crisis was marked by the rapid expansion in credit extended by several UK banks, including Northern Rock and HBOS (the acronym for the bank resulting from the merger of Halifax Bank and the Bank of Scotland), which relied heavily on interbank funding.[14]

The risks being taken by Northern Rock were evident many years before it failed, though UK regulators not only did nothing, they gave Northern Rock "a gold star." The Rock, as it was called, had been growing its assets annually, as noted in a House of Commons report, "by 20 percent plus or minus 5 percent for the last 17 years," leading it to becoming a member of the FTSE 100 (the hundred largest companies, in terms of market capitalization, listed on the London Stock Exchange).[15] From 1998 to 2006, its assets had grown more than sixfold—not quite the astonishing rate seen in Ireland, but nonetheless a rate that warranted close regulatory oversight. More alarmingly, the same report noted that deposits fell from 63 percent of assets in 1997 to 22 percent at the end of 2006. The significance of this is that retail deposits tend to be more stable in times of stress—if you will, the short-term, "smart, wholesale" money abruptly leaves a bank at the first sign of trouble, whereas at least a portion of retail deposits tend to be there for the longer term.

Northern Rock's exposure to the real estate market could not have been clearer to regulators—about 90 percent of its assets were mortgage loans, an enormous concentration. So the bank was lending long term, yet the financing was mostly in the form of very short-term funds, a good chunk of which was even overnight money. When its ability to borrow in interbank markets virtually disappeared in August of 2007, Northern Rock was in immediate deep trouble; the short-term funds it had been continuously rolling over were nowhere to be had.

Long before the run on The Rock began in September 2007, regulators should have been paying far closer attention to Northern Rock and most likely should have intervened in its decisions regarding growth. This was not happening; the bank was on a schedule to be reviewed only once every three years and wasn't due for another one until the end of 2009. The FSA, the single regulator for UK financial services (until 2010, when responsibility for macro-prudential or systemic regulation was shifted back to the central bank), was the sole regulator of Northern Rock and, astonishingly, viewed it as one of the safest banks in the United Kingdom. In fact, as late as June 2007, when the bank's share price had already declined by a third, a signal from the market of trouble, the FSA granted the Rock a Basel II waiver—the gold star mentioned earlier—basically allowing it to adopt the most sophisticated risk management approach allowed to banks, and the Rock's managers followed at the end of July, just days before its fate was sealed, with an increase in its dividend to 30.3 percent—allowed because it was determined that Northern Rock had an excess level of capital![16]

UK regulators did not seem to accord much attention to the growing fragility of a major bank. The Rock was not even supervised by those experienced with banks, but rather until June 2006, by a department of the FSA dedicated to insurance, and then moved to one department and then another before the run to withdraw deposits, so that three department heads at the FSA were alternately responsible for its supervision in the years leading up to its failure. Yet supervisors only completed about a quarter of the standard oversight work that should have been done.[17]

The House of Commons report (p. 34) concludes that Northern Rock was a clear case of regulatory failure:

The FSA did not supervise Northern Rock properly. It did not allocate sufficient resources or time to monitoring a bank whose business model was so clearly an outlier; its procedures were inadequate to supervise a bank whose business grew so rapidly. . . . The failure of Northern Rock, while a failure of its own Board, was also a failure of its regulator. As the Chancellor notes, the Financial Services Authority exercises a judgment as to which "concerns" about financial institutions should be regarded as systemic and thus require action by the regulator. In the case of Northern Rock, the FSA appears to have systematically failed in its duty as a regulator to ensure Northern Rock would not pose such a systemic risk, and this failure contributed significantly to the difficulties, and risks to the public purse, that have followed.

Yet Northern Rock, though perhaps the most extreme example, was not the sole problem bank in the United Kingdom. Others also had been pushing a strong pro-growth strategy similar to that of Northern Rock. There has been less investigation of these other banks, but in addition to their rapid rates of expansion, the need for recapitalization and/or take-over by other institutions is a telling illustration of the lack of adequate regulatory oversight.

For example, regulators failed to respond to an important warning from another major bank, HBOS, again indicating an extreme reliance on "light touch" regulation. In 2005 HBOS fired its chief risk officer (CRO).[18] This is the person whose primary and usually only responsibility in a bank is to measure and control risk, and to report to the CEO and the board of directors of the bank when dangerous risk-taking occurs. There may be innumerable reasons for sacking a CRO, but the most common reason in the case of a rapidly growing bank is that the CRO is blowing the whistle on risks and that the CEO does not want to hear the warning. As explained in chapter 3, senior management teams may be tempted to push growth to help pump up the share price and their own compensation and bonuses, effectively looting the bank. Supervisors should see the firing of a CRO as a red flag; they should have long discussions with the fired CRO, and use the event for a full-fledged review of the institution. In the case of HBOS, this did not happen. Worse still, the person who fired the CRO became deputy chairman at the FSA, which seems to indicate incredible faith in the market; private financial institutions evidently were viewed as only making good decisions, and even a CEO making what looked like a dubious decision is good enough for the regulatory agency!

As in Ireland and the United States, UK regulators failed to do their job. The UK Treasury report concludes as much:

While this document does propose a number of specific, targeted enhancements to the FSA's powers and amendments to the scope of regulation, the Government is clear that the financial crisis was not caused by a lack of powers with the UK's regulatory regime.[19]

As with the innumerable warning signs of a looming crisis in the United States in the 2004 to 2007 period, the Irish and UK cases show clear instances in which regulators were not doing their job and yet the public did not know about it until it was too late.

An Icelandic Meltdown

We could cite any number of examples of countries in which many financiers were taking absurd risks, but perhaps the most interesting story is where the crisis was the greatest relative to the size of the economy: Iceland. A sensible country known for its fishing and tourism, and often thought to have "good institutions" and a low degree of corruption,[20] Iceland was transformed almost overnight. Between 2000 and 2007, GDP doubled, real estate prices rose 135 percent, and equity prices jumped approximately sevenfold (the banks accounted for about three-quarters of the market), with household wealth tripling.[21]

As the alert reader might have guessed, the economic boom in Iceland was not due to a phenomenal increase in the price of fish. Essentially the entire country was turned into a highly leveraged entity, borrowing foreign exchange and gambling with the money. Iceland went from decades of state-ownership in the banking sector to rapid privatization during the 1998 to 2003 period. Unfortunately, and similar to some developing and transition countries, the banks were sold to those with close connections to (and financial supporters of) the political parties, and critically the private owners seemed to have little of their own funds at risk, having borrowed from one another's banks. Bank owners with no money at risk have an even greater tendency to gamble, as there is no downside risk (for themselves, as they can just walk away from their loans) but considerable potential for their own upside gain.

And gamble they did: by the first quarter of 2008, the assets of the top three Icelandic banks were about *eleven times* the estimate of the previous year's GDP—an expansion far more rapid that that which occurred in Ireland, even though the latter was already shown to be quite excessive. The assets of Icelandic banks grew at a fantastic (likely an all-time, world-record) pace, with the lion's share of their assets abroad, and mostly financed by foreign borrowing.[22] Icelandic banks had both a large foreign exchange mismatch (borrowing in one currency and lending in another), as well as a maturity mismatch (borrowing short term and lending long term). Similar to some US financial institutions, their banks pushed financial instruments on clients who did not seem to understand the risks they were taking).[23] Only about a third of their assets were funded with relatively stable deposits; the remainder of their funding was from overnight or other short-term funding. As was the case with Northern Rock, these banks too were engaged in Russian roulette, and again, not surprisingly, the gun went off with deadly results.

Fortunately, there has been an investigation and a Parliamentary committee that has concluded that the government in power at the time, the Central Bank, and the Financial Supervisory Authority of Iceland (FME) were negligent in the conduct of their jobs.[24] As seen in the Irish and UK financial disasters, Icelandic banks were engaging in phenomenally rapid portfolio growth (from 2004 to 2008 averaging 50 percent per year, or doubling in size about every 16 months). As explained in chapter 3, banks that want to grow rapidly can do so easily by rewarding their employees for growth without regard to risk, and Icelandic banks, according to a report by a Special Investigative Committee, had

. . . strong incentives for rapid growth . . . (including) the banks' incentives schemes, as well as the high leverage of the major owners. It should have been clear to the supervisory authorities that such incentives existed and that these incentives were reason for concern over this rapid growth. However, it is evident that the FME, the institution that bore the main responsibility for monitoring the activities of the banks, did not grow in the same proportion as the banks and its practices did not keep up with the rapid changes in the banks' practices.[25]

The report makes clear that the banks were not only growing rapidly, but as noted above, borrowing in foreign currency to leverage themselves further (in one year, the top three banks together borrowed abroad in an amount just larger than the size of the country's GDP!), borrowing short term, and engaging in excessive loan concentration, effectively hitting the "trifecta" for the top causes of bank failures. On loan concentration, the report notes:

The largest owners of all the big banks had abnormally easy access to credit at the banks they owned, apparently in their capacity as owners. . . . in all of the banks, their principal owners were among the largest borrowers. . . .When the bank [Glitnir] collapsed, its outstanding loans to Baugur and affiliated companies amounted to . . . 70 percent of the bank's equity base . . . . When Landsbanki collapsed, Björgólfur Thor Björgólfsson and companies affiliated to him were the bank's largest debtors. Björgólfur Guðmundsson—[this was Björgólfsson's father] was the bank's third largest debtor. In total, their obligations to the bank . . . [were] higher than Landsbanki Group's equity.[26]

The report even provides details on how regulators let things become out of control in the banks. It notes "During a hearing, an owner of one of the banks [Mr. Guðmundsson], who also had been a board member of the bank [chairman of the board, in fact], said he believed that the bank 'had been very happy to have [him] as a borrower.'"[27] The regulators, however, should have been decidedly unhappy. When banks lend to their owners, these loans either directly or indirectly (the report argues directly) support the equity the lenders have in the bank, leading to a dangerous situation. That is, if the reader were to buy control of a bank with loans from that same bank, his or her net investment in the bank might be zero or negative, which heightens to the extreme the incentives of shareholders to press for higher risk investments, as explained in chapter 2; such shareholders would have nothing to lose if the bank collapsed and lots to gain if the gambles succeeded. With these "insider" loans, controlling shareholders can push losses onto other shareholders, creditors, and, of course, taxpayers, which is why regulations in many countries both insist that purchases of bank equity by strategic owners not be financed by loans, and impose strict limits on loans from a bank to its directors. The report makes it clear that this was occurring in the Icelandic banks, and faults the regulator for not seeing the obvious abuse:

The operations of the Icelandic banks were, in many ways, characterized by their maximizing the interests of the larger shareholders, who managed the banks, rather than running solid banks with the interests of all shareholders in mind, where due responsibility was demonstrated towards their creditors. . . . In a letter to the Investigation Commission, Stefan Ingves, Governor of the Central Bank of Sweden, makes it clear that unclear ownership, along with the banks' rapid balance sheet growth had led to a dangerous situation and that the Icelandic government did neither seem to fully grasp nor understand how to deal with it. [28]

What makes this situation potentially fraudulent is that the CEO can approve loans to shareholders for purchasing stock, which pushes the stock price up, leading to a larger bonus for the CEO. Astute readers will notice the recurring game: find a way to push up the share price so that executives can justify large bonuses (e.g., misleading accounting and hiding problems off balance sheets in some US banks) or, as in the Icelandic and Irish cases, loans to insiders (a gambit that was used in the South Sea Bubble of 1720). Either way, some group of insiders profit at the expense of others—small shareholders, workers who lose jobs without the juicy pay packages, uninsured creditors, and taxpayers.

How could these abuses not be noticed, especially as they were very old ploys used by bankers often in the past? Investigations are ongoing, and the former Icelandic prime minister's trial is advancing as we go to press. The distinguished Icelandic economist, Thorvaldur Gylfason, cited earlier, adds that an investigation, including of some politicians, as of mid-2010 has revealed that ". . . of 63 Members of Parliament, 10 owed the failed banks €1 million or more each at the pre-crash exchange rate of the króna; their personal debts range from €1 million to €40 million. The average debt of the ten MPs, including the leader of the Independence Party, his deputy, and five other party comrades, was €9 million."[29] One of the bank owners declared bankruptcy in the amount of $750 million, adds the Special Investigation report, of which $500 million was owed to the bank he owned and on whose board he served as a director.

Regulators stood by while these events were happening. One of the members of the Special Investigation Commission, Sigridur Benediktsdottir, has stated in public talks that in numerous cases the Commission documented that regulations on insider lending and loan concentration were violated, and that the FME decided that if the practice had persisted for some time, not to enforce the rules.

Was regulation lax because the politicians were benefiting and liked the system the way it was, or was it lax because the regulator was embarrassed at having let the situation get out of control and then did not want to attract attention? We do not know, though Gylfason noted that the banks were the largest contributors to the ruling parties. Was regulation lax because the banks influenced regulators? We do not know the answer to that either, though banks were successful in hiring regulators at generous salaries from the regulatory agencies, and some "referee bias" could have played a role.[30] We also do not know if sensible enforcement of regulation could have prevented or significantly reduced the cost of this crisis. What we do know is that it was not tried.

Notes on Other Crises

Unfortunately, regulatory failings did not end with the crises in the United States, Ireland, the United Kingdom, and Iceland. In Spain the commercial banks seem to have been well regulated, and it is the home of a proposed solution to crises. Many have noticed that crises often come after booms because bankers and others get carried away during the "good times" and forget that a slowdown is inevitable—in other words, they forget that trees do not grow to the sky, as stated earlier.[31] What is the solution offered by the Spanish authorities? Force the banks to set aside some of their profits in good times—when the economy is growing strongly, for example—which will automatically slow their lending and one might hope prevent it from becoming excessive. However, the housing bubble in Spain was among the largest in industrial countries, so someone had to be lending money to people buying homes and developers building them. As it turned out, the *cajas*, similar to the US S&Ls, supplied the fuel for that boom, yet they seemed to escape regulation. Spain was in second place in Europe after Ireland in the growth of credit, as lending by the *cajas* and the commercial banks to households and nonfinancial firms jumped from about 70 percent of GDP in 1997 to about 170 percent in 2008.

The case of Spain further illustrates the problem of regulatory avoidance. When regulations establish limits on activities, it can make that activity especially profitable, and so engender forces that work for the evasion of the limits. For example, if banks are required to hold a certain ratio of reserves to deposits and/or capital to assets, another entity that functions like a bank but is not regulated as a bank, and therefore does not face these requirements, has the advantage that it can do business with lower costs. This is essentially the story of how "nonbank banks," such as money market mutual funds, were able to take some of the banking business from US commercial banks. In Spain the *cajas* evidently avoided coverage by countercyclical provisioning requirements, and in many cases they were connected to provincial governments in Spain, so political intervention—leaning on the banks to lend to politically connected property developers in the region—likely was a factor as well.[32] Again, this is not a new problem; regulators should expect that once a regulation affects banks—limits their profits—that they would try to avoid it. In any boom, credit from banks one way or another will be part of what is fueling rapid growth or price appreciation, so the claim that regulators did not know what was occurring is not plausible. We suspect that Spanish banks will be found to have participated in the credit boom as well, notwithstanding the provisioning requirements, but as this book was being finalized that was not clear.

In another example, in several eastern European countries, people financed their mortgages in foreign exchange. The practice—like the foreign exchange mismatch of Icelandic banks—might seem harmless, but in reality it is potentially devastating. If the interest rate in foreign currency is low, the loan might appear inexpensive. Still, such a loan is risky. If the local currency depreciates in value relative to the currency in which the loan is denominated, then the borrower must pay more in local currency terms, making the loan more expensive. This risk might be fine for those individuals or firms that receive income in the foreign currency. However, often that is not the case. The residents of many eastern European countries were only borrowing in foreign currency to obtain a lower interest rate. Why pay 10 or 12 percent in local currency interest when it is possible to borrow in euros or Swiss francs at only 3.5 percent—and thereby be able to afford a larger house or have more funds available for other uses? The problem with this strategy is that when local residents receive their incomes in domestic currency, they are playing Russian roulette—and if they play it long enough, the gun will go off and they will lose. Only if they stop playing (i.e., repay the loan) before the gun goes off (the currency devalues and they now owe much more money) will they win. Bank Supervision 101 teaches the danger of this strategy.

Even banks in relatively staid centers, such as Sweden, Austria, and Switzerland, got into trouble extending loans to eastern European residents, who were planning on their country joining the eurozone, meaning that the possibility of a devaluation of their currency—and a consequent jump in the cost of their mortgages—would no longer be possible. Regulators in both the home and host countries should have been asking whether it was wise to make this bet, but apparently they were not.

More generally, western European regulators should have been asking about all the securities their banks were buying. These securities included the mortgage-backed securities and collateralized debt obligations that embodied all manner of risk debts—not just the riskiest parts of US subprime loans, but even some Icelandic icing on the cake (debts of those overleveraged Icelandic banks). Of course, European regulators protest now that the securities were AAA-rated or other highly rated securities, and that the fault lies with the Americans selling the toxic securities. However, while there is no shortage of blame to be allocated, as already discussed, these securities were paying a healthy premium over other comparably rated securities, and as stated in chapter 3, the shortcomings of their ratings had been discussed in bank publications for about a decade. We will say again: higher returns usually entail higher risks.

Why were European regulators not asking more questions about these securities? It was clear to many that their banks were buying them to reduce their capital requirements, in line with the incentives from the Basel Committee. Academics had criticized the risk-based capital requirements pushed by this Committee for some time, and the incentive that they created to shift out of some assets and into others.[33] Thus it is difficult to believe that regulators did not understand the game that was being played. Regulators might have shared the view of their Irish and British counterparts that private financial intermediaries would look after themselves, or it might have been the case that those banks were lobbying the regulators successfully. European taxpayers now get to pay for the negligence of their regulators.

Failure Is Not Inevitable

The legacy of regulatory failures might lead us to the conclusion that it is too difficult to make regulation work, and that we need some simple but draconian restrictions on financial firms that will require little supervision or at least be easier to supervise. As argued in chapter 2, financial regulation is quite difficult, and we do not think that a simplistic approach can work. Consider one of the earliest and simplest forms of financial regulation: a ban by the religious authority (both in Catholicism and Islam) of charging interest (and the later prohibition on charging interest at "excessive" levels).

The simple strategy of banning an activity (in the case of usury, the penalty was jail, ostracism, and eternal damnation for violations) has always failed. Bankers come up with new instruments that allow the providers of funds to be compensated for the risks they bear; and usury limits led to the rise of Jewish bankers (not likely an intention of the restrictions) in Renaissance Italy because they were not governed by the regulations of the Catholic Church.

Or consider Regulation Q, a part of the Glass–Steagall Act of 1933, which prohibited banks from paying interest on US demand deposits. In a very low interest rate environment, there was no incentive to evade this rule. Then, as market interest rates rose, the impact of this restriction was readily evaded, in early years with gifts to those opening up such accounts and then later and more notably with the growth of money market mutual funds and the eurodollar market (i.e., the market for dollar-denominated accounts outside the United States). The same approach to regulation was also behind other parts of the Glass–Steagall Act, such as the separation of commercial and investment banking, a stricture that failed long before the act was repealed and would fail much faster with current technology, especially as most countries do not separate these parts of banking into distinct legal organizations. So a "simple rules" approach will not work, since finance can so readily adapt to such rules.

However, there are at least three reasons why a council of despair is not the lesson to be drawn from these examples. First, the events that precipitated the crises in different countries unfolded slowly. Regulators made mistakes and then watched, and the incentives they created slowly destabilized the financial system over years. There was time to take corrective actions. Second, the regulatory failures cited in the last chapter and in this one were readily apparent *once the requisite information was disclosed.* This was not rocket science. It was not difficult to understand the risks being taken by Anglo Irish Bank, Northern Rock, HBOS, and numerous other institutions, once sufficient information was made available. Nor was it hard to see US regulatory failings—especially once it is apparent that many were leveraging themselves highly, banks and borrowers alike. We will return in chapter 8 to propose ways to ensure more accurate disclosure and how to ensure that regulators do their jobs.

Third, and the subject of the balance of this chapter, not every country experiencing an economic boom suffered a crisis. This suggests at least the possibility—in addition to good luck—that some regulators might have had a positive impact.

Consider Australia, which experienced a boom in real estate, with prices in early 2010 up by 211 percent relative to their levels in 1997.[34] However, it is not clear how much of this increase represents a bubble. At least part of the increase can be accounted for by strong immigration flows and a variety of restrictions on building in many urban areas. From mid-2010 to mid-2011, however, housing prices fell by about 2 percent.[35]

How has the banking industry survived the global financial crisis and the recent decline in local real estate prices? One ingredient could have been the earlier (2001) failure of a large insurance company (HIH), which produced a hard-hitting review—written by John Palmer, former head of the Canadian regulatory agency (the Office of the Superintendent of

Financial Institutions, or OSFI)—of Australian financial regulation. Similar to the Honohan report on Ireland's regulatory failings, Palmer largely faulted Australian regulatory authorities for not taking simple measures to reign in an excessively risk-loving intermediary.

APRA, the Australian regulator, followed virtually all of the recommendations of the report. In reaction to rising real estate prices, ARPA started doing stress tests with "Texas-size" losses, that is, loss estimates on the order of those seen in Texas and California during the US real estate crisis in the 1980s; doubled the capital requirements for mortgage insurers; and increased banks' capital requirements for high loan-to-value mortgages.[36] So following monetary policy and regulatory tightening, real estate prices declined in real terms in 2005 to 2006 and again in 2009, the latter representing the effects of the crisis in interest spreads in international financial markets. Monetary policy in Australia resumed tightening in 2010, in response to another surge in real estate prices, and then the most recent decline occurred.

How did Australian banks avoid the explosion of financial compensation that fed risk-taking in the United States and some European countries? The answer to this is not clear and likely depends on several factors, on which even experts in Australian finance could disagree. One relevant feature of Australian regulation is the Four Pillars Policy, an unofficial policy of government since 1990s, which prohibits the four largest banks from merging or acquiring one another. The result of this policy seems to have checked the urge for rapid growth on the part of the big banks; they have a fairly comfortable oligopoly and do not have to worry about being swallowed up by a competitor—which in turn likely was a factor in limiting the spread of the volume-based compensation model discussed in chapter 3. It is interesting to note—and likely in part because their growth was restrained during the run-up to the crisis—that the four large Australian banks in 2009 to 2010 are in the small group of a dozen or so banks, as of the first half of 2010, that are AA rated. They are also in the list of the top 30 banks in the world by assets. But the key point is that the limits on bank growth seemed to play a role in the restraint on compensation: not being able to pursue growth at any cost, Australian banks were not rewarding growth alone.

We do not know what is the optimal limit on the size or number of banks in the United States, let alone in Australia, so we are not endorsing this particular limitation. Other ways of restraining compensation, such as greater disclosure of how the banks are rewarding risk-taking, might have been preferable. Australia's success in avoiding a crisis thus far might also be due to its enforcement of regulation; authorities might have learned a lesson as a result of the HIH failure. A question that Australian taxpayers should ask, in view of the expensive crises in many other countries, is that if better enforcement has been part of their country's success, how can they be sure that better enforcement will continue? Like bankers, regulators might have a tendency after a long period of stability to relax; for regulators, this would be seen in more lax enforcement of the rules, and/ or a failure to anticipate the new ways that bankers were using to evade old rules and take new risks. What will keep regulators vigilant? And, if regulators for some time resist being influenced by the home crowd (the banks), how can voters be sure that this will continue?

Canada also offers us important lessons. Despite a decline in GDP roughly equal to that of the United States, Canadian banks also avoided the worst effects of the crisis of 2007 to 2009, with smaller losses, a more limited decline in their share prices, and more modest increases in real estate prices, which were up only about 70 percent in the twelve years before the crisis. These better results reflect a variety of factors, including some differences in regulation and the structure of the Canadian financial system, as well as some differences in enforcement.

For example, Canadian borrowers wanting to take out a mortgage in excess of 80 percent of the value of the home are required to buy mortgage insurance on 100 percent of the value of the house (not only on the excess above 80 percent, as in the United States), and must pay this cost up front at purchase.[37] In contrast to the United States and Ireland, mortgage interest paid is not tax-deductible, so Canadian borrowers are likely to borrow less to finance home purchases, and to avoid borrowing on their home to finance consumption purchases.

Canadian borrowing also is circumscribed by the fact that loans are "full recourse," meaning that the creditor can try to go after other assets or income, even after default; in a number of US states, such as California, this is not the case, making it more likely that borrowers will "walk away" from their houses. Interestingly home ownership rates in the two countries differ only slightly: in 2006, 68.8 percent of the population of the United States, and 68.6 percent of Canadians, owned their homes.[38] Subprime lending, as it is practiced in the United States, is rare in Canada.

Canadian banks face several regulatory constraints in terms of their supply of credit. Regulators imposed an overall leverage restriction (a 20-to-1 cap on the ratio of assets to capital) on the nation's banks, and (unlike in the United States) this requirement includes all off balance sheet holdings of the banks. As noted earlier, even if US banks extended explicit lines of credit to an SIV, they could still economize on their capital by securitizing some of their assets. In Canada, this was not possible, and not surprisingly, the extent of securitization of mortgages was less than half that in the United States. This difference in how regulations were enforced was critical: on the surface, Canadian banks appeared to be highly leveraged, with assets averaging about 19 times their capital, compared to what appeared to be significantly lower ratios for US banks. But, for some US banks, ratios were in fact often closer to 30 to 1, as a result of the off balance sheet entities they created to hold a massive portion of their portfolio.[39]

Part of the difference between the Canadian and US banking markets also might have been due to the structure of their markets, which in turn reflect a variety of differences in their institutional environments. Canada has a long history of nationally branched banks, and the top six banks account for over 90 percent of banking assets.[40] Canadian banks therefore are more likely to fund themselves with deposits, rather than relying on less stable, short-term financing from markets (the strategy that blew up Northern Rock, Bear Stearns, and Lehman); on the eve of the crisis, each of the top six Canadian banks funded two-thirds or more of their assets with deposits, about double the ratio for Citibank at that time. Canadian banks also succeed in competing with money-market mutual funds, as the banks themselves in fact own many of these mutual funds. One driving force for securitization—avoiding the concentration of lending typical of a system reliant on smaller, local banks—was not present. The diversified branch networks of Canadian banks not only gave them a solid deposit base but also a geographically diversified portfolio of loans. Investors wanting to hold a diversified portfolio of Canadian mortgages need only buy the bonds or shares of Canadian banks—the extra step of bundling a diverse set of mortgages has already been accomplished. Of course, the stricter interpretation of leverage requirements also removed the motive to move loans to off balance sheet entities.

Although there was no formal policy similar to that of the "four pillars" in Australia, the dominance of the six banks had been stable for decades, and one important source of competition in US financial markets—that between commercial and investment banks—was missing in Canada. As discussed in chapter 3, in the United States, it is plausible that since the late 1990s greater risk-taking, fueled by a compensation system that rewarded growth, spread from the hedge fund industry to investment banks and then on to commercial banks. In Canada, the typically more risk-loving investment banks were owned by the usually more conservative commercial banks, and foreign competition had been limited. Again, the point is not to advocate a particular structure—though the lessons from Australia and Canada surely merit further study—but rather that a key result was another country in which the incentives in finance did not "go crazy," and blow up the sector.

In the case of both Australia and Canada, financial structure, macro policies (especially for Australia), and regulation and its enforcement could explain the superior performance of their banks in the crisis. It is important to realize, however, that these factors are not immutable and do not immunize either country against a crisis. The weakening of banks in other countries might easily push Australian and Canadian banks into thinking that they can expand internationally now. Historically, including in the 1990s cases of Spanish banks in Latin America and of European banks in transitional countries, the first wave of an expansion internationally by banks often led to losses. Also debt levels and housing prices are rising in both countries, and they are experiencing increased capital inflows—in part due to their relatively superior performance.

Most important, how are the regulatory systems in Australia and Canada performing at present? Because of the limited disclosure by their regulatory agencies, no one outside those agencies is in a position to assess their performance until well after the fact, when it is too late. Consequently neither we nor the taxpayers in each country have a way of knowing what is happening. Because of the possibility that regulators may be subject to the same bias as sports' referees, we think that it would be unwise to count on continued good performance without some mechanism to ensure accountability. Given the abundance of examples of regulatory failure and the paucity of cases of regulatory success, we will discuss in chapter 8 how to hold regulators more accountable so that we do not have to rely on luck or personalities in regulatory agencies to hold down the costs to society of financial failures. First, we turn to an earlier US crisis, one that led to a regulatory reform that was supposed to end all crises. Understanding why those reforms did not work is important in recasting regulation today.

6

Been Down This Road Many Times Before

What experience and history teach is this—that nations and governments have never learned anything from history.

—Friederich Hegel (1832), From *Lectures on the Philosophy of History*

A timeline that lays out major events in the history of financial regulation in the United States is quite revealing, but also downright disturbing. Whenever there has been a crisis originating in the financial sector, the governmental response has become all too predictable—establish more regulators and grant them more and broader powers (see figure 6.1). This approach has not worked over the past two centuries. The most obvious outcome of the cumulative reforms following crises is an overly complex and inefficient regulatory regime. More troublesome, regulators have frequently used their powers—or failed to use those powers—in ways that trigger the next crisis.

The authority to expand the structure and scope of regulation originates in the Constitution, allowing the federal government to "coin money and regulate the value thereof." These seven words have enabled the federal government after winning several early battles with the states to create what has now become an elaborate Rube Goldberg–style financial regulatory regime. That outcome in and of itself would be fine—if it worked. But it doesn't.

Each time there is a financial crisis, the Congress is eager to reassure people that it will make things better. The Congress passes new legislation and claims that it will cure the problem and prevent another recurrence. The President then signs the legislation into law, stating that with the financial reforms being put in place, "never again" will such a terrible and destructive event occur. With the enactment of the Dodd–Frank law,

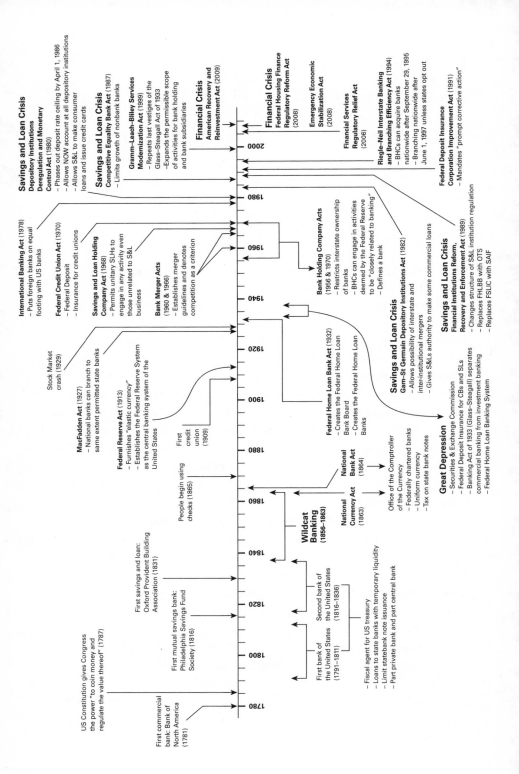

discussed in the next chapter, President Obama immediately declared, "because of this law, the American people will never again be asked to foot the bill for Wall Street's mistakes." Before signing the legislation, he added that "There will be no more taxpayer-funded bailouts. Period."[1]

The basic premise following each and every crisis is that the implementation of the new law will produce financial reforms that bring about a permanently better performing and more stable financial system. This repetitive practice of simply creating more regulators with more and broader powers after each crisis doesn't work. History tells us that as memories begin to fade, there is still another crisis. This cycle of crises and reforms must be broken. It is time to establish once and for all a regulatory system that adapts to an ever-changing financial marketplace so as to minimize, if not completely prevent, the likelihood and severity of crises.

This chapter provides examples from the past two centuries of how financial reforms following crises failed to prevent, and too often encouraged, the next crisis. The same old approach of establishing more regulators with greater powers over an ever larger portion of the financial system is fatally flawed—one crisis after another is followed by one financial reform after another. We show in chapter 7 that recent reform efforts in US legislation and in international agreements since the crisis continue this failed strategy of adding more regulations, building additional regulatory agencies, and granting the Guardians of Finance greater discretionary power.

Crisis . . . Financial Reform . . . Crisis . . . Financial Reform . . .

Our discussion of several historical financial crises and governmental reforms in response to them will necessarily be relatively short and omit many important details. We mainly focus on the rationale used for establishing new federal regulatory authorities following several distinct periods of financial turmoil. Simply creating more regulators after each crisis has not prevented future problems. We devote special attention to the savings and loan debacle in the 1980s because, like the most recent crisis during 2007 to 2009, it started in the real estate sector. Most important,

◀ Figure 6.1
Some major financial events in the United States since 1781

we explain that just like in the recent crisis, regulatory authorities contributed to problems or failed to take appropriate and timely action to contain them.

A Solution to Banking Problems: Create National Banks and the Office of the Comptroller of the Currency?

Prior to the establishment of the Office of the Comptroller of the Currency (OCC) in 1863, all US banks were chartered by the states. (Early on there were private banks operating without charters, but that situation did not last all that long.) In response to financial problems at state-chartered banks and fiscal demands of the Civil War, the National Banking Act of 1863 was enacted, establishing the OCC. The rationale was that with a federal regulator granting charters to banks that were required to issue a uniform currency, and a tax levied on state-chartered banks issuing different currencies, the country would be left with a single currency, national banks, and fewer, if any, banking problems. In addition, by requiring national banks to acquire government securities as backing for the uniform currency, government would receive help in raising funds to finance the war.

The result was that America established a uniform currency, but state banks survived and banking crises still occurred. State banks continued operating by adopting a new business model that involved offering checkable deposits to avoid the tax on issuing different currencies to obtain funding for making loans. Since then, both state- and federally chartered and regulated banks have existed side by side—a situation known as dual banking. Despite the introduction of national banks and a new federal regulator, both types of banks experienced serious banking problems in later years. The severity of banking crises in fact increased during the closing decades of the nineteenth century and the beginning decade of the twentieth.

A Solution to Systemic Banking Problems: Create the Federal Reserve System?

Following the Panic of 1907 and the prominent role of JP Morgan in organizing a response to bank insolvency, Congress established the Federal Reserve System (the Fed) in 1913. During the Panic of 1907, Morgan alone decided which banks received the private-sector support that he orchestrated and which did not. There was strong opposition to ever again allowing one person to have such power over the banking industry, which led to support for establishing the Fed. Early in its history, America had experimented with two successive central banks (The First and then the Second Bank of the United States). By 1836 the opponents of such an institution had defeated attempts to renew its charter. When it was time to establish, yet again, a central bank, the authorities chose not to call it the Third Bank of the United States—perhaps because such "branding" would not have signaled the formation of a secure and enduring institution.

Many compromises had to be made to overcome the historic US suspicion of a central bank, and one of the unique features was the joint public-private nature of the Fed, as well as its centralized-decentralized structure. The 7 governors of the Federal Reserve Board are appointed by the president and confirmed by the Senate, whereas the 12 presidents of the Federal Reserve Banks, which are curiously distributed throughout the country (reflecting political deals behind the Federal Reserve Act of 1913), are appointed by the boards of each of those banks. Three directors of those boards are bankers in that district appointed by member banks, three are from the nonbank private sector but also appointed by member banks, and three are appointed by the board to represent the public interest. (All national banks are required to be member banks, while state-chartered banks may choose to obtain membership.) The district banks are private, and member banks own nonvoting stock in each, but dividends are limited by law to 6 percent per year.[2] Since 1935, monetary policy decisions are made by a committee (the Federal Reserve Open Market Committee) composed of the 7 governors and 12 district bank presidents (the NY Fed president always has a vote, plus 4 of the other presidents, on a rotating basis), but regulatory decisions are made solely by the Board of Governors. Confusingly, each of the district banks has supervisors who, in conjunction with Board supervisors, oversee the member banks in their district, but the district supervisors report to Board staff in Washington, DC.

The Fed was designed to be the solution to the problem of bank runs that can unnecessarily destroy healthy banks. As noted in chapter 2, bank runs can be driven by panic and spread in a contagious manner to other banks. If depositors at one struggling institution panic and start to withdraw their funds, depositors at other, perfectly safe banks, might also panic and run to withdraw their deposits. Solvent banks could be driven to insolvency due to a forced sale of assets at fire-sale prices in a vain attempt to satisfy demand for funds by depositors.[3] The Fed was created, in part, to stop runs on healthy banks and the banking system. It would do so by always providing loans, or liquidity, to solvent but illiquid banks experiencing depositor runs or, in short, by serving as a lender of last resort.

The Fed didn't do its job in the 1930s, making the Great Depression longer and deeper than it otherwise might have been.[4] If the Fed fails to fulfill its mission of injecting liquidity into the banking system during a period of panic behavior on the part of depositors, the situation could lead to a liquidity freeze and credit crunch as banks are forced into a destructive competitive scramble to obtain cash to meet depositor withdrawals (or to cover short-term liabilities as happened during the financial crisis during 2007 to 2009). This is what happened when the Fed failed to serve as a lender as last resort during the early 1930s. As a result there were widespread runs and more than 8,800 banks failed in the 1930 to 1933 period. In response to this dire situation, President Roosevelt within days of assuming office in March 1933 declared a bank holiday to put a halt to the runs, closing down insolvent banks and convincing the public that the banks that were reopened a week later were safe and sound. He then signed legislation that June establishing a federal deposit insurance system, effective the following year, which promised to protect bank deposits up to $2,500 per person. The coverage limit was subsequently increased several times so that by 2010 it had reached $250,000 per person per bank. The Great Depression occurred despite the existence of both the Fed and the OCC; not surprisingly, even more federal financial agencies and more rules were established.

A Still Better Solution to Preventing Bank Runs and Costly Bank Failures: Create a Federal Deposit Insurance System?

In response to the Great Depression and the failure of the Fed, Congress created a new agency, the Federal Deposit Insurance Corporation (FDIC), in 1933 to prevent bank runs. Its purpose was to instill sufficient confidence in depositors that they would never again question the safety of their deposits, and thus have no incentive to run on banks, regardless of their view of the financial condition of the banks. The FDIC would cover losses of depositors up to a stated limit in bank failures. Its exposure to losses increased dramatically following the adoption of federal deposit insurance. The ratio of private bank equity capital-to-total assets fell from 13 percent to less than 6 percent between 1934 and 1945, and never again came even close to reaching a double-digit ratio. Such a large reduction demonstrates that when federal deposit insurance supplemented private equity capital as a buffer against losses to be borne by depositors, government discipline had to largely supplant market discipline to contain excessive risk-taking by banks.

As part of financial reform in response to the Great Depression, the Federal Home Loan Bank Board (FHLBB) was established to charter and regulate federal savings and loans. State-chartered depository institutions failed more frequently and imposed greater losses on depositors than banks chartered by the federal government, so it was considered prudent to extend the federal charter to savings and loan associations, which at the time were the primary suppliers of credit for housing. These institutions were considered particularly important because a national policy was taking shape to promote home ownership.

The Federal Savings and Loan Insurance Corporation (FSLIC) was also established at the same time as the FDIC to protect—subject to the same limits initially and over time—the depositors of savings and loan associations. The National Credit Union Administration (NCUA) was established shortly afterward to grant federal charters to credit unions for the same reason as savings and loans, and roughly three decades later, a separate federal deposit insurance fund for depositors of credit unions, the National Credit Union Share Insurance Fund (NCUSIF), was created.

These new federal regulatory agencies overseeing depository institutions helped further fill the regulatory landscape but did not prevent still more depository institution failures and huge losses associated with them. Both the FDIC and the FSLIC in later years would become so overwhelmed by costly depository institution failures that they would become insolvent, with the latter being shut down and replaced with a new insurance fund for savings and loans, which was eventually merged into the insurance fund for commercial banks. The failures would turn out to be so costly that taxpayers would be forced to help cover some of the losses. The FHLBB would also be eventually replaced by the Office of Thrift Supervision (OTS), which after a time was merged into the OCC. Due to the financial crisis during the 1930s, the scope of federal regulation was also extended to other aspects of the financial marketplace.

A Solution to Inadequate Securities Disclosure and Underregulated Investment Banks: Create the Securities and Exchange Commission?

Financial reforms did not end with a newly established federal deposit insurance system and new federal depository institution regulators. In view of the stock market crash in 1929, the Securities and Exchange Commission (SEC) was established a few years later in 1934 with the mandate to ensure through regulations and enforcement actions that issuers of securities disclose all material information when offering them for sale to the general public. Firms raising funds by selling securities to the public were henceforth being required to provide all pertinent information about themselves for individuals to make more informed investment decisions. Firms could thereby be held more accountable and more responsible for the securities they sell just as we are proposing that financial regulators should be held more accountable and more responsible for actions they take or don't take to protect the public.

During this period the Glass–Steagall Act, which prohibited the mixing of commercial banking and investment banking, also became law. The premise underlying this law was that conflicts of interest between the two businesses would exist and create potential financial problems. After its enactment, the two types of financial firms could no longer operate under a common ownership; commercial banks continued to be regulated by bank regulators, whereas investment banks became subject to the regulatory supervision of the new SEC. Despite the addition of still another federal regulator, both types of financial firms would encounter serious problems. Although Glass–Steagall is judged by some to have been a great success, and it did survive for five decades before being eroded by competitive forces and finally reversed by the Gramm–Leach–Bliley Act of 1999, still three of the five biggest, stand-alone investment banks, established in response to Glass–Steagall, would eventually fail (Bear Stearns and Lehman Brothers) or have to be absorbed (Merrill Lynch). Moreover, along with the establishment of the SEC and the other federal regulatory authorities, the federal government saw a need to address severe problems in the housing sector at the time.

A Solution to Promoting Home Ownership: Create New Federal Housing Institutions and a New Federal Housing Regulator?

Since the housing industry virtually collapsed during the 1930s, with total housing starts falling 70 percent,[5] the National Housing Act of 1934 created the Federal Housing Administration (FHA). The purpose of this new federal agency was to increase the availability of mortgage credit by providing government insurance for private mortgages and thereby stimulate the revival of the housing industry. This was followed by the creation of the Federal National Mortgage Association (FNMA or Fannie Mae) in 1938 to provide an additional impetus to mortgage activity by authorizing it to purchase FHA-insured mortgages. This new agency provided liquidity to home mortgages by providing a secondary market for them, which enables mortgages that have already been issued to be bought and sold. Saving and loans, and other home-lending institutions, were thus in a far better position to manage their balance sheets by now being able to sell the mortgages they originate to Fannie Mae.

Some years later, in 1970, the Federal Home Loan Mortgage Corporation (FHLMC or Freddie Mac) was established. Increasing home ownership throughout the country had for a time become a national goal, and Freddie Mac further increased the availability of mortgage credit with the expansion of the secondary market by also purchasing conventional mortgages (those mortgages that meet standards for purchase by Fannie Mae and Freddie Mac). Importantly, however, in view of recent events, at the time Freddie Mac only purchased mortgages in which the borrower either put 20 percent down or, in the event of a lower down payment, purchased private mortgage insurance.

At the same time that Freddie Mac was created, the Emergency Home Loan Finance Act of 1970 authorized Fannie Mae to buy conventional mortgages under the same down payment terms. (Two years earlier, in 1968, Fannie Mae was split into two separate entities: (1) a private stock corporation to focus on supporting the availability of conventional mortgages and (2) a new federal agency, the Government National Mortgage Association (GNMA or Ginnie Mae), to concentrate on purchasing

FHA-insured mortgages as well as Veterans Administration (VA) and Farmers Home Administration (FmHA) insured mortgages. Fannie Mae and Freddie Mac, both of which are chartered by the federal government—and thus referred to as government-sponsored enterprises (GSEs)—have since 1970 competed with one another with respect to the purchase and securitization of conventional and privately insured mortgages, while Ginnie Mae has focused on the purchase and securitization of government-insured mortgages. (Both GSEs were place into conservatorship by their regulator in 2008.)

As regards regulation, Freddie Mac was regulated by the FHLBB since its establishment in 1970 until 1989, when the FHLBB was replaced by the Office of Thrift Supervision in response to the savings and loan crisis during the 1980s, and then for several years by the US Department of Housing and Urban Development (HUD). Fannie Mae was regulated by HUD, and its predecessor entities, from its creation in 1938 until 1992. In the latter year the newly created Office of Federal Housing Enterprise Oversight (OFHEO) took over the regulation of both Fannie Mae and Freddie Mac. OFHEO was then merged in response to the most recent financial crisis that began in the summer of 2007 into the Federal Housing Finance Agency (FHFA) in the fall of 2008, which became the new and most recent regulator for the two GSEs. Ginnie Mae and FHA are federal agencies and oversight is provided by HUD.

All these developments coincided with an increase in housing activity over the years and contributed to a record high home ownership rate in recent years, though it is interesting that without providing for the tax deductibility of mortgage interest payments, non-recourse to a borrower's other assets and income in the event of default on a mortgage, and other less favorable treatment of housing, Canada has achieved a fairly similar rate of home ownership at roughly 65 percent of all occupied housing units being occupied by the unit's owner . Disturbingly, however, regulatory oversight of the two GSEs in particular and the real estate activities of financial firms more generally eventually contributed to a systemic failure of the regulatory and supervisory system, a failure that gave rise to the worst financial crisis since the Great Depression. Canada, at least through the most recent crisis, clearly demonstrates that a country can achieve a similar homeownership rate as the United States, but at the same time avoid a financial collapse in the process.

Summing Up

Figure 6.1 summarizes the regulatory structure in terms of a historical timeline. A notable feature is the burst of reform during or after wars (1812, 1863) and especially associated with crises, such as the Great Depression of the 1930s and the Savings and Loan Crisis of the 1980s. Clearly, a fairly elaborate federal regulatory structure had been put in place over the century and a half before the mid-1970s, albeit on a piecemeal basis after fighting several financial wars, to promote a well-functioning financial system. By the 1970s the Fed, OCC, FHLBB, HUD, and FDIC were all well-established federal agencies with several decades of regulatory experience. In addition they were supported by the financial regulatory authorities in each of the fifty states.

Despite this seemingly impressive and comprehensive structure, regulators were about to confront another financial crisis that would lead to still more expansive reforms. Between 1980 and 1995, 5,182 commercial banks, savings and loan associations, and credit unions failed. These depository institutions held $908 billion in assets and imposed losses on three relevant deposit insurance funds and US taxpayers of $192 billion (or roughly $330 billion in 2011 dollars), excluding losses to stockholders and uninsured creditors. We therefore devote time to discussing what happened during this turbulent and challenging period. The main focus is on savings and loans (S&Ls), since they account for more than 80 percent of the losses; as in the most recent and even worse financial crisis, the problems started in the housing sector.

Savings and Loans: A Case Study of Financial Regulatory Failure[6]

Widespread reports of inflated and misleading financial statements, intensive lobbying of financial firms, politicians, and regulators, numerous and costly failures of financial firms, millions of layoffs of hard-working people, numerous congressional hearings, and criminal and civil investigations. Sound familiar? For those with short memories, it's the most recent financial crisis of 2007 to 2009. But for those who are a bit older, it's also the savings and loan crisis of the 1980s.

In the early 1980s, nearly four thousand saving and loans throughout the country were unprofitable and insolvent on a market value basis. A decade later, nearly one-third of these institutions had been seized by regulatory authorities and either liquidated or sold to healthier institutions. Taxpayers had to help cover the $153 billion cost to resolve these failed institutions because the FSLIC, the industry-supported federal deposit-insurance fund set up to protect depositors, had itself become insolvent due to the huge losses.

This dire situation was the first but not last major breakdown of the new and expanded federal regulatory and deposit-insurance system that was established a half century earlier during the Great Depression. Ironically, the federal regulatory system was designed to promote a safe and sound savings and loan industry, but in fact it contributed to the crisis. The deposit-insurance system moreover was designed to ensure that any losses from failures would be borne by the industry-supported insurance fund, not taxpayers. Despite all assurances by the federal government to the contrary, as the savings and loan crisis unfolded, that too did not happen. In early 1989 President George H. W. Bush announced that taxpayer funds would be necessary to clean up the mess once and for all. (Nearly twenty years later, his son, President George W. Bush, would make a similar announcement regarding the banking industry.)

Shockingly, the losses of the 1980s were far greater than those borne by depositors of failed banks during the 1930s, which was before the establishment of federally chartered savings and loans, the FHLBB, and a federal deposit-insurance system. For at least four decades, no single industry had ever faced such a deep and widespread crisis as the savings and loan industry did in the 1980s. Not a single state of our nation was without a failure during this turbulent period. Taxpayers had never been required to bear such a large sum as that eventually required to cover the losses of so many failed firms in a single industry.

The financial turmoil, moreover, involved all the federally insured depository institutions. Indeed among the failed institutions throughout the 1980s and into the early 1990s were 1,273 savings and loans with assets of $640 billion, 1,569 commercial and savings banks with $264 billion of assets, and 2,330 credit unions with $4 billion of assets. However, the worst problem clearly resided with the savings and loan industry. These institutions suffered an annual failure rate 3 times the rate for business firms and 12 times the rate for banks during the period 1980 to 1984. As the crisis unfolded and spread to other depository institutions, the

FDIC like the FSLIC also became insolvent. Fortunately for taxpayers, the FDIC's insolvency, unlike the case of the FSLIC, was short-lived and remedied without direct taxpayer expenditures. Only the government insurance fund for credit unions, the NCUSIF, remained solvent throughout this turbulent period.

What caused these costly failures, and were the financial reforms enacted in response to such costly failures successful? The time is particularly opportune to address these questions given that the most recent financial reform that has been undertaken, in the form of the Dodd–Frank Wall Street Reform and Consumer Protection Act of 2010, is also a response to a housing-related crisis and is the most sweeping reform since the Great Depression. As discussed in chapter 7, it adds still another level of complexity to the existing federal regulatory structure in response to yet another and even more devastating financial crisis than the savings and loan crisis. Since about 130 other countries have also suffered financial crises since 1980 and many of these countries, like the United States, have or are currently undertaking financial reform, such an assessment should help provide further evidence as to whether the current course numerous governments are pursuing is sufficient to prevent, or at least reduce the severity of, future financial problems.

We now examine two distinct phases of the crisis, stressing that regulatory and legislative decisions exacerbated the breadth and depth of the problems. During the first phase, from the late 1970s until the early 1980s, savings and loans were devastated when a ticking time bomb was set off by a rapid rise in interest rates. At its core, the interest rate problem reflected regulatory and policy decisions that imposed untenable restrictions on savings and loans. The second phase was characterized by a deterioration in asset quality from the mid-1980s to 1989 brought on by expanded investment opportunities provided by the federal government in its effort to transform the industry into more bank-like institutions, which had largely avoided the interest rate problem. The regulatory reforms to facilitate the transformation allowed savings and loans to "gamble for resurrection," which drove the savings and loan industry deeply into the red, requiring a bigger government bailout and even more elaborate regulatory reforms. Finally, in 1989, a law was passed, the Financial Institutions Reform, Recovery and Enforcement Act (FIRREA), that provided funds for a new temporary agency, the Resolution Trust Corporation (RTC). The purpose of the RTC was at last to resolve all the remaining insolvent savings and loans. In addition, due to a job badly done and to appease the public, FIRREA replaced the FHLBB by the Office of Thrift Supervision (OTS)—though the same employees were retained—and the FSLIC was replaced by a new insurance fund for savings and loans, the Savings Association Insurance Fund (SAIF), and placed under the administration of the FDIC. (SAIF was later merged into the deposit insurance fund for banks, the Bank Insurance Fund [BIF]). If regulators had been fired, there might have been some accountability, but merely reshuffling the agencies and retaining an alphabet soup of regulators was instead the chosen course of action, Indeed Heisel and Vartabedian (2008) report that during the more recent financial crisis of 2007 to 2009 a top regulatory official allowed a financial institution to backdate a capital infusion, which allowed the institution to report that it was "well capitalized." However, two months later, the institution failed at an estimated cost to the FDIC insurance fund of $8.9 billion. The same official reportedly had been demoted because of his role in the collapse of another financial institution during the S&L crisis, which at the time was the biggest institution failure ever.[7]

Ticking Time Bomb

Savings and loans were among the most heavily regulated firms in the country at the beginning of the 1980s. These federally chartered institutions were forbidden by law to make adjustable-rate home mortgages because it was decided by the federal government that these types of mortgages would expose home buyers to higher payment risk and thus possibly even to foreclosures should interest rates rise. (Supposedly, the story goes, when a prominent US Senator saw his mortgage payment increase because he had an adjustable-rate mortgage from a state-chartered savings and loan, which that particular state had allowed; he persuaded a majority of his congressional colleagues to impose a moratorium on the offering of all such mortgages by even state-chartered institutions, a moratorium that was relatively short-lived.) Savings and loans were not even allowed to make loans more than one-hundred miles from their home office, despite any geographical diversification benefits, because this protected local institutions from competition from other savings and loans outside their immediate geographic area. Nor could these institutions originate most loans that commercial banks could make, such as commercial real estate loans or loans to businesses, despite any product diversification benefits. However, this limited the potential for any destructive competition between these two types of depository institutions. It also helped justify two separate regulatory authorities for the two industries operating under separate business models. In an effort allegedly to make these institutions safe and sound, the restrictions imposed on their portfolios concentrated their risks and left them with a funding mismatch (borrowing very short term to lend long term) that left them ripe for failure in the event of an adverse upward shift in short- relative to long-term interest rates. Savings and loans were not even allowed at the time to offer their customers demand deposits or use the word "bank" in their title largely due to opposition from commercial banks.

The range of activities in which savings and loans were allowed to engage at the beginning of the 1980s was strictly limited by law and regulation almost entirely to fixed interest rate home mortgage loans. This required them to keep narrowly focused on their mission to help promote home ownership. At the same time, the mortgages were funded by relatively short-term deposits whose interest rates were also fixed by law and regulation. At the beginning of the 1980s, for example, savings and loans earned an average of 4 percent on home mortgages and paid 2 percent on deposits. Thus, for every $100 of home loans they made, they received $2 in net interest income. This was virtually their only source of revenue, out of which they paid salaries and other expenses as well as taxes.

This traditional and apparently simple business model, however, was about to encounter severe difficulties. Reacting to inflationary conditions in the late 1970s, the Fed changed its operating policy, focusing much more on the rapidly expanding money supply rather than on interest rates. As a result of the subsequent monetary tightening to control inflation, interest rates rose abruptly, with short-term rates rising much faster than long-term rates. The $2 in net interest income earned by savings and loans quickly vanished as they found it necessary to raise the interest rate paid on deposits in response to the new and higher interest rate environment. This action—which enabled the institutions to retain more deposits and avoid having to sell assets at fire-sale prices—was belatedly facilitated by the federal government when it eliminated the ceiling on deposit rates they could offer. If these institutions had not been able to raise the rates paid, depositors would have withdrawn their deposits and put them into unregulated financial intermediaries like mutual funds, or what are now considered a part of the shadow banking system (i.e., the more lightly regulated but bank-like part of the financial system), offering the higher interest rates. Still, many but far fewer depositors did make the switch.

The once workable business model no longer worked once interest rates rose. Almost every institution saw its profits turn to losses and, on a market value basis, most institutions became insolvent as the market value of its home mortgages fell below the market value of the deposits funding them. (The home mortgages had predominantly fixed rates, whereas the rates paid on deposits were fairly flexible.) Holding loans on the balance sheet that were put there in earlier years and earning low, fixed interest rates was no longer so attractive when similar interest rates on new loans had skyrocketed.

Nevertheless, despite the long-standing existence of a deposit rate ceiling and the delay in its removal, allowing savings and loans to pay market interest rates on its deposits prevented the far more serious and widespread deposit withdrawals that would have forced them to sell their home mortgages at huge losses to obtain liquidity. The federal government considered it better to permit savings and loans to suffer reduced earnings by raising the interest rate they had to pay to retain deposits than to suffer even larger losses from the forced sale of home mortgages. The overall federal governmental strategy being pursued at the time was designed to buy time for savings and loans until the structure of interest rates returned to a more normal level and shape. The expectation, or perhaps more likely the hope, was that this reversal would occur sometime soon and restore profitability to the industry before capital was entirely depleted.

This example shows that the Fed's interest rate policies created a serious problem for the heavily regulated and supervised depository industry. In general, federal government regulators must continually adapt and react to contain any excessively disruptive impacts on depository institutions from changes in financial markets, both domestic and foreign. In this particular case, the Fed reacted to contain growing inflationary pressures. However, as the savings and loan crisis demonstrates, the broader impacts of such reactions should be more carefully examined and appropriate adjustments made in regulations in a timelier manner. Given the business model of savings and loans at the time, the potentially disastrous side effects of the Fed's reaction to inflation should have been widely anticipated by the federal regulatory authorities. In this case the adverse effects were confined to a fairly narrow segment of the entire financial system—commercial banks were better diversified at the time both to credit risks and interest rate changes—and thus less disruptive than proved to be the case in the most recent financial crisis in 2007 to 2009 when credit flowed freely and on fairly generous terms into the housing sector as the Fed lowered interest rates too much and kept them low too long.

The Savings and Loan Industry Plunges into Insolvency

The first phase of the savings and loan crisis—roughly 1980 to 1985—was the result of laws and regulations that imposed too rigid a business model on institutions, permitting them to offer only fixed rate, long-term home mortgages funded by deposits tied to short-term rates. Although there were many other less risky ways to fund home mortgages in the late 1970s—from hedging interest rate risk in the forward, futures, and options markets to offering adjustable rate mortgages—savings and loans were largely forbidden to use these alternatives. Only after the industry imploded did the government relent and allow their use.

When interest rates rose and the savings and loan industry plunged into market-value insolvency, the second phase of the savings and loan crisis began. The regulatory authorities had a straightforward game plan that they were supposed to follow. They were expected to seize savings and loans known to be insolvent and then choose the least expensive way to deal with them. This would involve either liquidating them or finding other healthier institutions to acquire them, by providing financial support if necessary.

One binding constraint, however, prevented the authorities from resolving all the insolvencies in this manner. Compared to the number and depth of the insolvencies, the FSLIC had insufficient funds to fulfill its assigned task. By the early 1980s, saving and loans throughout the country were insolvent by about $110 billion, while the fund was reporting only $6 billion in reserves. The FSLIC, in other words, was insolvent on the basis of its contingent liabilities associated with all the insolvent institutions. Yet its auditor, the US General Accounting Office (GAO—now the Government Accountability Office), did not require this large liability to be recorded until 1986. It was only then that the GAO fully revealed the depth of the insolvency of the FSLIC to the public. By then, nearly 500 institutions were publically reporting that they had negative capital on the basis of generally accepted accounting principles (GAAP), the standard framework that commercial banks and businesses use to present their financial accounts. Yet these institutions were still open and operating, and many with such negative capital had been open and operating in this condition for years.

As a result the federal government—a major contributing culprit to the crisis by its failure to fulfill its responsibilities to promote a safe and sound savings and loan industry and to resolve failed institutions in a timely manner—was left to manage a huge insolvency proceeding in which it had a relatively simple, but unpleasant, choice. Either it could require taxpayers to cover the approximately $110 billion to resolve the insolvent savings and loans at the time or, with the hope that the term structure of interest rates would fall and shift in such a way as to eliminate the immediate crisis, it could implement ways to postpone recognizing, if not actually avoiding, the embedded market-value losses. Under the circumstances it is not surprising that Congress chose the latter course, without public opposition from the administration or the FSLIC's auditor, the GAO. Needless to say, the course chosen by Congress also had the full support of the savings and loan industry.

Congress specifically enacted two major laws in reaction to the crisis that allowed it and the regulators to ignore the severity of the crisis. The first law was the Depository Institutions, Deregulation and Monetary Control Act in 1980 and the second was the Garn–St Germain Depository Institutions Act in 1982. Neither new law, however, provided additional funds to allow regulators to resolve insolvent institutions. Instead, the laws were an attempt to buy time for a turnaround in the financial situation by lowering the minimum level of capital that a savings and loan was required to hold to satisfy regulatory requirements. This enabled institutions immediately to report a far healthier financial condition than otherwise. But it also forced regulators to devise other solutions to the problems they still faced. There was, however, no public outcry from regulators for the failure to be granted additional funds to help deal with the enormous problems it was required to resolve.

The laws also lowered enforcement standards for those institutions still near insolvency despite the lower capital requirements, and they gave regulators authority—and presumably with the implied message that it be used—to permit new accounting forms of regulatory capital. Many savings and loans widely known to be insolvent, even on the basis of accounting standards already in use, were therefore allowed to report publicly otherwise. Some benefited enough to be even allowed to report a capital level that met the minimum requirement. Indeed the amount of capital that institutions reported on the basis of regulatory accounting practices (RAP) exceeded that reported on the basis of GAAP. (Just as in the most recent financial crisis, investors paid the most attention to capital reported on the basis of tangible accounting principles, or owner-contributed equity capital less selected intangibles, rather than regulatory-based measures of capital.) Ironically, the federal government subsequently sued several major accounting firms for "overstating" the financial condition of savings and loans that failed, even though regulators themselves counted items as capital that were not allowed by those same accounting firms.

In short, Congress was granting authority to, and thereby in effect telling, regulators to "paper" over the problem and to engage in regulatory forbearance (i.e., to not enforce existing regulations and supervisory guidelines). Even though Congress was unwilling to provide funds to the FSLIC, federal regulators did not publically complain. Instead, they sought to buy sufficient time until savings and loan profitability could be restored with the return to a more normal interest rate environment. It was hoped that when this happened, institutions would have found ways to improve profitability through the new and expanded powers provided for in the two laws enacted in the early 1980s. These new laws allowed savings and loans to become more like commercial banks, which were not anyway near as hard hit by the precipitous rise in short-term interest rates at that time. This reluctance to provide funds would resurface in the most recent crisis. In this case the Congress seemed averse to considering a temporary takeover and then sale of big banks due to the huge fiscal cost at the same time that there was substantial concern about the growing size of the federal budget deficit.

Gambling for Resurrection

Lower capital requirements for savings and loans were allowed, as already noted, in the laws enacted in 1980 and 1982. These institutions also were permitted to diversify into commercial real estate loans, direct equity investments, commercial loans, and other kinds of loans that commercial banks could already make. The savings and loans were also allowed to offer variable-rate mortgages and to make loans nationwide. At roughly the same time, an increasing number of states granted broader lending and investment opportunities to their own state-chartered savings and loans, sometimes even far broader than the opportunities authorized for federally chartered institutions. All these developments came too late and at a time when hundreds of savings and loans were already insolvent. This situation gave rise to the second phase of the savings and loan crisis.

Although the new changes brought about by new federal laws allowed savings and loans to reduce their interest rate risk, the changes exposed savings and loans to new risks. After being granted broader powers, many institutions began making commercial real estate loans and investments, new activities in which they were relatively inexperienced. The Economic Recovery Tax Act of 1981 by providing tax benefits spurred much of this activity. As savings and loans moved into the commercial real estate market, commercial banks also increased their commercial real estate loan business, making the market still more competitive. These additional factors also gave rise to the second phase of the crisis, as savings and loans diversified away from home mortgages, and as has happened in the past, a rush by intermediaries to plunge into new markets was met with losses, both deliberate (some banks looted their shareholders, as described in chapter 3) and unintended.

Perverse incentives were created for many institutions by the new, looser regulatory restrictions. Specifically, open but still insolvent savings and loans and even those near insolvency had an incentive to take excessive risks, or "gamble for resurrection," a term coined by R. Dan Brumbaugh Jr. in his early and important book on the problems of the thrift industry during the 1980s.[8] The reason is that these institutions would reap the rewards if everything went well and the deposit insurance fund would bear the losses if everything went wrong. Even the most deeply troubled savings and loans that were left open could attract more deposits to grow by offering higher rates because of federal deposit insurance. The higher rates paid would moreover accrue in the accounts of depositors and require no cash outlays by the institutions. This enabled them to avoid the discipline of the marketplace and the need to rely on internally generated profits. The additional funds raised could be used to acquire excessively risky assets or even used to pay higher salaries to management. Of course, state and federal authorities' duty to taxpayers was to keep the perverse incentives in check by appropriate regulation and supervision.

Competition, inexperience, and perverse regulatory incentives—all of which were clearly predictable and increasingly more obvious as problems began to develop—led to serious problems. Even more severe problems arose as the result of regional recessions and the Tax Reform Act of 1986. The law more than eliminated the tax benefits for investing in commercial real estate that savings and loans had received only a few years earlier. These developments caused commercial real estate values to fall dramatically. In particular, regulatory flip-flops on the part of the federal government also contributed to the savings and loan crisis. For example, in 1981 and 1982, Congress provided savings and loans with an incentive to invest in commercial real estate, and then in 1986, Congress eliminated the incentive, leaving the savings and loans with a poorly performing asset.

The important lesson of the savings and loan crisis is quite clear. We urgently need some way to hold regulators accountable for their behavior, since, as already noted, apparently one cannot entirely rely on them to enforce regulations, or even Congress or the GAO to compel them to do so, especially when things get difficult for a large number of institutions.

Commercial Banks Did Not Entirely Escape Problems

What was happening to commercial banks during the saving and loan crisis? They largely avoided problems until the late 1980s and early 1990s. At that time commercial banks, like savings and loans earlier (which should have alerted bank regulators to an impending problem), experienced significant deterioration in asset quality from commercial real estate, which is also the case for many banks during the most recent financial crisis. As a result of this deterioration in asset quality, there were numerous bank failures that cost $37 billion to resolve and drove the FDIC into insolvency for two years. If it were not for the savings and loan crisis, the banks' problems would have been the focus of far greater public attention. Furthermore, if a few large banks had failed or required federal government support, the problems could have been even greater than those of the savings and loans, which indeed was the case less than two decades later.

The deterioration in bank performance was the result of a series of difficulties first involving loans to developing countries in the early 1980s, then loans for highly leveraged transactions in the mid-1980s, and finally commercial real estate loans in the late 1980s. The process that led to this sequence of difficulties had many characteristics similar to the savings and loan crisis. Banks faced geographic banking restrictions that were not removed until the enactment of the Riegle–Neal Interstate Banking and Branching Efficiency Act of 1994. They were also restricted in their ability to engage in securities, insurance, and real estate activities. The enactment of the Gramm–Leach–Bliley Act of 1999 removed the final restrictions to allowing banks to engage in securities and insurance activities. Until these laws were enacted, banks were impeded in their ability to diversify their operations, both with respect to their product offerings and geographical locations in which those products could be offered. They now, albeit belatedly, were provided with both potentially new profitable and risk-reducing opportunities.

As deterioration in the banks' condition overwhelmed the funds available to the FDIC, just as in the case of FSLIC a few years earlier, the banking regulatory authorities adopted some of the same forbearance techniques that had been used for the savings and loans. For instance, banks known to be insolvent were allowed to remain open in the hope that they would be able to recover and spare the deposit-insurance fund further losses. In addition the traditional and more backward-looking accounting techniques used by many banks allowed several large banks to avoid reporting some losses.

Unlike the savings and loans in the late 1970s and early 1980s, however, the banks benefited from actions taken by the Fed. Its response to combat the recession in 1990 to 1991 was to pursue an expansionary monetary policy, with the result that short-term interest rates fell relative to long-term interest rates. This enabled banks to restore profitability through greater net interest income. For several years, just as happened in 2010, banks were able to earn profits by purchasing Treasury securities with federally insured deposits rather than making more traditional business loans. Thus the Fed's policy that changed in the late 1970s and early 1980s precipitated the savings and loan crisis, whereas its policy change during 1990 to 1991 helped the banks avoid potentially even larger losses. Given that the Fed is responsible for monetary policy, financial stability (in its role as lender of last resort), and regulating banks, as seen, these different roles do not always work in unison to produce desirable outcomes for all financial firms over time.

Summary and Conclusions

The 1980s savings and loan crisis and associated commercial bank problems form an important backdrop in evaluating the general notion that federal government regulation as it has been conducted over time can be effective in preventing banking crises or reducing the severity of such crises when they occur. Even before the 1980s, the United States had over time built up one of the most elaborate regulatory and supervisory regimes in the world. Yet throughout the 1980s and into the early 1990s, the United States experienced a lengthy financial crisis that involved an unprecedented number of depository institution failures and highly costly resolutions. At the time there was a "prompt corrective action" regime in place in which savings and loans were required by law and regulation to meet a 5 percent minimum capital requirement. If the required capital ratio fell to 3 percent, the institutions were subject to strict supervisory control. If the required capital ratio fell to zero or less, institutions were to be seized by the appropriate regulatory authorities.

Nonetheless, during the early 1980s when hundreds of savings and loans became insolvent, Congress—with full knowledge of the extent of the problem—lowered capital standards and jettisoned prompt corrective action measures. Laws and regulations were also changed by the federal government so that institutions were subject to lower minimum capital requirements at the same time as there was a liberalization of the items that could count as capital, even items that were not allowable under GAAP, thereby providing institutions with the ability to grow in size without additional capital. The overall effect was to allow institutions with negative capital, properly measured, to remain open and operating, in many cases for several years. Thus in postponing the recognition of the problem, Congress made the cost of resolving it much greater—as much as five to six times what it would have been.

To deter excessive risk-taking with depleted owner-contributed equity capital, one would expect growth in assets of savings and loans to be relatively modest during the 1980s. Total assets at all savings and loans, however, doubled from $604 billion in 1980 to $1.2 trillion in 1986, which represented 41 percentage points more than the growth of GDP over the same period. Such rapid growth in overall credit, and even more rapid growth by the insolvent institutions, was fueled by incentives provided by the federal regulatory authorities and occurred under their watchful eyes. Furthermore it was largely funded by institutions offering relatively high interest rates on deposits. Of course, it was well known that the only way institutions could hope to pay the higher rates and still earn profits was to acquire assets that promised to yield still higher rates, which means ever riskier assets. Yet, in view of the high rates, regulators did nothing for far too long.

The basic change in regulation that occurred in the 1980s was that first there was a heavy reliance on various restrictions, such as strict capital requirements, interest ceilings, and portfolio limits, and then a switch as the financial marketplace changed to a reliance on prudential measures, such as regular examinations and supervisory oversight and prompt corrective action requirements. Both approaches to regulation, however, proved to be a dismal failure in adequately limiting problems. It is important to note that this change in regulatory approaches to better regulate financial institutions was not accompanied by a corresponding change in the accountability of regulators. The result was that the federal government basically spent a decade making the situation worse and blaming others. Sounds familiar, doesn't it? Recall that in response to the crisis in the housing sector in the Great Depression, the federal government tried to strengthen the savings and loan industry to help promote home ownership. When in response to market forces the federal government-directed, housing-lending savings and loans industry collapsed in the late 1970s and early 1980s, the federal government turned to Fannie Mae and Freddie Mac to help promote home ownership, only later to see these two GSEs subsequently be placed into conservatorship by their regulator after having grown rapidly for several years with relatively little owner-contributed equity capital.

The core lesson to be learned from these historical crises is the need for skepticism about the benefits of simply creating more regulators and granting more powers to them after every crisis, and especially the efficacy of crisis-driven, financial reform. What is truly and finally needed is to hold the regulatory authorities accountable to the public. The old approach has simply not worked; it is time for a new approach.

7

More of the Same: Post 2007–2009 Financial Crisis Regulation

What is desired is something having a good sound, but quite harmless, which will impress the popular mind with the idea that a great deal is being done, when, in reality, very little is intended to be done.
—Charles Adams Jr., president of Union Pacific Railroad, 1887

This time is no different. In response to the worst financial crisis since the Great Depression, the US government established more regulations, created new regulatory bodies, and granted the Guardians of Finance more and broader power, without addressing the core defects in the financial regulatory system that produced the crisis. The Dodd–Frank Wall Street Reform and Consumer Protection Act of 2010 (Dodd–Frank) is certainly the longest reform law ever passed, and it gives regulators complete discretion with respect to bank capital standards, liquidity, requirements, and numerous other financial policy considerations. Furthermore, since the financial crisis was global in nature, the Basel Committee on Banking Supervision (BCBS) also weighed in with a third and updated version of its guidelines on banking regulation for countries to adopt. The new bank capital and liquidity framework, referred to as Basel III, was announced by the BCBS in September and ratified by the Leaders of the G20 in November 2010.

The purpose of this chapter is to assess whether Dodd–Frank and Basel III truly represent a break from the past and will improve the safe and sound operation of financial systems. To do so, we describe and analyze some of their components in detail. The key question is whether the reforms at long last address the main weaknesses in the financial regulatory approach to preventing financial crises that we have identified in previous chapters?

The short answer is no. Admittedly, parts of Dodd–Frank may actually do some good at the margin, but overall, it is an astonishingly weak and insufficient response to a crisis that has made the record books. Put bluntly, it represents more of the same old discretionary approach that regulators everywhere favor so much. The obvious loser is the public, because the "reforms" perpetuate the same lack of regulatory account-ability that contributed to the crises in the first place. Basel III is no bet-ter. While it consists of higher capital and liquidity requirements that are phased in over several years and some other bells and whistles, Basel III still fundamentally relies on risk weights, ratings models, and rating agen-cies—though with promises from regulators that they will now put these to better use going forward than they did in the past.

Charles Adams would have been proud of both Dodd–Frank and the Basel III "reforms." It looks to the public like "a great deal is being done," but in reality, "very little is intended to be done." Of course, regulators, who largely write and implement reforms, are proud to take credit for their work, that is, until the next crisis when denials and finger-pointing begins. After a discussion of these most recent regulatory efforts, we turn in the concluding chapter to some reforms that we think might actually work (and thus worry a modern Charles Adams).

The Dodd–Frank Wall Street Reform and Consumer Protection Act

Dodd–Frank certainly sets a new record in terms of length. At 2,319 pages, the law far exceeds the combined length of all major pieces of federal financial legislation over the past century. The length is truly astounding in view of the fact that the 1913 law establishing the Federal Reserve was only thirty-one pages long. Even the more recent Gramm–Leach–Bliley Act of 1999 (the GLB Act), which prohibits commercial firms from owning banks and vice versa, was only 145 pages long. In view of its length, who was surprised when reports began to circulate that virtually no member of Congress had read the entire bill before voting on it? It's almost as though the spirit of railroad magnate Charles Adams were at work, devising a palliative that sounds good and is sure to impress the "popular mind."

Beyond its length, Dodd–Frank is complex, vague, and grants regula-tors more discretionary power without enhancing the ability of the public and their elected representatives to govern the regulatory apparatus.[1] Of the 330 rule-making provisions, 208 do not even impose any deadlines for issuing the rules, and the law mandates more than 60 studies and a hundred congressional reports. Upon its enactment, the various financial regulators had to get busy reading, interpreting, and writing the hundreds of new rules to implement the new law (as shown in table 7.1). Thus the true impact of Dodd–Frank is essentially delegated to the Guardians of Finance. As the regulators study and interpret the law, needless to say, an army of lobbyists will be quite busy earning its pay by trying to shape the eventual outcome so that it is more favorable to its many and diverse clients. Some have even cynically described Dodd–Frank as the "Financial Lobbyist Full Employment Act of 2010."

Dodd–Frank certainly does not reduce the complexity of the U.S. regulatory apparatus. As figure 7.1 shows, it is virtually impossible for anyone

Table 7.1
Provisions in Dodd–Frank that expressly reference rule-making, by agency

Agency	Mandatory provisions	Discretionary provisions	Total
SEC	46	51	97
Board of Governors	25	42	67
CFTC	21	31	52
CFPB	17	25	42
FDIC	7	8	15
Other individual agencies	4	10	14
Two agencies	8	10	18
Three or more agencies	20	5	52
Total	148	182	330

Source: Curtis W. Copeland, "Rulemaking Requirements and Authorities in the Dodd–Frank Wall Street Reform and Consumer Protection Act," CRS Report for Congress, November 2010.
Note: The "other individual agencies" include the Secretary of the Treasury, the Federal Trade Commission, and the Comptroller of the Currency. The "two agencies" provisions include rules to be issued by the CFTC and the SEC, and by the FDIC and the Board of Governors. Provisions requiring rules to be issued by "all primary financial regulatory agencies," "each federal primary financial regulatory agency," "the appropriate federal banking agencies," or "the prudential regulators" were treated as issued by three or more agencies. Other "three or more agencies" provisions listed the agencies required or permitted to issue rules (e.g., "Board of Governors of the Federal Reserve System, the Comptroller of the Currency, the Federal Deposit Insurance Corporation, the National Credit Union Administration Board, the Federal Housing Finance Agency, and the Bureau of Consumer Financial Protection").

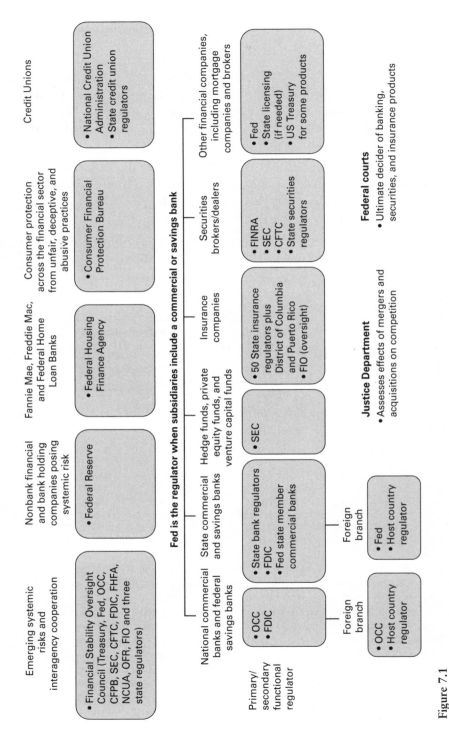

Figure 7.1
The US regulatory regime: Multiple, overlapping, inconsistent, and costly regulation

other than trained regulatory experts to discern any noticeable difference between the new and old regulatory structures. Consolidation has occurred in the private banking industry, but obviously not in the financial regulatory industry. The only consolidation that takes place is the merger of one regulator (the Office of Thrift Supervision, OTS) into another (the Office of the Comptroller of the Currency, OCC). However, this merger is offset by the creation of a new regulator, the Consumer Financial Protection Bureau, which is discussed below. The new structure remains an inefficient hodgepodge of overlapping regulatory agencies that reflects the gerrymandering fashion in which financial regulation has evolved in the United States. Charles Adams could not have done better.

We are not arguing that a single financial regulatory authority does better than multiple authorities as discussed in chapter 5 and our earlier book, *Rethinking Bank Regulation*, but excessive complexity could hinder effective regulation and may reflect political, rather than economic, objectives. For example, more regulatory agencies imply more congressional oversight committees. This may be desirable to some members of Congress, and explain their reluctance for greater consolidation because more oversight committees necessitate more committee chairs benefiting from campaign contributions.

We next explain several specific components of Dodd–Frank and assess its likelihood of success in preventing a future crisis. As will become clear, the law leaves considerable discretion to the regulators, just as in the past. While this may be fine, what is not so fine is the continued practice of allowing regulators to exercise that discretion without any accountability to the public, especially given their past record of poor performance.

Finally, we turn to Basel III, which not only will influence the shape of regulation in the United States, but in much of the rest of the world. While it takes modeling complexity to a new height, Basel III retains the same weakness as Dodd–Frank, a total reliance on unelected regulators who are given a wide berth to regulate as they see fit without any meaningful accountability. History tells us what the outcome of that approach has been: one crisis after another, followed by one unsuccessful reform after another.

A New Guardian of the Financial System

Dodd–Frank established a new Financial Stability Oversight Council (FSOC) whose stated purpose is to identify, monitor, and address any systemic risk posed by large, complex financial firms, as well as the financial products and activities commonly found at many financial firms throughout the country. In short, the FSOC is the new financial police force on the block. It consists of fifteen members: nine federal financial regulators, one independent member with insurance expertise, and five nonvoting members, including three state regulators. The Secretary of the Treasury serves as chairperson, or chief of financial police.

In addition to its other responsibilities, the FSOC is responsible for identifying systemically important nonbank financial firms for regulation by the Fed. The law is silent as to how to measure systemic risk and therefore how the FSOC is to fulfill this duty. It is also authorized to make recommendations to the Fed on standards for systemic risk firms, including capital and liquidity requirements. The exact standards are left to the discretion of the Fed. Of course, as has been the case in the past with reform legislation, the Fed remains unaccountable for whatever happens based on the standards it sets. The Fed also is authorized to require that firms identified as posing systemic risks conduct all their financial activities in an intermediate holding company that will be regulated like a bank holding company (a BHC, an example of which is Citigroup).

To support the FSOC, a new Office of Financial Research (OFR) is established within the Treasury Department, which "sounds like a great deal is being done." Its responsibilities include promoting best practices for financial risk management, monitoring and reporting changes in systemic risk, and evaluating and reporting on stress tests for banks. Strange, isn't it—adding still another layer of bureaucracy to perform the same types of activities that have always been an ongoing responsibility of the financial regulatory authorities? But the important question is: Will the OFR now accomplish what all the other regulators collectively failed to accomplish in the past? We think not.

Rather, the OFR seems like a device to "impress the popular mind" but, in reality, to do nothing to truly protect the public. After all, the OFR is located within the Treasury Department, not within an independent agency, and this makes it more vulnerable to political pressures. Does anyone really believe that the OFR is going to hire a sufficiently large group of top-notch lawyers, accountants, financial economists, and individuals with private-market experience at close to market wages, organize them into effective teams, grant them unencumbered access to data, make them independent of financial market influences, have them assess the state of financial regulation, and then deliver an objective assessment to the public at large—an assessment that could conflict with the views of the Secretary of the Treasury, the chairs of the Fed, SEC, OCC, and all the other regulatory bodies? Charles Adams must be laughing and cheering.

At first glance, other features of the FSOC might also seem like good ideas. For example, to the extent that the individual regulators previously failed to devote enough attention to systemic risk because each was focused too narrowly on its own segment of the financial system, then the FSOC could play a beneficial, coordinating role. Dodd–Frank now mandates that financial regulators meet and act as a group so as to devote far more attention to systemic risk and impose stricter prudential standards on those firms giving rise to systemic risk. The new council will in theory ensure that this happens by adding an additional layer of oversight above and beyond the individual regulatory agencies themselves (i.e., more complexity). Yet the FSOC membership consists of nearly all the same regulatory agencies that were in charge prior to the crisis and that not only failed to prevent the crisis but actually contributed to it.

An apt analogy for the college classes we teach would be a system in which the grading was turned over to the students. The students might take their responsibility seriously, critique one another's performance, and accurately assess one another's strengths and weaknesses. But we don't think that's likely. They won't want the stigma of criticizing each other, and since they constitute the group that will determine the grades, the likely outcome is that they will all end up with high grades. We suspect that same bias in the FSOC. We recall all the assurances by regulators in many countries; we heard them explain time and again how they were on top of the risks in the years leading up to the crisis. So why should we have confidence that they will take their jobs seriously now?

Is the added value of the FSOC an improved opportunity to communicate? It's hard to believe that regulation was ineffective in terms of crisis prevention because the regulators didn't all belong to the same council . . . or couldn't pick up a phone to speak with their counterparts at other agencies. After all, an interagency body already exists: the Federal Financial Institutions Examination Council (FFIEC), established in March 1979. The FFIEC consists of the Fed, the FDIC, the National Credit Union Administration (NCUA), the OCC, and, before it was abolished, the OTS. Despite the existence of the FFIEC, three financial crises—the savings and loan and commercial bank crises as well as the most recent crisis—took place under its watch. The experience gained over time by members working together for a common purpose based on a common approach to detecting problems did not appear to be of much help since the third crisis was far more severe than the previous two crises. It is therefore not clear that yet another council will be much of an improvement with respect to preventing another financial crisis. Meanwhile the Secretary of the Treasury and Chairman of the Fed have long had a practice of regular meetings, often weekly, supported by numerous contacts at many levels of their respective staff.

The case for the FSOC seems to rest on the assumption that the crisis was characterized by activities that were hard to detect or that fell between the jurisdictions of different agencies. This argument holds a bit of truth; as described in chapter 4, AIG was regulated as a savings and loan holding company supervised by the now-abolished OTS, as well as by a state regulator, with OTS the weakest link in the pre-crisis regulatory chain. But the Fed also had indirect jurisdiction. It just wasn't paying attention or, if it was, it didn't act. After all, it was the Fed's decision to allow banks to enjoy lower required capital ratios when they purchased credit default swaps from firms such as AIG that gave those firms and others the ability through excessive leverage to help blow up the financial system. The Fed did this without any due diligence over the providers of this form of insurance and did not protest that it needed the ability to oversee them before the crisis. Yet it still could have stopped allowing banks to enjoy lower capital ratios when they purchased credit default swaps, as their use and associated risk were skyrocketing.

There just is not much factual evidence that the crisis was driven by a failure to communicate or an inability to detect emerging problems. Regulators clearly knew about activities that precipitated the financial crisis. Consider, for example, that real estate assets at all FDIC-insured depository institutions accounted for nearly half of their total assets, or roughly $7 trillion, in 2007. This astronomical amount of outstanding real estate loans was due to double-digit growth rates during 2001 to 2007. At the same time housing prices were also growing at double-digit rates in many parts of the country. It is reasonable to presume that regulators were either fully aware of these particular facts or should have been aware of them—which is important because all depository institutions heavily involved in real estate would suffer if real estate prices were to collapse, which did indeed happen. Since real estate assets were also held by GSEs (Fannie Mae and Freddie Mac) with their own regulator, they too would suffer, which indeed they did.

Regulators also knew well that a large portion of all real estate assets had been securitized or were being held off-balance sheet, waiting to be securitized. So it is also reasonable to assume that regulators would have or should have been fully aware of the potential fallout from a collapse in real estate prices. If they couldn't focus on a widely held and huge asset class like home mortgages and think in terms of systemic fallout rather than damage to isolated individual depository institutions, then putting these people together on a new council is not enough, in our view, to change the decision-making process. Regulators must be charged with creating a better decision-making process to prevent, or at the very least, lessen the likelihood and severity of financial crises, and they must be accountable for seeing that it happens. While they are welcome to engage in self-assessment, taxpayers should want their performance to be evaluated on an ongoing basis by an independent group of experts reporting to and therefore accountable to the public. There are many checks and balances in our society but, as of yet, not a truly meaningful check and balance for our unelected, unaccountable financial regulators.

Dodd–Frank does authorize the FSOC to extend regulation to systemically important nonbank financial firms. Nonbanks, such as hedge funds, private equity firms, investment banks, and mutual funds, are part of the "shadow banking" system. These firms can become systemically important, that is, so big, important, or interconnected that their failure creates havoc as the effects spread throughout the financial system. Gorton and Metrick (2010) make the point that financial firms like investment banks, money-market mutual funds, and mortgage brokers—and financial instruments like repurchase agreements, asset-backed securities, and collateralized debt obligations—perform the same functions as banks (whose role in the financial system is diminishing) but that their regulation (compared to banks') is virtually nonexistent.[2] Publicly available data indicate that the shadow banking system has grown from roughly less than $3 trillion in 1980 to more than $40 trillion in 2010, and Gorton and Metrick argue that the recent crisis was in many respects centered in this fast-growing but largely ignored part of the financial sector. This is an important point because as the striking growth in the shadow banking system took place, the regulatory regime failed to adapt to the accompanying increase in risk. Did regulators not see that this major change was occurring? It was, after all, only trillions of dollars that were involved!

Although Dodd–Frank is correct to empower the regulatory authorities to regulate systemically important nonbank financial institutions, there are many questions about whether this will fix the root causes of the regulatory failures that fostered the most recent crisis of 2007 to 2009. For example, the spectacular growth of the shadow banking system from the 1980s through the crisis was not secret. It involved tens of trillions of dollars, more than the size of the entire commercial banking industry. What were the systemic, institutional failings in the regulatory apparatus that allowed this to happen? Have those defects been addressed by Dodd–Frank? We don't think so; instead, a system based on imposing required capital ratios and risk weights on banks not only encourages shadow banking, but raising those capital requirements, as discussed below, increases the incentive for banks to move risky assets into off-balance sheet entities. Also it is unclear which circumstances would trigger an extension by the FSOC to nonbanks, and how it would proceed in a timely manner to address looming problems.

Consumers Get Their Own Consumer Financial Protection Bureau

The Consumer Financial Protection Bureau (CFPB) was created to regulate all consumer financial products. Since the crisis saw a number of abusive practices, we certainly agree, as noted in chapter 2, that consumer protection is a real and legitimate goal of regulation. Of course, we also believe that more effort should be devoted to improving the financial literacy of consumers. The annual budget for CFPB was scheduled to increase from 10 to 12 percent of the Fed's budget as it ramps up to its operations to full force. This is a big enough budget to support a substantial amount of discretion to be exercised by the CFPB in regulating consumer financial products. The important point, however, is whether this discretion will be used wisely. It should be noted that although the CFPB is housed within the Federal Reserve, the Fed is not allowed to direct its activities, hire or fire its staff, or review or block its regulatory or enforcement activities.

The director of the CFPB is a regulatory czar over consumer financial products. Although the FSOC may issue a "stay" of a CFPB rule, this will require a two-thirds vote and the rule must endanger the stability of the entire financial system. We worry that this unprecedented amount of power given to a single individual could stifle financial innovation or otherwise lead to unintended and costly consequences for consumers. For example, will at some point a director be appointed who believes in concealing information from the public and mainly serves as a pawn of special interests? Or a director who believes in suppressing some products even though they may genuinely help consumers manage the risks that they face? In other words, the post-crisis pattern continues—another un-elected, unaccountable regulator has been created. Congress, even though it represents the public, alone clearly does not have the expertise to assess what is being done, and its exposure to lobbying efforts makes us less than sanguine about the positive results to be achieved by this new bureau.

The CFPB takes over the consumer protection functions and rule-making from OCC, OTS, FDIC, Federal Reserve, NCUA, HUD, and the CFTC. Apparently, since these regulators failed to do a good job, their responsibilities for consumer financial products and the associated employees are transferred to a new regulatory agency. Why should one expect CFPB to work better due to the consolidation of responsibilities within a single entity? We don't think it does much to addresses the core institutional weaknesses that failed to protect consumers.

The CFPB has vast powers. It may enforce federal laws intended to ensure fair, equitable, and nondiscriminatory access to credit for both individuals and communities. The CFPB may impose and keep fines, or distribute them to injured consumers. It is to conduct compliance exams for large banks (with more than $10 billion in assets) and covered non-banks, with the exams to be coordinated with FDIC, Fed, and state bank regulators. The CFPB may not "establish a usury limit" but may be able to indirectly regulate interest rates by finding a rate is "unfair." However, how all these things are to be done in an objective and defensible manner to the benefit of society is not explained. Again, the discretion is vast, but the accountability is virtually nonexistent.

Even the CFPB's most basic goals are quite vague, magnifying its discretionary powers. A new definition of "abusive" practice is added in the law: one that "materially interferes with the ability of a consumer to understand a term or condition of a consumer financial product or service; or takes unreasonable advantage of (A) a lack of understanding on the part of the consumer of the material risks, costs, or conditions of the product or service; (B) the inability of the consumer to protect the interests of the consumer in selecting or using a consumer financial product or service; or (C) the reasonable reliance by the consumer on a covered person to act in the interests of the consumer." After reading this, is it clear to you how the CFPB will go about identifying which practices are abusive and which are not? We didn't think so, but don't worry. Just have faith that the CFPB will ensure that financial firms will only provide those products and services to people who fully understand that they really want them!

The bottom line is that the creation of this new regulator fails to address the key weaknesses identified in the earlier chapters. After all, the Fed had widespread consumer financial and prudential regulatory powers and did not use them. Thus creating a new regulatory agency within the Fed hardly seems like a sound response. Some might view it as "looking good" but, "when in reality, very little is intended to be done." Others might stress that since the fundamental flaw with the US regulatory system is the inability of the public to govern the financial regulatory apparatus because it cannot obtain an informed, expert, and impartial assessment of financial regulation, creating another unmonitorable regulatory czar with broad discretionary powers is unlikely to have positive ramifications for the public at large.

What happens under Dodd–Frank if all else fails and there is indeed another systemic problem? It is to that issue that we now turn.

No More Taxpayer Bailouts: Too Big to Fail Firms Will Now Be Allowed to Fail

Banks need to be allowed to fail just like firms in any other sector of the economy. But the government steps in when banks fail to prevent runs that could rapidly spread to healthy banks. The existence of federal deposit insurance has virtually eliminated the tendency of depositors to run because their deposits are now insured (as long the public has faith in the credit worthiness of the federal government, and depositors are paid promptly when a bank fails). Deposit insurance also avoids the unnecessary losses that might be associated with a "fire sale" of bank assets to meet deposit withdrawals. This limits the losses to uninsured depositors and other creditors—and taxpayers. If runs are eliminated by the existence of the FDIC and liquidity is provided to illiquid but solvent banks by the Fed, then one would expect insolvent banks to be allowed to fail. The procedure that is supposed to be followed in such situations is that the FDIC is to seize insolvent banks and then either transfer the institutions to healthier banks or liquidate them and sell off the assets, choosing the least costly alternative course of action.

This arrangement has worked fine for small banks over the years, those "too small to save," but it has been a dismal failure when it comes to big banks. As some banks grew enormously over time, the government simply stood idly by and watched them grow. When several of them were at or near insolvency during the recent crisis, the government chose to bail them out. These banks were deemed "too big to fail (TBTF)." Having let them grow so large, the government by default could then only claim it had no other choice but to rescue them.

Dodd–Frank has created a new mechanism for the orderly liquidation of such systemically significant financial companies. This includes bank holding companies and those companies whose financial activities constitute 85 percent or more of consolidated revenues. The law specifically excludes Fannie Mae and Freddie Mac. Reform of these two systemically important financial firms awaits another day, to be determined by recommendation of the Secretary of Treasury, based on a study the department is required to conduct regarding options for ending their conservatorship while minimizing the costs to taxpayers.

A so-called Orderly Liquidation Fund is established within the Treasury Department, but experience raises serious questions about whether it will work in practice. It is managed and to be used by the FDIC to liquidate failing systemically significant financial companies. Since it is not prefunded, the funds to cover the liquidation costs are to be borrowed from the Treasury and the debt repaid from the liquidated assets. In addition there are not to be any more taxpayer bailouts, required assessments (no indication in the law as to how they will be determined or how much they will be) are to be levied on BHCs with total consolidated assets of $50 billion or more, and systemically significant nonbank financial companies will be regulated by the Fed. Recall that when the federal deposit insurance funds for savings and loans and commercial banks were depleted in the past there were no funds initially forthcoming from either the Congress or the Treasury Department, and as a result regulators without complaining had to rely for a time on other inferior methods to deal with insolvent institutions. Should we expect that the Treasury will now be ready and willing to loan money to the FDIC to liquidate too big to fail firms if they become deeply troubled in the years ahead? Might the Treasury resist the FDIC's attempt to close big banks to be spared the political embarrassment and financial cost? This is not an imaginary possibility; governments around the world have sought to postpone the recognition of losses and in general, the lower the degree of checks and balances in government, the longer the charade can continue.

When a big financial company is failing, the Secretary of the Treasury, in consultation with the president, now has the ultimate authority to recommend the appointment of the FDIC as receiver. This appointment can proceed with the agreement of the Federal Reserve. The new procedure is meant for emergencies only, with most large financial companies still expected to be resolved through the normal court bankruptcy process.

Again, lots of discretion is granted, but without any meaningful public accountability and without any plausible reason for believing that this Fund will reduce the incentive problems created by TBTF. For instance, without both clear guidelines about when liquidation will occur and a clear, credible commitment that the government will actually follow the guidelines, private investors will continue to treat some institutions as too big to fail and hence not monitor their risk very rigorously. Why should they? The government will pay off a TBTF financial institution if the institution is insolvent. Thus the vagueness of the policy undermines its effectiveness. Furthermore, since the Secretary of the Treasury has the ultimate authority to recommend the orderly liquidation of a large financial institution, this may inject political considerations into the decision-making process. To assist the regulatory authorities in the resolution process, the systemically significant companies are required to submit "funeral" plans (i.e., plans for how a company should be wound down and eventually be disposed of in the event it becomes insolvent) that are to be updated over time to the regulatory authorities. How the decision will be made as to whether such plans are acceptable remains unclear.

We certainly support a more orderly liquidation process, as well as one that shields taxpayers from bearing any of the closure costs of failed financial firms. Not only has the resolution process been disorderly in some of the previous financial crises, but worse yet, taxpayers have borne a significant portion of the costs to resolve problems.

However, it is important to distinguish between establishing a new resolution procedure to address the issue of systematically significant financial firms and regulators actually following through in times of crisis in a fair and equitable manner to dispose of such firms when they become insolvent. Consider the following reality check. At year-end 2010, five big banks (JP Morgan Chase Bank, Bank of America, Citibank, Wells Fargo Bank, and US Bank) had $7.7 trillion in assets as compared to the $13.3 trillion in total assets at all FDIC-insured institutions. Are the federal regulatory authorities, in conjunction with the Treasury Department, really prepared to seize and then liquidate a single one of these big banks, should conditions dictate such action? In view of their past behavior, we think not, at least not without oversight by an independent group other than the regulators.

The situation is even more complicated when considering the biggest financial companies in the world. In mid–2010, there were twenty-four financial companies headquartered in ten different countries with $1 trillion or more in total assets. Four of these were US financial holding companies. Most of these companies are actively engaged in global activities, which would most likely inject political considerations into their closure. Dodd–Frank simply requires that a study be undertaken regarding international coordination and the resolution of systematically significant financial institutions. This is a gaping hole in addressing the too big to fail issue.

Another issue related to too big to fail arises from the fact that Dodd–Frank now requires that swaps, with some exceptions,[3] be cleared through a clearinghouse and those transactions be executed on a centralized exchange. These institutions certainly do help reduce opacity in the over-the-counter (OTC) derivatives market[4] and thus enables everyone to better assess counterparty risk. This facilitates both the regulatory oversight of this market and the discipline exerted on the market by its participants so as to more adequately contain systemic risk. However, the clearinghouse and central exchange themselves may become too big to fail, which will require that they be adequately supervised and regulated. Once again, who will watch over regulators and hold them accountable for performing this important task?

Summary and Conclusions about Dodd–Frank

In summary, Dodd–Frank fails to introduce the truly meaningful reforms essential to significantly reducing the likelihood and severity of another financial crisis. Some of its reforms are clearly well intentioned and may be helpful. But far too often, with respect to the more serious issues, the law requires more studies rather than reform, or leaves too much discretion to regulatory authorities to determine the most appropriate interpretation of the intent of the law. We see little more than a continuation of a troubling historical pattern. In the wake of every financial crisis, the government, with great predictability, acts with great flourish to pass a new financial reform law, admittedly with some positive elements, but that is mainly only impressive in the sense described by Charles Adams. Regulatory authorities have been given ever more discretionary power over our financial system, but still remain unelected by and unaccountable to society. Instead, a better mechanism than congressional oversight to hold regulators accountable is the type of reform that is needed. As noted in chapter 1, regulators like all people are susceptible to bias, so more and broader discretionary powers granted to them with no accountability seems a particularly dangerous way to proceed.

It is time to break from the past and create an informed, expert, and independent entity acting solely in the interest of the public to assess the condition of the financial system over time and the way in which it is being regulated, based on a broad and dynamic perspective. The public needs to have an independent, expert evaluation of what the regulators are doing.

Indeed, consider the views of the special investigator general, who was appointed to oversee the $700 billion Troubled Asset Relief Program (TARP) that was established in the midst of the recent crisis. The individual appointed to the position, Neil Barofsky, was by all accounts the only independent, reasonably well-informed voice stating his concerns about the implementation and effectiveness of TARP. According to him, his ". . . job turned into blunting the effects of their [the Treasury Department] bad decisions."[5] Mr. Barofsky also stated that a TARP-funded program was a "colossal failure" and that "TARP's most significant legacy may be the exacerbation of the problem posed by 'too big to fail,' particularly given the manner in which Treasury executed the bailout. . . ."[6] Not surprisingly, the Treasury Department disagreed with his assessments.

Mr. Barofsky resigned in March 2011 after serving more than two years. His important but relatively narrow and temporary role and his public assessments of what happened related to that role underscore our major point about holding all the Guardians of Finance accountable in an ongoing and more comprehensive manner by creating a permanent overseer, namely a Sentinel.

Given that there are over two thousand pages describing the law, there are clearly other parts of the law that may be of interest to the reader. We briefly comment on some of these other parts in an appendix to this chapter. In some cases the law has the potential to make things worse, reflects political considerations in the treatment of some customers of depository institutions, and ventures into areas where reform may not be necessary. We now turn to a discussion and assessment of Basel III.

Basel I and II Didn't Do the Job, So Now Basel III

The Basel Committee on Bank Supervision approved capital guidelines on September 12, 2010, which were presented and agreed to at the G20 Seoul Summit in November 2010. The most recent incarnation of the Basel Capital Adequacy Accord, or Basel III, provides guidelines agreed upon by the central banks and bank supervisory authorities of the twenty-seven member jurisdictions.

The first Basel accord, Basel I, was adopted in 1988. Over time, however, it became clear that Basel I was a failure because it did not adequately measure various risks of banks. At the same time it contributed to greater securitization, which played a major role in the recent crisis, so as to more easily satisfy the capital requirements set for banks under Basel I. As a result of these developments, Basel II was developed in 2004 and implemented in the European Union that year. The United States had issued the final regulations for its implementation in April 2008, but the financial crisis and economic recession diverted attention elsewhere and Basel II was never fully implemented. It was widely realized that Basel II, which relied on risk models and credit ratings, was another failure and in need of a major overhaul. This gave rise to Basel III.

The purpose of Basel III is to correct all the deficiencies in Basel II. Once implemented, it is argued, Basel III will remedy the failures uncovered by the previous capital and liquidity requirements imposed by the bank regulatory authorities and which contributed to the 2007 to 2009 global financial crisis. In addition, since the United States is one of the member countries and Dodd–Frank defers to the banking regulators for setting such requirements, Basel III will undoubtedly be implemented in this country.

Minimum Capital Requirements and Phase-in Timetable

Basel II took six years to negotiate, and was based on quantitative risk models and ratings, both of which were dismal failures, as seen in the recent global financial crisis. Not surprisingly, the response to this crisis was to increase the capital and liquidity guidelines for banks. International banks and some governments complained, however, and the full implementation of the more stringent guidelines has been extended to January 1, 2019.

Table 7.2 summarizes the various guidelines of Basel III and when each takes effect. If you are dumbfounded by its complexity, not unlike the formidable figure for the new US financial regulatory structure discussed earlier in this chapter, don't worry, our point has been made. The table moreover does not even include an additional countercyclical buffer[7] of common equity or loss absorbing capital that is to be implemented according to national circumstances. Adding the countercyclical buffer to the minimum total capital plus conservation buffer means that if all the elements are implemented, the total minimum capital requirement could be as high as 13 percent in 2019. It is important to emphasize that these are risk-based capital guidelines that did not work in the past and are to be implemented over time, which means there is ample opportunity for (less stringent?) modifications during the phase-in period. In addition to the risk-based capital guidelines, there is also a minimum non–risk-based capital guideline, or leverage ratio, of at least 3 percent.

At this point you are most likely wondering whether the numerous and complex risk-based guidelines will work. We don't think so because they rely heavily on quantitative risk models that will, in turn, rely heavily on historical data. Yet relatively recent and new financial instruments will necessarily have limited historical data and therefore require highly questionable assumptions about the risk of these instruments and the degree to which they are correlated to other financial instruments. Thus the models

Table 7.2
Basel III: Capital guidelines and phase-in time line

	2011	2012	2013	2014	2015	2016	2017	2018	2019
Minimum common equity capital ratio			3.5%	4%	4.5%	4.5%	4.5%	4.5%	4.5%
Minimum capital conservation buffer						0.625%	1.25%	1.875%	2.5%
Minimum common equity plus capital conservation buffer			3.5%	4%	4.5%	5.125%	5.75%	6.375%	7%
Minimum tier 1 capital			4.5%	5.5%	6%	6%	6%	6%	6%
Minimum total capital			8%	8%	8%	8%	8%	8%	8%
Minimum total capital plus conservation buffer			8%	8%	8%	8.625%	9.25%	9.875%	10.5%
Capital instruments that no longer qualify as non–core tier 1 capital or tier 2 capital			Phased out over 10-year horizon, beginning 2013						
Liquidity coverage ratio	Observation period begins 2011				2015 introduces minimum standard				
Net stable funding ratio		Observation period begins 2012						2018 introduces minimum standard	

Source: Basel Committee on Banking Supervision.
Note: All dates are as of January 1.

are best employed as useful inputs and guides for assessing the safety and soundness of banks, not as definitive metrics.

As the recent financial crisis more than amply attests, the lack of appropriate data limits the effectiveness of quantitative models. All of the largest US financial institutions had risk-based capital ratios that exceeded the regulatory requirements. These institutions on the eve of the crisis were therefore deemed by the bank regulatory authorities to be well capitalized. Yet the government injected government funds, or Troubled Asset Relief Program (TARP) capital, into them.[8]

In addition to the various capital requirements, Basel III introduces a new liquidity standard due to the liquidity problems many financial institutions experienced during the crisis. The guideline consists of a short-term coverage ratio, mainly government securities and cash, and a long-term structural ratio, which is to address liquidity mismatches between liabilities and assets.

Will this new feature do the job? The new liquidity standards might help, but we are very skeptical that they will have a big impact without enhanced governance of the regulatory agencies implementing these standards. There was clear evidence before and during the financial crisis that some of the biggest financial institutions in the United States were relying heavily on short-term funding. This was public information, and regulators did know or should have known that serious financial difficulties would arise if there was a need for institutions with this type of liability structure to obtain liquidity on short notice. As explained in chapter 4, the fragility of this funding arrangement was repeatedly identified by FDIC supervisors in the years before the crisis. But they did not respond to their own analyses despite laws requiring them to act promptly to correct growing risks. While this new liquidity law might be desirable, the bigger question is what will compel regulators to act in the public interest when implementing this and other laws?

Overall Summary and Conclusions

It has been shown that Dodd–Frank (1) has lots and lots of pages with very little meaningful content that promises to make things better, (2) requires hundreds of rules to be decided upon by regulatory authorities so that almost everything needs to be argued and interpreted, which provides a rich feeding ground for lobbying, and (3) delegates enormous power to a group of unelected, unaccountable regulatory officials. Basel III has also been shown to come up short when it comes to meaningful reform. The Basel approach ultimately relies on requirements based on risk models and credit ratings, the interpretation and implementation of these requirements by financial institutions, and all of which in turn relies on regulators, who like sports referees are subject to various biases. Once again, we are back to the key weakness; we need to be able to monitor and evaluate the performance of regulatory officials on an ongoing basis.

The major conclusion is that Dodd–Frank and Basel III do not address the fundamental weaknesses identified in earlier chapters. These weaknesses are that systemic flaws with the institutions associated with designing, executing, and adapting financial regulations are root causes both of financial crises and financial systems that allocate capital inefficiently. From this perspective, bad financial regulations are mere symptoms of a defective system, one that fails to choose and implement policies that promote the safety and sound operation of the financial system. Moreover, under the pre- and post-Dodd–Frank world, the public and its elected officials can't compel the regulatory apparatus to act in the public interest because they can't obtain informed, expert, and independent assessments of the state of financial regulation absent an independent institution with (1) the requisite human capital skills and resources and (2) the power to obtain the information necessary for assessing the state of financial regulation. Right now there is a monopoly of information, expertise, and power within the hands of unelected, unaccountable regulators. Much of the information possessed by regulators is deliberately withheld from the public in a cloak of secrecy. For example, Bloomberg and Fox Business Network requested information from the Fed regarding its lending during the recent crisis under the Freedom of Information Act (FOIA). When the Fed failed to provide the requested information, Bloomberg and Fox sued to compel disclosure. A federal judge ruled against the Fed in its effort to block disclosure and the requested information was released nearly three years later.[9] Surely there should be a better way to keep the public informed of, and thus be in a better position to evaluate and influence, important actions taken by a regulator other than by filing costly and time-consuming legal suits, affordable by only a relatively few. Besides, whose interests is the Fed serving if it resists complying with FOIA requests and requests from members of Congress, who had introduced resolutions seeking similar information as requested by Bloomberg and Fox, until forced to do so by a federal judge? Despite such behavior, the Fed has been given even more discretionary power over an ever larger segment of the financial system. Neither Dodd–Frank nor Basel III corrects these weaknesses.

Appendix: Additional Aspects of Dodd–Frank

Investors Get More Protections, and New Constraints Are Put on Financial Firm Compensation

Not surprisingly, the new law expands even the layers of bureaucracy within the individual regulatory agencies. It creates, for example, within the SEC an Office of the Investor Advocate; an Investor Advisory Committee, composed of twelve to twenty members who serve four-year terms; and an ombudsman appointed by the Office of the Investor Advocate. Another imaginative solution! Add another office and a new committee, and bring in more people to compensate for the failings of the other parts of the agency.

The SEC is also authorized to issue "point-of-sale disclosure" rules when retail investors (individual investors) purchase investment products or services. The disclosures are to include concise information on costs, risks, and conflicts of interest. It is hard to imagine how this can possibly be done to fulfill the letter of the law. It may instead facilitate more litigation.

The SEC is also authorized to impose regulations requiring "fiduciary duty" by broker-dealers and investment advisers to their customers. Moreover a firm bundling together and/or originating asset-backed securities is required to retain at least 5 percent of the credit risk, so that it has "skin in the game." However, securities backed by "qualified residential mortgages"—which will be defined by (surprise!) regulatory authorities—are exempt from these credit retention requirements.

Furthermore the Office of Credit Rating Agencies (OCRA) is established within the SEC to regulate, oversee, and discipline nationally recognized statistical rating organizations (NRSROs). The law—at last—requires greater transparency and disclosure of rating procedures and methodologies. Investors are granted the right of legal action against credit rating agencies that knowingly or recklessly fail to investigate the quality of data provided to them or fail to obtain analysis of the information from a neutral, independent source. The rating agencies are now to be treated as experts when assigning grades to asset-backed securities and therefore subject to the same legal liabilities as law and accounting firms.

So far, sounds good, but don't ignore the reaction and powerful influence of private firms on the regulatory bodies. The credit-rating agencies responded to this new law by refusing to allow their ratings to be used in the offering circulars for asset-backed securities. This action led to the freezing of the market for these securities in July 2010. As a result the SEC initially indicated that it would not bring enforcement actions against issuers that did not disclose ratings in prospectuses as required under its rules for only six months. It then extended the stay of enforcement actions indefinitely in January 2011, and credit rating agencies are not subject to legal liability as of the writing of this book.[10] Despite the intent of Dodd–Frank, this example clearly demonstrates not only the discretionary power of regulators but also the power of recalcitrant financial firms to influence regulators so as to block potential adverse actions against them.

Why, given the greater disclosure requirements and the right of action now accessible to investors, is there even a need for OCRA and NRSROs? Most important, doesn't this simply continue to instill a government blessing on the credit rating agencies and thereby lessen the market discipline that is imposed on them?

Last, new rules are established for shareholder nonbinding "say-on-pay" and golden parachute votes, compensation committee member independence, expanded proxy disclosure (pay vs. performance), incentive compensation clawbacks in cases of corrected and restated financial results, and enhanced compensation disclosure for financial institutions. Exactly how these rules will play out should be interesting to watch. Can one really rely on the SEC to determine and enforce the most appropriate compensation rules to produce the best results for society, given its past performance?

All these reforms once again require that regulators identify emerging problems in a timely manner and take appropriate and timely action to address them. This approach has been repeatedly tried and it has failed. The SEC was previously charged with overseeing credit rating organizations, yet it failed to do so. Why should the establishment of a new office within the SEC suddenly increase its ability or willingness to the job it was always assigned?

The unaddressed and much bigger issue remains. Who has the necessary information and the incentive to hold regulators accountable on an ongoing and public basis? This is crucial now that they hold more power than ever before.

Given the Failure of AIG, What Happens to the Insurance Industry?

The new law creates the Federal Insurance Office (FIO) within the Treasury Department to monitor the insurance industry and identify regulatory issues or gaps that could contribute to systemic risk. In addition the FIO is to conduct a study and submit a report to Congress within eighteen months, or by year-end 2011, that will address ways to modernize the system for regulating insurance companies (one of its numerous mandated studies). State regulatory authorities are still responsible for licensing and regulating insurance companies, except for those deemed to be "covered financial companies," the "too big to fail firms," which are then also subject to regulation by the Fed. We consider the new office an attempt to appease those who were angry over the failure of AIG and its subsequent takeover by the federal government. We also suspect it may be an initial move toward transferring greater supervision and regulation of the insurance industry from the states to the federal government.

The FIO is clearly not a significant player in identifying and addressing systemic risk within or involving the insurance industry. If it hadn't been for the capital relief obtained by AIG through the most recent government bailout, the credit default swap business would have remained much smaller. Besides, it was the Fed that made a momentous decision in 1996: it permitted banks to use credit default swaps to reduce their capital reserves.[11] Regulators treated the *securities* guaranteed by an issuer of the credit default swap as having the risk level of the issuer (or, more accurately, the counterparty) of the credit default swap. Thus a bank that purchased credit default swap protection from AIG on collateralized debt obligations (CDOs) linked to subprime loans would have those CDOs treated as AAA securities, for capital regulatory purposes, because AIG had an AAA rating from a nationally recognized statistical rating organization (i.e., from an SEC-approved credit rating agency). So banks used credit default swaps to reduce the amount of capital that they are required to hold and thereby freed funds to invest in more lucrative, albeit more risky, assets. And the FIO, had it been in existence, would not have been, just as it is not now, authorized to oversee the Fed.

Deposit Insurance Limits Increased

The new law raises the deposit insurance limit, from $100,000 to $250,000. But this should raise a red flag. The increase in the deposit insurance limit worsens moral hazard—the more deposits that are insured, the less incentive depositors have to monitor their bank's risk and the greater is the appeal of banks that promise high interest rates. Just the week before IndyMac Bank, a savings and loan heavily involved in real estate, was seized by regulatory authorities, it was paying among the highest interest rates on deposits in the country, not at all unusual for a bank sinking into insolvency. Such banks offer their high rates to attract more deposits, which they will use to purchase ever more risky assets with access to deposit insurance because the interest paid on the new deposits doesn't have to be paid out (as it would for bonds) but rather accrues in the depositors' accounts. The higher limits for insured deposits also means that the discipline exerted on banks by their uninsured depositors to contain excessive risk taking is further reduced. Indeed in mid-2010, after the limit was raised, insured deposits at banking institutions were nearly $800 billion greater than in 2007 As a result this particular aspect of the new law does not reduce the likelihood of another financial crisis without even more regulatory discipline to contain excessive risk taking by federally insured financial institutions. In this regard the case for our new oversight group is further strengthened.

It is interesting to note that the deposit insurance limits were made retroactive to January 1, 2008. The reason seems political: it primarily benefited the uninsured depositors of the failed IndyMac Bank, which was headquartered in California. And the Speaker of the US House of Representatives, who was heavily involved in the legislation, was up for re-election in California.

Although the timing of the date at which the new limits took effect may be a coincidence, it is widely known that members of Congress are not averse to assisting their constituents on occasion. The potential for political considerations to affect various actions taken by Congress as well as regulatory authorities is another reason for having an oversight group serve as a check and balance as to whether such actions are in the public interest.

States Now Serve as a Check on Selected Federal Regulatory Power

Dodd–Frank significantly reduces the ability of national banks and federal savings banks to circumvent state consumer financial laws by federal preemption of those laws. From now on, the state laws can be preempted, but only if they are discriminatory toward the federally chartered institutions, as compared to the state-chartered institutions. But this change may impede the ability of the national and federal institutions to offer uniform products across the county. It may also lead some of these institutions to withdraw from certain states if they deem it too costly or burdensome to comply with the state laws. However, the change also introduces an additional check by each of the additional states on the appropriateness of various products that the national and federal institutions may wish to offer consumers in their states.

The "Volcker Rule"

This is an example of a reform that may not be needed. Banks, bank affiliates, and bank holding companies are prohibited by the new law from engaging in proprietary trading, which occurs when a firm trades with its own funds, not its clients, for its own benefit, not theirs. The Volker rule, named after the former Fed chairman who proposed it, allows for some limited exceptions to the prohibition: banking entities may not acquire or retain any equity, partnership, or other ownership interests in, or sponsor, a hedge fund or private equity fund that exceeds 3 percent of the total ownership interests of an individual fund and that exceeds 3 percent of the tangible common equity of the banking entity for all funds.

But proprietary trading by banking entities was not the cause of the most recent financial crisis. And regulatory authorities have yet to define proprietary trading under the new law. The ruling may moreover lead some banks to move their proprietary trading activities overseas, and banks in less restrictive countries may gain a competitive edge. Furthermore systemically important nonbank financial companies are not covered by these restrictions, even though they compete with the banking entities.

Parent Companies of FDIC Institutions Are Required to Be a Source of Strength

The new law requires all holding companies (parent companies) owning FDIC-insured institutions to be a source of strength to these subsidiaries. The law also specifies that regulators may conduct assessments to determine the capacity of a holding company to provide a source of strength. These rules previously applied to bank holding companies—though they clearly were not enforced—but have been explicitly extended to holding companies of other federally insured depository institutions.

The source of strength doctrine, however, raises an interesting issue, especially so due to a legal case in 2010 involving the holding company of a savings and loan. The stockholders of the holding company allege that the officers and directors injected funds into their failing subsidiary institution, and knowingly threw good money after bad. There are, however, potential problems with the new law. If holding companies must be a source of strength for their subsidiaries, their officers and directors would like to be able to argue, if sued by shareholders, that regulators required them to inject funds into subsidiary banks to save them—even if such banks eventually fail. But that potentially exposes regulators to legal suits if they required a holding company to be a source of strength to an institution that eventually fails. Can regulators, if they are allowed to be sued, argue that there was a reasonable basis for believing the required injection of funds would save the institution? The new law fails to resolve this issue.

The law fails to note also that if the total assets of a holding company consist almost entirely of a subsidiary bank, it would appear that the holding company is not only unnecessary but may have been a structural ploy to avoid FDIC seizure and obtain more favorable treatment in the bankruptcy courts (see table 7.1). This is an issue that should have been raised and addressed years ago by bank regulatory authorities. It does, however, suggest that one might consider a trigger point at which bank assets are so large a portion of a parent's company assets that the holding company structure is deemed no longer necessary.

As table 7.3 shows, of twelve large holding companies, eight have bank assets that exceed 90 percent of their total assets. If one or more of the subsidiary banks encounter financial difficulties, it would seem that the parent's ability to serve as a source of strength would be significantly compromised.

Industrial Loan Corporations: What Are They and Why Are They in the Law?

The new law also ventures into areas of reform where reform may not be necessary and could in fact be viewed as overzealous and, worse, reflecting political agendas. A good example of this overreaching is in the area of industrial loan corporations (ILCs), also known as industrial banks.[12] These institutions are not new; they date back as far as 1910, even before the establishment of the Fed. In essence, they are institutions that, like banks, lend money and whose deposits are FDIC insured. At one time industrial loan corporations were charted in more than thirty states. Today they operate in only six: California, Hawaii, Indiana, Minnesota, Nevada, and Utah.

The "issue" today is that of the approximately forty industrial loan corporations still in operation, nine are owned by commercial firms. While the ILCs fall under federal and state regulation, the commercial firms that own them do not.

Commercial firms use the ILCs to service their customers. Harley Davidson, for example, owns an ILC that is probably in a much better position to assess the collateral value of a motorcycle than is a typical bank. As a result its ILC may qualify more people for motorcycle loans than would a bank. The parents of ILCs—Toyota, Target, and Flying J, among others—are better able to provide their customers with access to financial services and simultaneously supply capital and provide additional governance over their ILCs to ensure that they operate safely and soundly. Indeed no commercially owned industrial loan corporation has ever failed.

But Dodd–Frank imposed a three-year moratorium on new charters for commercially owned ILCs. It also required the Government Accountability Office (GAO) to issue a report that assesses the role and regulation

Table 7.3
Source of strength: Importance of banks to corporate parents, ranked by assets, 2009

	Name of bank holding company	Total assets (US$ billions)	Bank assets as a % of total bank holding company assets
1	Bank of America	2,225	70.5
2	JP Morgan Chase	2,032	77.1
3	Citigroup	1,857	58.9
4	Wells Fargo	1,244	90.8
5	US Bancorp	281	99.0
6	PNC Financial Services	270	94.2
7	Bank of New York Mellon	212	81.4
8	SunTrust Banks	174	95.8
9	Capital One Financial	169	96.8
10	BB&T Corporation	166	93.5
11	State Street Corporation	157	97.6
12	Citizens Financial	148	98.6

Sources: FDIC, Milken Institute.

of ILCs. The federal government will determine whether or not to subject these institutions to the Bank Holding Company Act of 1956 and the Gramm–Leach–Bliley Act of 1999, which prohibit commercial firms from owning commercial banks and savings and loans or to subject their commercial parents to supervision by the Fed. There has been a longstanding concern among some that allowing commercial firms to own banks is inappropriate, for fear of greater competition, especially by banks, and/or the emergence of large financial powers. These fears are not new; they led to limits on interstate banking and branching, which were only relaxed in 1994. There is also the issue of whether individual states or federal regulators should have final say over state-chartered financial institutions.

The question of ownership has become a major issue because some states charter industrial loan corporations, and allow them to be owned by commercial firms.[13] When Wal-Mart received Utah's permission to acquire an ILC, it faced such overwhelming opposition, and lengthy delay due to a moratorium imposed by the FDIC (the ILC had to obtain its stamp of approval), that the retail giant withdrew its application. The commercial firms that own ILCs are reported in table 7.4. The ILCs in almost every

Table 7.4
Industrial loan corporations compared to their parents (US$ billions, Q1 2010)

Industrial loan corporation		ILC		Parent company	% Parent company	
		Total assets	Total equity capital		Total assets	Total equity capital
GE Capital Financial, Inc.	UT	9.19	2.44	General Electric Capital Corp	1.18	1.98
BMW Bank of North America	UT	7.76	0.71	BMW (Germany)	5.51	2.63
Toyota Financial Savings Bank	NV	0.88	0.11	Toyota	0.27	0.10
The Pitney Bowes Bank, Inc.	UT	0.69	0.05	Pitney Bowes	8.29	18.40
Transportation Alliance Bank	UT	0.46	0.07	Flying J, Inc.	n/a	n/a
EnerBank USA	UT	0.29	0.03	CMS Energy	1.88	0.91
Target Bank	UT	0.11	0.01	Target Corporation	0.24	0.08
Eaglemark Savings Bank	NV	0.04	0.01	Harley Davidson	0.37	0.28
First Electronic Bank	UT	0.02	0.01	Fry's Electronic	n/a	n/a

Sources: Flow of Funds, Federal Reserve, Federal Deposit Insurance Corporation, Bloomberg, Milken Institute.

case account for a relatively small percentage of the total assets or equity capital of the parent commercial firm.

The decision as to what eventually happens to these institutions may be based more on political considerations than those that take into consideration the net benefits to society. Interesting enough, the ownership of banks by commercial companies is allowed in most countries around the world. The United States is out of step with these other and more permissive countries with respect to ownership flexibility.

8
Making the Guardians of Finance Work for Us

A dependence on the people is, no doubt, the primary control on the government; but experience has taught mankind the necessity of auxiliary precautions.
—James Madison, Federalist 51, 1788

The Guardians of Finance too frequently do not work for the public at large because the public lacks the institutional mechanism to compel financial regulators to do so. Around the world, there is no authoritative institution that (1) is independent of short-run politics, (2) is independent of the financial services industry, (3) has the power to demand and obtain information necessary for assessing and monitoring the Guardians of Finance, (4) contains the multidisciplinary expertise necessary for fruitfully processing that information, and (5) has the prominence to deliver such an assessment to the public and its elected representatives in a ongoing manner that materially affects the open discussion of financial sector policies. The absence of an institution with these five traits means that the public *cannot* effectively evaluate financial regulation and therefore *cannot* constantly oblige the Guardians to act in the public interest.

Current reforms largely sidestep the fundamental financial policy challenge facing all countries in all time periods: inducing the Guardians of Finance to work more effectively for all of us—the public at large. Reforms emerging from the US Congress, Basel, the United Kingdom, the European Union, and many other countries and organizations do not squarely address the deeply rooted, institutional weaknesses in the regulatory apparatus that lead to so many critical problems affecting so many people. These reform efforts primarily provide fleeting palliatives, not enduring improvements to the process for selecting, implementing, evaluating, and reforming financial regulations.

We recommend the creation of an institution acting on behalf of the public—the Sentinel—to provide an informed, expert, and independent assessment of financial regulation. We design the institution to be independent of political and financial systems, to have information and professional skills necessary for assessing the full constellation of financial regulatory issues, and to have the legally granted status to help shape debate on financial sector policies. *Each* of these characteristics is necessary for improving the still seriously flawed financial regulatory institutions operating around the world today.

The Guardians of Finance Did Not Work for Us

The institutions associated with making and implementing financial regulatory decisions—those charged with ensuring the safety and soundness of the financial system—helped cause the crisis of 2007 to 2009. In the United States and several countries around the world, the Guardians of Finance (1) adopted policies that encouraged poor credit allocation decisions and excessive risk-taking by financial institutions and (2) maintained those policies over many years even as they learned of the increasing fragility of the financial system. In chapters 4 and 5 we provide numerous examples of authorities turning a blind eye to escalating risks, of not enforcing regulations, and of not using their powers to adjust to changing conditions in financial markets during the ten or so years before the full-blown crisis struck. These systemic institutional defects are not new. Chapter 6 shows that the US Guardians of Finance since the nineteenth century have followed an all too familiar pattern of selecting and maintaining policies that lead to a crisis and then responding by adding new rules, establishing more regulatory agencies, hiring more regulators, and granting the Guardians even greater discretionary power over an ever larger portion of the financial system. Chapter 7 demonstrates that this trend has continued.

Financial innovation, regulatory gaps, and insufficient regulatory power are not root causes of the crisis. These factors mattered, but alone they do not even come close to accounting for the worst crisis since the Great Depression. Although financial innovation fostered complexity in some crisis countries, there was no significant innovation in Ireland, eastern Europe, or Spain, and new financial products did not bring down the UK financial system either. Regulatory gaps between multiple regulatory agencies might have played a small role in the US crisis, but the existence of multiple regulators has been overplayed as an excuse for US regulatory inaction, and there were no regulatory gaps in several countries that experienced devastating crises but had a single financial regulator. Furthermore we find little evidence that a lack of regulatory power destabilized financial systems. Again and again, regulatory authorities frequently had the power to adjust policies and chose not to exercise it, so focusing on the impotency of regulatory authorities just doesn't ring true as an overarching source of financial system fragility.

Rather, a common explanation that cuts across all crisis countries is that there were severe defects in the institutions that chose destabilizing policies and maintained those policies as the financial sector deteriorated and eventually collapsed. The crisis is about defective regulatory and political systems that did not appropriately respond in a timely manner to clear and ever more numerous signs of escalating danger.

Moreover the Guardians of Finance frequently had ample time to adjust to increasing financial system fragility—this crisis is not essentially about unforeseeable shocks. This is not a situation in which a single regulator made a single mistake and then things blew up. Rather, many regulators made many mistakes, problems grew ever worse over years, regulators learned of or should have recognized the cumulating problems arising from their policies and from the obvious changes in the financial landscape, and yet the regulators chose not to respond until it was too late. While many individuals and institutions make mistakes now and then, several regulators over many years did not adjust their policies even as widespread information accumulated that their mistakes were increasing the fragility of the entire financial system. Why were US regulators not reporting on the alarming increases in leverage at financial institutions, or the shift of trillions of dollars of assets off of banks' balance sheets? Why were Irish regulators willing to sit around for two-and-a-half years waiting for a reply to a letter they sent to Anglo-Irish bank expressing concerns about its meteoric growth in size? Why were UK regulators giving Northern Rock a blue ribbon for its risk management and allowing it to increase dividends three months(!) before it failed? Clearly, these examples demonstrate a generalized defect. The Guardians of Finance did not work effectively to protect citizens in many countries. Merely adding more regulatory powers without correcting the problem of regulatory abdication in the face of clear risks accomplishes little of lasting value.

Why Don't the Guardians of Finance Work for Us?

The public cannot always compel regulatory authorities to act in society's best interest because the public does not have the information, expertise, or an independent institution focused solely on its interests with the information and the expertise to evaluate financial regulation effectively. Although regulatory agencies sometimes have information and expertise, they are not independent of the influences of short-term politics and the financial services industry. Without informed, expert, and unbiased assessments of the financial regulatory system, the public and its elected representatives will have a correspondingly difficult time governing financial regulators.

Information

The public simply does not have access to the information necessary for evaluating financial regulation. For example, the public did not know that the FDIC was identifying problems in numerous banks years before the crisis and choosing not to act. The public did not know that banks were reducing their capital to cover losses through the purchase of credit default swaps from increasingly fragile institutions. The public did not know that the SEC was incapable of fulfilling its widely trumpeted goal of supervising investment banks, or that the OCC was taking actions to *facilitate* lending abuses. As one article put it,

The O.C.C. is a coddler, a protector, an outright enabler of the institutions it oversees . . . .. Back during the subprime bubble, for instance, it was so eager to please its "clients"—yes, that's how O.C.C. executives used to describe the banks—that it steamrolled anyone who tried to stop lending abuses. States and cities around the country would pass laws requiring consumer-friendly measures such as mandatory counseling for subprime borrowers, or the listing of the fees the banks were going to charge for the loan. The O.C.C. would then use its power to either block or roll back the legislation.[1]

Similarly UK taxpayers did not understand that their vaunted FSA was not paying attention to the obvious risks building up in Northern Rock, just as Irish taxpayers likely thought that their regulatory authority was actually overseeing the financial industry and not ignoring one of the biggest housing bubbles in history. Unfortunately, Icelandic residents had a similar, misplaced faith in their regulators. In many countries the public did not know about the size and the systemic nature of risks associated with the derivatives market, or the outlandish nature of the big bets that were being made with these instruments.

More generally, the public lacks effective mechanisms for obtaining detailed information on what regulators and financial institutions are doing. Indeed *The Wall Street Journal* in an article titled "Systemic Risk Stonewall: Some bailout questions the Fed still hasn't answered" noted that "[O]n the key facts behind the bailouts of 2008, regulators have stonewalled the public, the press and even the inspector general of the Troubled Asset Relief Program." The article adds that "[T]wo years after the bailouts and more than a month after President Obama signed into law new authority for the government to prevent 'systemic risk,' Washington still won't tell us what this term means, yet alone how it will be measured."[2]

The Fed was also adept at blocking and delaying efforts by the judiciary and legislative branches of the US government to obtain information. In May 2008, Bloomberg News reporter Mark Pittman filed a Freedom of Information Act (FOIA) request for Federal Reserve documents on its lending to banks. The Fed said it would respond in June but did not. Bloomberg sued in November 2008. In August 2009, Manhattan Chief US District Judge Loretta Preska ruled that the Fed must release the documents. The Fed appealed, and in March 2010, a three-judge appellate panel unanimously sided with Judge Preska. At that point Congress urged the Fed to comply. In April 2010, by a vote of 59 to 39, the Senate called on the Federal Reserve to identify the banks and other financial institutions that received loans. Ignoring the Senate, the Fed delayed and requested a review of the appellate panel decision. In August 2010, the panel denied the request. The Fed appealed to the Supreme Court, which in March 2011 ordered the Fed to release the records. But, even in complying with the Senate and the courts, the Fed released the thousands of documents in a nonsearchable PDF form, making it difficult for the public to examine them. There really is something remarkable about the Fed resisting requests and demands by the formally constituted branches of the US government to release information about the use of US taxpayer funds.[3]

Expertise

Barriers to obtaining information are not the only obstacles preventing sound evaluation of financial regulation. The public—along with presidents, prime ministers, and legislators—are not competent to make an expert assessment of financial regulation even if they managed to obtain information from regulators and financial institutions. As developed in chapters 2 through 5, no single individual has the capacity to monitor and assess the behavior of regulators.

It takes the *combined and coordinated* skills of financial economists, lawyers, forensic accountants, and other finance skills, including some with private sector experience, to analyze issues such as (1) the impact of capital regulatory policies with respect to credit default swaps on the risk-taking and fragility of banks, (2) the systemic risks associated with an opaque multi-hundred trillion dollar OTC derivatives market, (3) how regulations and financial innovations affect the behavior of Fannie Mae, Freddie Mac and ancillary financial institutions, (4) whether raising more funds through non–core financing vehicles poses a risk to the financial system, and (5) when the growth of structured financial products tilts the incentives of credit rating agencies in a dangerous direction.

It is not just a matter that the *average* citizen lacks the requisite skills to govern financial regulators. Indeed a collection of first-rate finance professors couldn't do it either. The complexity of the system is such that it takes a multidisciplinary team to assess financial regulation. But a lack of information and expertise are not all that thwart effective governance of financial policy. The regulatory authorities themselves are not independent of the entities they are charged with regulating.

Independence: Money-Induced Bias

One factor that biases financial regulatory policies is money. As emphasized in chapter 1, the financial services industry employs an arsenal of well-paid lobbyists to induce politicians to enact supportive laws and encourage politicians to pressure regulatory agencies to interpret and apply those laws in ways that are most supportive of the financial services industry. Much academic research and investigative reporting suggests that the financial services industry effectively shapes the design of financial sector policies. The evidence does not indicate that the financial services industry is the *only* factor shaping financial policies; financial institutions are not writing all financial regulations. Rather, the point is that the financial services industry exerts a disproportionately large influence on politicians who write and enact financial policies. These same politicians—tempted by campaign contributions and other means of encouragement from financial firms—often pressure regulators to interpret and implement those policies in a manner that aligns with the preferences of the financial services industry. From this perspective and according to considerable evidence from around the world, financial regulation is systematically biased in favor of the financial services industry and against the interests of the broader public.

A second factor that biases financial regulation is money—but in this case money directed at regulators, not politicians. While there might be straightforward under-the-table bribes, most analysts argue that influence is subtler.[4] As emphasized in chapters 1 and 4, not only do regulatory officials frequently raise their salaries by a factor of ten, if not more, by moving from their regulatory offices to private financial firms, but also those same firms sometimes play a role in selecting executives who run regulatory agencies. For example, the same financial institutions regulated by the Fed play a role in choosing the executives running the Federal Reserve Banks. It is simply incorrect to characterize the Federal Reserve as independent of the financial institutions that they regulate.

While there are issues at the Fed, the speed of the revolving door at the SEC makes one's head spin.[5] Annette Nazareth moved from her job as an attorney at Davis Polk and Wardwell law firm (which counts major banks among its clients) in the early 1980s to become the SEC director for regulating markets, and is now back at Davis Polk. Linda Chatman Thomsen also moved from her job at Davis Polk to the SEC, where she ultimately directed the Enforcement Division, before returning to Davis Polk. Paul Roye moved from the SEC to another law firm (Dechert), then back to the SEC where he supervised investment firms, and is now an executive at an investment firm, Capital Research and Management. Meredith Cross moved from the law firm of King and Spalding to the SEC, where she was involved in the regulation of corporate finance, then moved to the WilmerHale law firm, but went back to the SEC as head of the corporate finance unit. As a final example, Thomas Biolsi started as an examiner at the SEC, then moved to the compliance office at Prudential Insurance, then to PricewaterhouseCoopers, then to the SEC compliance office, and then back to Pricewaterhouse.[6] We are not suggesting that any individual behaved unethically, but many observers question the independence of the SEC and regulatory agencies more generally. For example, *The New York Times* reported in August 2010 that almost ". . . 150 people who had worked in financial regulatory agencies registered as lobbyists over the last year," and the *Times* added that this "boom in recruitment of former regulators by corporations and advocacy groups" reflects a desire "to influence how the newly enacted financial overhaul is translated into rules and regulations."[7]Legislatures in many countries reinforce this problem by holding pay in financial regulatory agencies far below that in the private sector.

The revolving door problem is further illustrated by noting where the 2008 Treasury team that used taxpayer money through the Troubled Asset Relief Program (TARP) to bail out the major banks now work: the top investment banks, AIG, and several other major financial institutions. The Treasury's former Chief of Staff, Deputy Assistant for Financial Institution Policy, Associate Secretary for Financial Institutional Policy, Under Secretary of Domestic Finance, Advisor to the Secretary on the Financial Crisis, Assistant Secretary for International Affairs, Under Secretary for International Affairs, and Associate Secretary for Legislative Affairs all moved from their government positions to the financial institutions over which they had just been shaping national policies. When the regulators readily become the regulated and the regulated, in turn, become the regulators, this might naturally reduce confidence that the Guardians of Finance are working for the public and not for their next employer.

Independence: Home Field Advantage

Regulators may also be biased in favor of the financial services industry, albeit subconsciously, because financial firms dominate the "crowd" surrounding the regulatory officials as they make policy decisions. As explained in chapter 1, sports teams win a disproportionately large proportion of their home games because referees, umpires, and officials systematically make calls that please the home crowd, especially on big, game changing calls. The officials are not prejudiced for one team. They are biased for the home team because they seek to please the home crowd. But, this is not just a sports phenomenon; it is a basic human characteristic.

Psychologists find that social connections and community exert a powerful influence on the decisions, behavior, and beliefs of individuals. People are innately drawn to the group's view. Moreover individuals genuinely adopt the beliefs of the group. It is not that the person grudgingly mimics the opinions of the community; rather, people's actual beliefs change, so that they sincerely believe in, and wholeheartedly embrace, the group's view. In short, human beliefs are shaped by the communities in which we participate—our views are shaped by the "home crowd."

In financial regulation the home crowd is dominated by the financial services industry. Besides the revolving door, regulators interact with the financial services industry on a daily basis. That's their job. But this also means that regulators participate in a "community" dominated by financial firms; they will face the jeers and complaints of this home crowd when financial firms do not approve of the "calls" made by regulators.

Thus financial officials may tend to favor the financial services industry, as the public is only sparsely represented within the crowd voicing its opinion to financial regulators. Those outside of financial firms will have a more difficult time shaping the decisions, behavior, and beliefs of regulators. The public is sitting in the upper bleachers and regulatory officials can scarcely, if at all, hear their cry, which naturally, and systematically, biases financial regulators in favor of the financial services industry, especially on big, game changing calls.

Simplistic Ideologies: Another Source of Systemic Regulatory Defects

Flawed ideologies can also produce systemic regulatory failures, where by "ideology" we mean the ideas and philosophies that shape regulatory choices. Ideological failures do not necessarily favor financial firms, but they can produce a lasting series of bad policies. The complexity of financial regulation makes it difficult to assess financial policies and correct flawed approaches to regulation. Thus a defective ideology could become an enduring source of regulatory blunders. Furthermore, if powerful politicians and regulators become personally identified with an ideology—and indeed rely on the broad acceptance of that ideology for their power and prestige, they might rigorously defend it regardless of any conflicting evidence.

The recent crisis illustrates the power of ideology. As demonstrated in chapters 2 to 5, Alan Greenspan and others around the world embraced, and in some cases embodied, a laissez faire approach to financial regulation. This approach too frequently involved an unrelenting push toward removing regulations without an adequate appreciation of how removing one or two regulations, from the complex soup of other policies and regulatory interventions, would affect the incentives of financial firms. At times, it seemed as if this extreme ideology morphed into a dangerous operational dogma: "the fewer regulations the better." While this is an exaggerated caricature, the Guardians made too many consequential decisions regarding the removal of regulations without satisfactorily assessing the effects of those decisions on the mixture of incentives facing the financial services industry.

The Guardians should have known better. Economists have long known that the extreme laissez faire view is internally inconsistent and, thus, harmful as a guiding policy prescription. As explained in chapter 2, it is a basic axiom of economics that eliminating a government regulation will not necessarily improve the economy if there are other government interventions, *even if all of the assumptions underlying the laissez faire ideology hold*. The hot and sour soup analogy stressed that the financial system is a complex blend of government and market failures. Removing one ingredient could upset the balance, even if that one ingredient is individually "distasteful." Similarly, adding one ingredient, that individually seems appealing, could ruin the mixture, and create incentives that induce socially destructive behavior by financial markets. Applying simplistic ideologies to the complex world of finance is a recipe for disaster.

Unfortunately, in the wake of the crisis, we now seem to be lurching from one simplistic, unqualified ideology—that private markets will look after society's interests—to an equally flawed, if not more perilous, ideology—that the Guardians will always act in society's interests, so let's give them more power to do so. As observed in chapter 6, countries historically increase the discretionary power of regulators following crises. As documented in chapter 7, that is exactly what governments are doing now. This is dangerous.

We argued strenuously in chapter 2 and at length in our earlier book, *Rethinking Bank Regulation: Till Angels Govern*, that empowering direct government oversight of finance is less successful at promoting economic growth and expanding economic opportunities than a regulatory system focused on competition, transparency, and establishing sound incentives within the financial services industry. But our work is not a call for laissez faire. Rather, our research stresses that the efficacy of any particular regulation depends on the other regulations in place and the precise institutional features of the economy. The evidence from chapters 4 and 5 indicates that officials in several countries failed to appreciate the complex incentive effects of financial regulation, which too often encouraged financial firms to seek immediate growth and bonuses with little regard for long-run stability.

To develop sound regulatory policies, countries must resist the comforting allure of simplistic ideologies and embrace the inherent complexity of financial regulation. Socially beneficial financial reforms *must* involve a full assessment of the complex incentive effects associated with changing financial policies. But the public does not have a mechanism for obtaining an informed, expert, and impartial assessment of financial regulation. Therefore the public does not have the basis for challenging the efficacy of Guardian policies or the validity of their ideologies; nor does the public have the capacity to compel regulators to act in the public interest. In short, the regulators are saying, trust us, but pay the bill if things go wrong.

Current Reform Efforts Do Not Fully Address the Root Causes of the Problem

The situation is precarious: the only institutions capable of assessing the financial regulatory institutions are the financial regulatory institutions themselves, and they are not effectively designed to act in the public's long-run interests. The public and its representatives simply have nowhere to turn for an informed assessment of financial regulation conducted by experts that are neither influenced by short-run political pressures nor by the narrow interests of the financial services industry.

Successful and lasting reform requires addressing a core cause of the systemic malfunctioning of financial systems—poor governance of the Guardians of Finance. Simply tinkering with regulatory glitches that characterized the most recent crisis of 2007 to 2009 will leave this root cause of the problem firmly in place and able to strike again in the future.

But policy makers are not addressing this root cause of the crisis. In chapter 7 we argue that the bulk of regulatory reform efforts emerging from the United States, the Basel Committee, and other leading countries and institutions do not address this major but correctable defect with financial regulation. While the Dodd–Frank Act of 2010 is long, it is vague and accomplishes little meaningful reform—as perhaps intended by some. The vagueness of the Act means that lobbyists have intensified their work to shape the actual implementation of the complex law, such that one might rename the Dodd–Frank Act the "Financial Lobbyist Full Employment Act of 2010." As we detail in chapter 7, there are few reasons to believe that had this Act been enacted in 2000, rather than in 2010, things would have turned out much different.

In chapter 7 we also raised questions about the ultimate efficacy of Basel III. Besides the capital regulations stressed above, one of the ideas widely touted in current reform proposals is that the crisis was caused by the focus of regulators on "microprudential" issues, meaning that their tendency was to look at risks one institution at a time and not to focus on the entire financial system. As a result an emphasis on macroprudential risks, meaning to look at all of the risks across institutions in the system, is now in vogue. We certainly agree that attention to macroprudential risks is sensible, but the last crisis could have been prevented or at least its severity lessened by enforcing microprudential regulations. Moreover, the problem with the current popular solution is that it is hard, and by no means clear, that experts can come up with effective ways to detect and address macroprudential risks in a timely manner. For many decades microprudential risks received more attention precisely because experts could largely agree on how to measure them. Macroprudential efforts are partly focused on building up capital in good times—so-called countercyclical capital requirements. The belief is that it is during booms that banks take more risks, and that this is when they should be building up their capital buffers (or their provisioning for bad loans) for when the economy slows and loan losses grow. The logic is compelling, but for the reasons noted in chapters 2 and 3, we think that maintaining a healthy skepticism about the miracle powers of capital to prevent problems is wise and supported by ample experience. Besides the technical challenges associated with macroprudential regulation, this too ignores the core question—determining the appropriate macroprudential regulations, and interpreting and implementing any new rules is not straightforward. Giving authorities more tools or similar tools dressed up with different names does not solve the pressing issue of accountability, of creating checks and balances on the

Guardians of Finance. As argued in chapter 5, banks will have incentives to evade new rules, and society has an overriding interest in ensuring that regulators remain vigilant.

While the European Union announced the creation of three pan-European watchdogs to oversee financial regulation, these do not fully address the core weakness in the financial regulatory apparatus either. The three new watchdogs will oversee supervision in the banking, insurance, and securities markets sectors, respectively. The supervision and regulation of individual companies and markets will be conducted by the national supervisory agencies. These new "European Supervisory Authorities" will harmonize technical standards and mediate disputes between national regulators. Furthermore a European Systemic Risk Board, which will be composed of each of the central bank governors from the 27-member countries, will warn of impending threats to financial stability. These reforms might improve financial sector policies by improving coordination across countries and providing a vehicle for supervisors to communicate about risks and other problems. However, it is not yet clear that these reforms will tackle the fundamental institutional weaknesses identified by our analyses, for it is uncertain whether the European Systemic Risk Board will (1) be able to obtain information about financial regulations, financial markets, and financial institutions and (2) have the resources, technical skills, and most notably the independence to assess that information and provide an unbiased assessment to the public and the authorities. Since the regulatory authorities in each country will be on the Board, one could envision an agreement not to criticize one another, and some members may be bound by national legislation that prohibits them from sharing information gathered by their home agencies. So, although promising, the verdict is still out on the efficacy of these new institutions. European taxpayers (and those holding the bonds of the countries) are right to be concerned that this new system might not work as intended in practice.

The Sentinel

Contours

In light of the evidence presented above, we sketch a proposal for a new institution to improve the system for selecting, interpreting, implementing, and adapting regulations. We call this new institution the "Sentinel," since it will act as the public's sentry over financial policies and regulations. As James Madison argued in the quotation from the Federalist Paper that opens this chapter, "auxiliary" arrangements are sometimes necessary for strengthening the public's ability to control government officials and induce them to work for us.

Our goal is not to provide a checklist of specific rules and regulations, but rather to improve the process through which countries choose them. The Sentinel will provide an informed, expert, and independent assessment of financial regulation that will both assist financial regulators and enhance the ability of the public and its representatives to govern financial regulators.

The Sentinel is a practical and workable proposal that addresses core defects in the regulatory system. Of course, the Sentinel is only one part of creating a sound financial regulatory apparatus. But the basic elements of the Sentinel are *necessary* for correcting fundamental flaws in financial regulation. We also recognize that it will be difficult to implement. But, without such reforms, society will not enjoy the essential and enduring benefits of well-functioning financial systems.

We first sketch the essential features of the Sentinel within the context of US institutions. While the general principles—such as transparency and checks and balances—translate to other political and cultural contexts, some of the specific elements will not. We emphasize key attributes of the Sentinel, recognizing that particular elements will need to be custom designed for the specific institutions of individual countries. We then describe how the Sentinel will improve financial regulation before discussing alternatives to the Sentinel and lessons for making the Sentinel work effectively.

The Sentinel's Power and Responsibility

The only power of the Sentinel would be to acquire any information that it deems necessary for evaluating the state of financial regulation. The law establishing the Sentinel must clearly and unambiguously assert that the Sentinel should be granted immediate and unencumbered access to any information it deems appropriate from any and all regulatory authorities and financial institutions. There must be clear and immediate penalties, including the loss of employment, for any official who withholds, obstructs, or in any way impedes the flow of relevant or requested information. The (nonproprietary) information collected by the Sentinel would be made publicly available, potentially with some delay and with due respect to the privacy of financial firms and individuals. Sentinel demands for information must trump the desires of regulatory agencies for secrecy; part of its purpose is to shed a cleansing light on financial regulation. While it is likely that some information gathered by the Sentinel would need to remain confidential, the histories of past crises and of this crisis suggest that officials have erred in the opposite direction, keeping too much information confidential. From regulatory failures contributing to oil spills and nuclear fuel leakages to those involving finance, the problem seems to be too much secrecy, not too much transparency.

The only responsibility of the Sentinel would be to deliver an annual report to the legislative and executive branches of government assessing the degree to which financial regulations foster the safe and sound operation of the financial system. The Sentinel would have no official power over the central bank, the regulatory agencies, or financial markets and institutions; put another way, the Sentinel would not affect the power and responsibilities of the central bank or financial regulatory agencies, and it would have no regulatory power whatsoever. The Sentinel will simply provide an informed, expert, and independent assessment of the full constellation of regulatory practices, across all segments of the financial services industry—including banks, securities markets, the shadow banking system, derivatives, rating agencies, insurance companies, executive compensation, and the composition and operation of boards of directors.

This "sunshine" regulatory approach—obtaining information, evaluating that information, and disseminating an expert assessment—has a long and promising history, as discussed in McCraw's (1984) impressive book on regulation.[8] This approach is also fully consistent with the notion of checks and balances incorporated into the political philosophies of several countries. The Sentinel will reduce the probability that unelected, unaccountable, and largely unchecked officials enjoy too much discretionary power of financial regulation that can produce real harm to societies if not used properly.

The Sentinel's Organizational Design

We seek to organize the Sentinel to align the incentives, professional ambitions, and personal goals of its staff with the interests of the public, and then provide the Sentinel with the necessary resources, authority, and prominence to inform and frame financial policy deliberations. Toward this end, we outline three organizational features, using the United States as a point of reference.

First, the Sentinel would be as politically independent as possible. The most senior members of the Sentinel—a public sector entity—would be appointed by the president and confirmed by the Senate for staggered and appropriately long terms. As with the Board of Governors of the Federal Reserve System, the goal is to limit the short-term influence of politics on the Sentinel. Furthermore the Sentinel's funding must be independent of the annual budget battles that regularly threaten the ability of regulators to carry out their charge. We recommend granting the Sentinel a small percentage of Federal Reserve's revenues (net of Federal Reserve expenses), over 90 percent of which is typically handed over to the US Treasury, or otherwise that the Sentinel be given the power to impose a tiny fee on financial institutions.

Second, the Sentinel would be independent of private financial markets. Senior members of the Sentinel would be prohibited from receiving compensation from the financial services industry and lobbying groups for a significant time period after completing their tenure at the Sentinel. The precise definition of a "significant time period" is debatable (and even differs among the authors, ranging from at least five years to forever). What is crucial is to select an interval that both shuts the revolving door for a lengthy period of time, if not permanently, and materially reduces the home field advantage enjoyed by the financial services industry.

Third, besides having the power to obtain information, the Sentinel would have the resources to process that information and contribute an influential message on financial regulation. Sentinel salaries must be market-based to attract the most highly skilled individuals, especially in light of the restrictions on private sector employment just noted, and the Sentinel must be large enough to house financial economists, accountants, lawyers, supervisors, and regulators, and—critically—senior professionals with private financial market experience. Since those individuals with the expertise to evaluate the state of financial regulation would also be individuals with lucrative opportunities in the private sector, countries adopting this proposal need to understand that staffing the Sentinel with sufficiently talented individuals will require a dramatically different compensation schedule than currently contemplated in public sector jobs. Still the payback would be substantial in view of the anticipated reduction in the likelihood and costs of future crises and the anticipated increase in the efficiency of resource allocation.[9]

These three organizational features will help make the Sentinel a prominent institution, with an influential voice on financial policy issues. The Sentinel's importance will primarily arise *not* because of its statutory mandate to deliver a high-visibility report. Rather, the Sentinel's evaluations will matter *because* of its independence, expertise, and information available to it.

The Sentinel's Unique Role

Given the existing array of regulatory agencies, quasi-regulatory bodies, and other oversight entities, do we really need another official institution?

Yes. No other entity currently has the incentives, power, or capabilities to perform the role of the public's sentry over the full constellation of financial sector policies. No other entity has five crucial characteristics for successfully ameliorating core deficiencies in financial regulation: independence from short-run politics, independence from financial markets, the power to acquire the necessary information for evaluating financial regulation, the resources necessary for conducting a comprehensive evaluation of financial regulation, and the prominence to deliver such an evaluation effectively to the public and its elected representatives.

No existing financial regulatory institution has a high degree of independence from both political and market influences. Incentives matter in regulation too. In capitals around the world, lobbyists shape legislation, the revolving door between industry and regulatory agencies spins often and rapidly, and the financial services industry typically enjoys a home field advantage in influencing the decisions of officials. While there are good reasons for having highly skilled individuals with private sector expertise help in regulating the financial sector, there are equally good reasons for worrying about the close connections between regulators and industry. The Sentinel would be uniquely positioned to provide an impartial assessment of financial regulation and thereby enhance the debate on financial policies.

No existing entity has the information and expertise to challenge major regulatory agencies on financial policy matters and ignite an informed debate. A monopoly on regulatory power and information is dangerous. Consider, for example, the worrisome role of the Federal Reserve, which

(1) directly supervises and regulates major financial institutions, (2) is largely independent of elected representatives and the public, and (3) is influenced by financial markets directly, since banks help in choosing the presidents of the Federal Reserve Banks,[10] and indirectly, since there are close connections between officials working at the Fed and people employed by the financial services industry. Such power in the hands of officials with limited public accountability *and* with close links to the financial services industry breaks the democratic lines of influence running from the public to the design and execution of policies that determine the allocation of capital. The Sentinel would eliminate this monopoly on information and expertise.

While many regulatory agencies have auditing and inspector general departments, the Sentinel would be quite different. These internal departments typically assess whether a *particular* regulatory agency adhered to its rules and procedures. The Sentinel would instead conduct an independent evaluation of the key risks emerging in the *overall* financial system and how these are being met by the full array of financial regulations and supervisory practices, continuously assessing financial regulations in a forward-looking context. The Sentinel would not replace internal evaluators at regulatory agencies; it would play a different, complementary role, and again would have no regulatory power.

Desirability of the Sentinel: Informed Debate

First, the Sentinel would enhance the quality of discourse and debate on consequential financial policies. Several examples illustrate the Sentinel's potential impact. What would have happened if a Sentinel had highlighted the FBI's 2004 fraud report in mortgage finance and the fact that the Fed was not responding to it? We suspect that at the very least there would have been calls for the Fed to gather more information to justify its inaction. What would have happened if an Irish Sentinel had highlighted the dangers of Anglo-Irish's astronomical growth and the banking system giving out mortgages with virtually a 100 percent loan-to-value ratio, at ten times (or more) borrowers' income, while the financial regulator stood by just watching? What would have happened if a British Sentinel had pointed out that Northern Rock's risk management strategy only worked under very optimistic assumptions, and that the FSA was not seriously supervising the bank? We suspect that such actions by prominent sentinels would have dramatically increased the probability that regulators would have adapted their policies to address the growing fragility of their financial systems to the benefit of the public.

There are many more examples of how the Sentinel, by fostering an informed discussion of financial policies, would have reduced the likelihood of the crisis of 2007 to 2009 and improved the operation of the financial system. As stressed in chapters 2 and 4, this crisis was partially caused by the tragic mixture of a dynamic financial system—overwhelmed with credit default swaps, collateralized debt obligations, and other financial innovations—and a stagnant regulatory regime that did not adapt to changing conditions and instead encouraged excessive risk taking. A Sentinel, by constantly reassessing financial regulation and publicizing its concerns, would have reduced the likelihood that such perverse incentives would fester for so long and thus be able to cause so much harm. Similarly, in an innovating, growing economy, the impact of the same regulation can change, so regulations must be constantly reassessed and revised to maintain sound incentives. By enhancing the *ongoing* analyses of financial regulation, the Sentinel would improve the design of financial policies.

While regulators and others could refute the Sentinel's analyses and persuade policy makers to reject its recommendations, the Sentinel would *permit* an informed debate and hence increase the likelihood of adopting sound policies and decrease the likelihood of maintaining harmful ones. For example, while the Fed was or should have been aware of the destabilizing effects of its capital regulatory policies many years before the onset of the crisis, the public and Congress would have found it difficult to obtain this information and discuss alternative policies with the Fed. Similarly the public and Congress would have found it difficult to identify the SEC's decision to weaken its ability to supervise investment banks on a consolidated basis and hence the public's ability to challenge these decisions. While the Fed and SEC were aware of the growing incentive problems in credit rating agencies during the boom in structured financial products, it would have been difficult for the public to obtain the requisite information and conduct the appropriate analyses necessary to challenge the decision of the Guardians of Finance to do nothing about the resultant emerging and escalating systemic risks. A Sentinel would have reduced the probability that regulatory authorities around the world would have ignored the compensation explosion, made so many mistakes, and maintained those failed policies in the decade before the 2007 to 2009 global financial crisis.

By enhancing the quality of debates about financial policy, the Sentinel would also reduce the chances that a simplistic ideology would dominate financial policy decisions. Because financial regulation is so complex, regulators, politicians, and the public will naturally search for simplifying ideologies, rules of thumb, filters through which to understanding the multifaceted, confusing world of finance. But, as stressed throughout this book, such simplicity has its costs. The Sentinel would have the capacity—and mandate—to challenge various approaches to regulation. This would provide a mechanism for questioning the legitimacy of regulatory ideologies. *Because* it is a natural human tendency to seek out simplifying mechanisms for dealing with a complex world, we propose the Sentinel as an institutional device for reducing the potentially pernicious effects of oversimplification. The Sentinel would provide the basis for comprehensive and informed discussions of the inherently complex, multifaceted issue of financial regulation.

While transparency and open debate are sometimes uncomfortable and even inefficient, they are better than the alternative. Ask any Icelandic, Irish, or British taxpayer, not to mention all those unemployed in those and many more countries! Just as many governments create commissions to examine complex and consequential issues, such as the recent commission on the fiscal challenges facing the United States, we are proposing the creation of a Sentinel to examine the extraordinarily complex and extremely consequential issue of financial regulation. But this must be an ongoing assessment that seeks to identify problems with financial regulation *before* they trigger a crisis or seriously hinder the efficient allocation of capital. Just as such independent commissions can foster very healthy debate on a complex issue, the Sentinel will have the ability to challenge existing institutions and thereby contribute to more informed discussion that should lead to better outcomes.

Desirability of the Sentinel: Boost Governance and Regulatory Performance

The Sentinel would push the policy debate toward a focus on the general welfare of the public and away from the narrow interests of the powerful and wealthy. As an extra group of informed, prying eyes, it would reduce the ability of regulators to obfuscate regulatory actions and would instead make regulators more accountable for the societal repercussions of their actions.

As emphasized by a vast literature, financial institutions devote substantial sums of money and time to shape financial policies, regulations, and supervisory practices to serve their private interests. As emphasized by an equally vast literature, narrow political constituencies work tirelessly on tilting the financial rules of the game so as to collect a greater share of the economy's resources. Consequently it is vitally important to have an independent and capable group devoted to the public interest to provide an objective assessment of financial policies. As a prominent institution, the Sentinel's reports would help reduce the influence of special interests on the public's representatives. While the Sentinel itself may be imperfect, it would *reduce* the probability that socially damaging and reckless policies would be selected and maintained.

Moreover the Sentinel would be uniquely positioned to improve the performance of existing regulatory agencies. At the simplest level, knowing that the Sentinel is going to scrutinize their actions would increase the performance of regulatory agencies, reducing complacency. The mere existence of the Sentinel might have reduced the dubious actions and inactions of several regulatory bodies during the most recent crisis.

For instance, recall the evidence from chapter 1 on monitoring sports referees, umpires, and game officials. When a baseball umpire knows that a digital system is reviewing balls and strikes, the bias disappears! It is not that the digital system catches and corrects decisions by the umpire. Rather, simply knowing about the digital review eliminates the umpire's systematic bias in favor of home team pitchers and batters. Similarly, in football, the mere existence of instant replay—the enhancement of transparency—reduces the home bias in calls made by officials during the game, *before* they are reviewed. Monitoring improves the performance of the officials.

The Sentinel will also provide a type of "instant replay" and hence improve the performance and decisions of the Guardians *before* the Sentinel reviews them. The mere existence of the Sentinel will reduce the home field advantage enjoyed by the financial services industry.

Furthermore, by having no official power over either the regulatory agencies or financial markets and institutions, the Sentinel would be less constrained in its assessments than an organization with direct supervisory and regulatory responsibilities. For example, if a regulator gives the OK on a particular practice, the regulator might later find it difficult to reverse or adjust its decision as new information becomes available. The regulator might have the very human fear of losing credibility with the regulated entity. Or, as in the Irish case, if the regulator discovers unsafe practices that have been ongoing for some time, there might be a tendency to delay regulatory intervention , as that would highlight past regulatory laxity. In contrast, the Sentinel would face fewer such conflicts. The Sentinel would make it more likely that bad policies are identified and changed in a more timely manner. As a second example, while one regulatory agency (e.g., the Fed) might steer clear of criticizing another agency's actions (e.g., the SEC's) to avoid triggering cross-agency battles, the Sentinel would be less reticent. In conversations with regulatory officials in several different agencies, many concurred: nobody would dare criticize another regulatory agency because of the severe bureaucratic repercussions. The Sentinel would have the responsibility of commenting on the performance and policies of all regulatory institutions, with positive implications for the governance of financial regulation.

Alternatives to, Critiques of, and Reflections on the Sentinel

We now discuss alternatives to the Sentinel, respond to critiques of our proposal, and highlight its key limitations. Many of the alternatives are more accurately described as valuable additions to the Sentinel, not as substitutes for it. None of the alternatives has the key characteristics of the Sentinel: independence, capacity, authority, and the prominence to affect the national, and indeed international, discussion on financial regulation. We further argue that the Sentinel is not a cure for all ills plaguing financial regulation, but it is necessary for addressing core weaknesses in the regulatory apparatus.

Alternatives
Some might claim that the United States is already moving to adopt a Sentinel. The Dodd–Frank Act established the Financial Stability Oversight

Council (FSOC) to gather regulators around a table, foster communication, and eliminate regulatory gaps. The same legislation creates an Office of Financial Research (OFR), which might in theory act like a Sentinel.

We could not disagree more. As explained in chapter 7, there were already ample formal and information mechanisms for sharing information and coordinating policy actions across regulatory bodies. Moreover, as noted in chapter 4, the crisis does not primarily reflect the lack of communication across regulatory agencies. In terms of the OFR, it is housed within the US Treasury and the organizational structure does not do anything to slow the revolving door. Again, critical ingredients of a Sentinel—independence from political and market influences—are missing. Since the OFR, which will likely be on a standard, civil service pay scale, is unlikely to have the resources to assemble a highly skilled group of financial economists, accountants, lawyers, regulators, and private financiers, they will not have the coordinated teams of experts necessary for evaluating the full array of financial sector issues in a comprehensive and compelling manner. These are no substitutes for the Sentinel.

Some might argue that governments already have constructed mechanisms to hold regulators accountable. For example, the US Government Accountability Office (GAO) has broad oversight capacity of agencies and departments of the government, so in theory it could fulfill the role of a Sentinel-like agency in the financial sector.

We are skeptical. The GAO is a creature of Congress, depends on Congress for its budget, and covers every conceivable sector and issue, from agriculture to health to national defense to veterans' affairs. Furthermore its staff is on a civil service pay scale. For regular staff (the equivalent of a senior economist with say ten years' experience) the salary scale limit was $155,000 in 2010. For the Senior Executive Service, pay is capped at $179,900; pay at the Federal Reserve Board tops out at $205,000. Although these pay levels look attractive compared with per capita GDP in the United States ($47,400 in 2010), they are a fraction of what relatively junior staff can make at top banks. It will be difficult to attract and maintain seasoned financial experts to the GAO, or a similarly structured institution.

Existing institutions simply do not have the human capital skills to accomplish the mandate of the Sentinel even if they had the power to obtain the requisite information, which they do not, nor the political independence, which they typically lack as well. GAO and similar agencies in other countries could set up a special financial watchdog unit, but its pay would have to be many times current levels—and the head of the unit would have to have both pay and stature above that of the head of the agency. We think it would be harder to get someone of sufficient stature and expertise to take a position reporting to the head of the GAO. In addition the unit would need a separate budget—one would not want its work on financial institution risk, for example, to be constrained by obsolete computer technology—and separate procedures designed to minimize bureaucratic delays, as these will also hurt its ability to attract first-rate staff. Finally, the unit would need access to all of the information collected by financial regulatory agencies. Practically speaking, this access would not happen if there were the possibility that it might circulate within a larger agency (how would the head of the unit keep information from the head of the agency?). With all of these requirements, we think that the Sentinel needs to be a separate entity, as described above. Setting up the Sentinel within another agency is creating the conditions for its failure, and its mission is too important to hinder in this way.

Similarly there is little reason to have much confidence that international institutions, such as the Bank for International Settlements or the International Monetary Fund, can fulfill the role of the Sentinel. There are many reasons why they cannot be relied on to do so. As noted in chapter 4, these institutions are not politically independent; they are not independent of financial markets, as the revolving door spins easily between these institutions and financial firms; they do not have the power to demand information from national regulatory authorities; and major countries are unlikely to listen to international agencies, rather than to their own regulators. For example, consider the efforts of William White, the former chief economist of the BIS, and his deputy Claudio Borio. As early as 2003, they began to warn of a growing real estate bubble, and by 2007, they noted the dangers of securitization.[11] They did not have access to detailed supervisory reports on what was occurring in US banks, and they did not have access to a multidisciplinary team of accountants, financial economists, lawyers, and experts with private sector experience to assess the ramifications of securitization for different components of the financial sector, major financial system, or the global economy. This kept their prophetic research at a more abstract—and hence less influential—level. In the end, one of their bosses, Alan Greenspan, who did have detailed supervisory reports and a vast staff of experts, was saying that all was well. The BIS research did not have the prominence to contribute substantially to financial policy debates within the United States.[12]

Other strategies focus on improving the operation of existing regulatory agencies without adding a new institution. Some suggest raising the pay of financial regulators as a mechanism for attracting and retaining highly skilled people. Professor Edward Kane of Boston College, as part of a package of comprehensive reforms, has suggested both raising regulators' pay and, most important, deferring more of it—similar to a bonus or large pension. The regulator would lose some or all of the deferred payment if there were shortcomings in his or her regulatory actions. Moreover Kane proposes an expansion of the oath of office for supervisors, and his proposals include a "duty of vision," in which supervisors pledge to adapt their surveillance to discover the ever changing risks in finance, and a duty of accountability, meaning that the supervisor would disclose sufficient information so that he/she could be held accountable.[13]

Perhaps these strategies would help, but they do not substitute for the existence of an independent institution that evaluates financial regulation on behalf of the public. We are not opposed to higher pay in regulatory agencies, as this might help attract superb people and slow the revolving door. But raising pay without changing incentives is an insufficient strategy for improving financial regulation. Similarly, establishing and enforcing contracts that seek to induce regulators to adopt the views of the public is a valuable and commendable goal, and a potentially useful component of the financial reform tool kit. But we sincerely question whether this is workable in a complex environment. Getting the incentive contracts wrong could induce regulators to impose draconian limits on bank behavior, or other interventions, that would choke off economic growth and curtail opportunity—exactly the opposite of the benefits of finance that were discussed in the first chapter. So while we would be glad to see more work on how such contracts could be written, since increased accountability still is critical, we favor establishing the Sentinel now. Put differently, we certainly would not want compensation contracts and promises of better behavior to substitute for the Sentinel as a response to woefully defective financial regulatory systems.

Critiques

Some might argue that we just don't need a Sentinel, and that the regulatory agencies do a good job of interpreting and implementing regulatory policies for the public at large. From this perspective, defects in the financial regulatory apparatus have played minor roles in precipitating the crisis of 2007 to 2009, the 130 or so financial crises in the last few decades, and the poorly functioning financial system that all too frequently collects savings with one hand and passes it along to political and social cronies with the other. From this perspective, these are not systemic, institutional failures with financial regulation; rather, regulators make mistakes, as do all humans—there are earthquakes, tsunamis, and global financial crises. A Sentinel will not do much good, but it will cost a lot of money.

We disagree. Yes, accidents happen. Yes, people make honest mistakes. But chapters 3 through 7 show that there are systemic defects with the financial regulatory apparatus that contributed, and continue to contribute, to the malfunctioning of financial systems.

Some might even directly critique the essential ingredients of the Sentinel, including its power to demand information. At conferences and in private communications, some who work, or worked, in regulatory agencies have argued that regulators might respond by being careful not to leave a paper trail, so that they would not have to turn over information to the Sentinel. For instance, we have been told that existing regulatory agencies circumvented laws meant to enhance transparency. For example, if the law states that any meeting of five out of the ten executives of a regulatory agency requires the taking of formal minutes, then the chief executive might only talk with three other executives, eliminating any written record of their deliberations. Indeed regulatory agencies use all sorts of strategies to limit transparency and accountability. Recall the description of how the Federal Reserve successfully weaved around attempts by the legislative and judicial branches of government to obtain information on the use of taxpayer funds for several years.

But this seems like an argument *for* a Sentinel with the power to acquire any information that it deems necessary. If in reality unelected regulators with enormous power can successfully make themselves unaccountable to the public and its representatives, then we must quickly change this dangerous reality.

Others directly challenge the value of creating an independent entity since this independence could actually hurt its ability to assess financial regulation. Since the Sentinel would not regulate financial firms, it would miss out on any "soft" information—impressions, understandings, and insights that emerge from conversations and close relationships with financial market participants—that naturally accrue to regulators during the course of their work.

This distinction between the Sentinel and Guardians is exactly what we want; we do not want to replicate the work of the regulators. Distancing the Sentinel from financial institutions reduces the influence, both through the revolving door and through the home field advantage, of the financial services industry. Yes the Sentinel will miss out on valuable "soft" information. Thus the Sentinel is not the "decider"; it is not a regulator and it cannot repeal any regulatory decision. Its function is to enhance debate by delivering an independent assessment, which *permits* a truly informed public discussion.

At presentations, several senior staff members from regulatory agencies have questioned the goal of enhancing the governance of regulatory agencies. They have even argued that there is "too much democracy," complaining that politicians interfere too much in financial regulation. The implication is that (1) regulators know best and (2) they will choose what is best for the public if only the politicians would leave them alone.

Too much evidence suggests that the Guardians do not always act in the best interests of the public to simply leave them alone and assume that they know best. While democracy is messy and inconvenient, the goal of the Sentinel is to provide an auxiliary institution that will make it work better. Not only will it inform debate, hold regulators accountable, and enhance regulatory performance, it will also reduce inappropriate political interference in the operation of regulatory agencies by shining a disinfecting light on the entire apparatus. Thus the Sentinel will actually reduce the types of annoying interventions by politicians that provoke complaints by those working to make regulation work well.

Others claim that many countries are not ready for this proposal. Their regulators do not want to be held accountable; their financial industry does not want tougher regulators; and their voters are not ready to tolerate the levels of pay that would be necessary to make the Sentinel effective. This is certainly possible, but we hope and believe that this is not the case in all countries. Indeed, just as we turned in the manuscript of this book to our publisher, we found an English translation of the 2011 report of the Swedish Fiscal Policy Council, which notes the grave threat to fiscal balances posed by the financial system—a lesson learned all too well in the recent crisis—and recommends a Sentinel-type body whose responsibility would be to produce a report twice a year highlighting the systemic risks in the financial system, yet without other powers. Although that report did not discuss other aspects of a Sentinel agency, such as how to keep it independent, how to attract those with sufficient skills, and what information to require, the Swedish proposal is close in spirit to our recommendation. Ireland also has formed an independent fiscal council that will look for contingent liabilities that might lead to enlarged future fiscal deficits. This is similar to a Sentinel, but unfortunately the Irish agency does not (yet) plan to attract the financial talent needed to spot the most likely source of contingent liabilities, that is, excessive risk-taking in the financial system.

For the many countries not yet ready for a Sentinel, we simply ask: If not now, when? Do we need even more costly crises to be willing to hold regulators accountable? Do we prefer the alternative of giving ungovernable Guardians ever more power and simply hoping—against all available evidence—that next time they will work for us?[14]

The Sentinel Is Not a Panacea

We propose the Sentinel as a mechanism for *improving* financial regulation, while fully recognizing that alone it is insufficient to guarantee a well-functioning regulatory system. Since financial regulation is complex and political, there will be mistakes, officials will embrace flawed ideologies, and both money and the home field advantage will unduly continue to shape financial policies. These maladies will persist regardless of whether there is a Sentinel. But the goal is not to achieve a perfect, flawless system; the goal is to improve the financial regulatory apparatus.

The Sentinel would *help*. It would reduce the incidence and duration of regulatory mistakes. It would force regulators to be more accountable for their actions and shine a disinfecting light on the entire financial policy process. It would, therefore, make regulation less prone to the influences of the financial services industry and reduce the likelihood that one or two powerful individuals with a defective ideology could exert undue influence on financial regulatory policy. Perhaps most important, it would *permit* an informed debate about financial regulation. Such a debate is currently impossible because unelected, unaccountable, and unmonitorable regulators with close ties to the financial services industry have a virtual monopoly on the information and expertise necessary for assessing financial regulation. We are very open to suggestions for improving the Sentinel, as well as to alternatives to the Sentinel, as long as they do not rely on the angelic intentions of politicians and bureaucrats and as long as they provide an effective mechanism for enhancing the public's governance of the Guardians of Finance. The Sentinel alone is not enough, but such an institution is *necessary* for creating a well-functioning financial system. Although an effective Sentinel will require higher salaries than public sector pay in most countries, an effective Sentinel will be far cheaper than a financial crisis.

Conclusions

There are serious defects in the institutional apparatus that selects, implements, and reforms financial policies. Until we fix those deficiencies, the public will not derive the economic benefits associated with a well-functioning financial system—enduring improvements in living standards and expanding economic opportunities for society at large. The global financial crisis was not simply the result of too little regulatory power, unclear lines of regulatory authority, toxic financial innovations, or unsustainable international capital flows. All these were contributing factors. But, through acts of commission and omission, major financial regulatory institutions repeatedly designed and maintained policies that increased the fragility of the financial system and the inefficient allocation of capital. The financial policy apparatus maintained these policies even as they learned that their policies were distorting the flow of credit toward questionable ends. These same types of systemic failures also cause less dramatic, though potentially more costly, financial system inefficiencies. As we, and others, have shown, countries often choose financial policies that tilt the flow of credit toward the economically and politically powerful and away from those with the best projects and entrepreneurial ideas.[15] These regulatory choices slow long-run economic growth by distorting the allocation of capital and promote income inequality by helping the rich and powerful while curtailing the economic opportunities of everyone else.

The public and elected officials do not have effective mechanisms for compelling the Guardians of Finance to act in the best interests of the public largely because they cannot obtain informed, expert, and independent assessments of financial regulation. In the absence of such sound assessments, the public cannot effectively govern the Guardians of Finance. As suggested by James Madison, the people cannot simply rely on the angelic intentions of financial regulators and, given the complexity of finance, the great challenge is developing auxiliary institutions to induce the regulatory apparatus to operate in the best interests of the public.

The Sentinel is our proposal for improving fundamental defects with the financial regulatory system. Unlike existing institutions, the Sentinel would be independent of both political and market influence. While the vast majority of regulators might act, or might want to act, in the best interests of the public, just as most sports referees want to make the right call, it is nevertheless valuable to have an informed, expertly staffed institution—without potential conflicts of interest—assessing the performance of official agencies and the efficacy of financial policies. Unlike existing institutions, the Sentinel would have the prominence, information, and expertise to evaluate the full array of financial markets and institutions and to question existing regulatory agencies. It is anti-democratic, and downright economically dangerous, for a group of unelected, largely unchecked, regulatory officials to have a monopoly on the information and expertise necessary for assessing financial regulations. By providing an independent, expert perspective, the Sentinel would encourage the Guardians of Finance to work for us.

Glossary

Checkable deposits Deposits at banks on which the owner can write checks to make payments.

Collateralized debt obligations (CDOs) Debt securities that are collateralized with other securities, such as mortgages and possibly other forms of debt. When CDOs include other CDOs, they are termed CDO-squareds. See structured finance.

Credit default swaps Insurance-like contracts written on the performance of a security or bundle of securities. For example, a purchaser, bank A, buys a credit default swap from issuer B on security C. If security C later has a predefined "credit-related event," such as a missed interest payment, a credit downgrade, or a bankruptcy filing, then issuer B must purchase security C from purchaser A at face value to compensate for the loss in value.

Credit spreads Difference between two interest rates, usually the difference between a "risk free" or the lowest risk interest rate, such as the rate on short-term government bills, and the rate that a risky borrower has to pay.

Derivatives Securities whose value is derived from the value of an underlying instrument or agreement. The underlying asset might be a stock, bond, or almost any other "promise to pay" that depends on some well-defined event.

Dual banking Existence of both national and state-chartered banks in the United States.

Equity tranche Securities (e.g., mortgages) that are pooled together and their payments made in a pre-determined priority to groups or tranches. The first group to get repaid would be the safest, or highest rated, the second group or tranche would be riskier—it only is paid after income is taken to pay the holders of the first tranche; and the last group to be paid is the equity tranche, which takes the highest risk and receives the highest promised return.

Hedge funds Funds that are not open to smaller individual investors but only either to institutional investors or wealthier individuals. These funds can invest in a variety of assets and often will bet on the elimination of some distortion or price difference in a market.

Holding company A company whose assets primarily consist of stock in other companies.

Material loss reviews   Reviews issued in the United States by the Federal Deposit Insurance Corporation (FDIC), the Federal Reserve, and the Treasury Department in the event a bank has failed and led to costs for the deposit insurance fund in excess of $25 million or 2 percent of the bank's assets. See the FDIC Office of Inspector General (http://www.fdicoig.gov/mlr.shtml) for examples.

Metrics   Measures, or definitive models.

Mortgage-backed securities   Securities that pool typically hundreds or thousands of mortgages together, and then pay the holders of the securities out of the cash flows generated by the mortgage payments.

Net capital rule   A 1975 rule of the US Securities and Exchange Commission for determining the minimum capital standards at broker-dealers.

NINJA loans   Mortgage loans that require no information on income, jobs, or assets, and also were dubbed no-documentation or no-doc loans because the loan documents in a typical mortgage were not checked for accuracy. Borrowers could, of course, lie about their incomes (these were dubbed "liar loans") and also mortgage brokers, who were paid on commission based on the size of the loan, had the incentive either to encourage borrowers to engage in this practice or even to re-write the loan documentation writing in a higher income level and loan amount.

Option-ARMS   Option adjustable rate mortgages are mortgages in which not only does the interest rate adjust over the life of the mortgage, in accordance with some formula, but also the borrower has the option during the initial years of a mortgage to pay less than the principal and interest due, with the unpaid amount added on to the size of the mortgage.

Over-the-counter derivatives   Derivative instruments that trade bilaterally between parties rather than over an exchange.

Quantitative risk models   Mathematical models of various risks. For example, at any point in time banks are interested in estimating their expected losses (on individual loans and on their entire portfolio of loans), which depend on the probability of default, the loss given default per dollar of the exposure (the amount of the loan outstanding), and the loan exposure at the time of default. Each of these components can be estimated by using available data, applying assumptions about probability distributions and data on what has happened in the past.

Securitization   Process of bundling loans and other assets together and then selling those assets. A bank could, for example, securitize its loans in this manner, receiving cash for the loans sold, and so be able to use the funds received to make more loans. For the purchasers of securities, this process allows them to the extent that the assets in the securities are not highly correlated, to acquire exposure to such assets with less risk than purchasing individual loans or securities.

Shadow banking system   Financial firms—such as investment banks, money-market mutual funds, and mortgage brokers—and financial instruments—such as repurchase agreements, asset-backed securities, and collateralized debt obligations—that perform the same functions of banks but whose regulation (compared to banks') is virtually nonexistent.

Structured" finance[1]   Whereas securitization refers to the pooling and selling of assets, "structured finance" involves some prioritization of the claims on the pooled income, so that some are more likely to be repaid than others.

Structured investment vehicle, or SIV   Entities, often established by banks, but with a minimal amount of capital, that hold assets (frequently purchased from the bank that set up the SIV) funded by issuing short-term debt, such as commercial paper or repurchase agreements.

Subprime lending   All mortgage loans that are not prime. In the United States a prime mortgage is typically one in which the borrower has a credit score of 660 or above, and the loan-to-value ratio is less than or equal to 80 percent (so that the borrower has put in a down payment of at least 20 percent). In this case a subprime loan could be any loan either where the borrower has a credit rating below 660 or puts down less than 20 percent of the value of the home.

Usury   Originally referred to the practice of charging interest on loans, which formerly was banned by the Catholic Church and still is prohibited in Islam. Over time usury has become associated with the practice of charging an excessively high rate of interest.

Value-at-risk models (VAR) models   Models of estimated profits and losses of financial intermediaries that can be used to estimate with a pre-specified probability (e.g., 1 percent) what a bank might expect to lose in a single day. Unfortunately, in the recent crisis these models were based on optimistic data and assumptions, and so wildly understated banks' losses.

Notes

Chapter 1

1. Opening statement of Senator Carl Levin, 2010, US Senate Permanent Subcommittee on Investigations Hearings on *Wall Street and the Financial Crisis: The Role of High Risk Home Loans*, April 13.

2. Timothy Geithner, 2008, "Reducing Systemic Risk in a Dynamic Financial System," Remarks by the President of the Federal Reserve Bank of New York at *The Economic Club of New York*, June 9.

3. Alan Greenspan, 2010, "The Crisis," *Brookings Papers on Economic Activity*. Also see Ben S. Bernanke, 2010, "Monetary Policy and the Housing Bubble," Speech at the Annual Meeting of the America Economic Association, Atlanta, Georgia (January 3); Ben S. Bernanke, 2009, "Four Questions about the Financial Crisis," Speech at Morehouse College, Atlanta, Georgia (April 14); Ben S. Bernanke, 2009, "Financial Reform to Address Systemic Risk," Speech at the Council of Foreign Relations, Washington, DC (March 10); Henry Paulson, 2009, *Financial Times*, January 1, 2009 (Krishna Guha); Robert Rubin, 2010, Testimony before the Financial Crisis Inquiry Commission, April 9; Christopher Cox, 2008, "Testimony Concerning Reform of the Financial Regulatory System," Testimony before the US House of Representatives Committee on Financial Services, July 24.

4. M. Nakamoto, and Wighton, D., 2007, "Citigroup Chief Stays Bullish on Buy-Outs," *Financial Times*, 9 July.

5. On Bernanke and Paulson, see David Wessel, 2009, *In Fed We Trust*, New York: Crown.

On Cox, see Christopher Cox, 2008, "Testimony Concerning Reform of the Financial Regulatory System," Testimony before the US House of Representatives Committee on Financial Services, July 24; Christopher Cox, 2008, "Testimony: The State of the United States Economy and Financial Markets," Testimony before the US Senate Committee on Banking, Housing and Urban Affairs, February 14.

On insufficient power, see Christopher Cox, 2008, "Speech by the SEC Chairman: Address to the Security Traders 12th Annual Washington Conference," May 7; Timothy F. Geithner, 2008, "Reducing Systemic Risks in Dynamic Financial System," Remarks at the Economic Club of New York City, June 9; Timothy F. Geithner, 2009, "Treasury Secretary, Written Testimony before the House Financial

Services Committee," March 26; Timothy F. Geithner, 2009. "Treasury Secretary, Written Testimony, House Financial Services Committee, September 23; Timothy F. Geithner, 2010, Treasury Secretary, Written Testimony, House Committee on Oversight and Government Reform, January 27, 2010; Henry M. Paulson, 2008, "Remarks by Secretary Henry M. Paulson at the Ronald Reagan Presidential Library," November 20; and Henry M. Paulson, 2008, "Treasury Secretary, Statement on Emergency Economic Stabilization Act Vote," September 29.

On regulatory gaps, see Timothy F. Geithner, 2010, "Treasury Secretary, "Remarks before the American Enterprise Institute on Financial Reform," March 22; Christopher Cox, 2008, "The State of the United States Economy and Financial Markets," Testimony before the US Senate Committee on Banking, Housing, and Urban Affairs, February 14.

6. Sometimes claims of policy maker impotence have required a rewriting of history. As beautifully told by David Wessel in his book, *In Fed We Trust*, Bernanke and Paulson sat together in September 2008 before a Senate subcommittee nine days after the failure of Lehman Brothers, the second major investment bank after Bear Stearns to fail. Reading from prepared testimony, Bernanke explained that "the Federal Reserve and Treasury declined to support the institution. . . . [because] we judged that investors and counterparties had had time to take precautionary measures" (p. 23). In the light of the upheaval following Lehman's failure, however, Wessel notes that "their later accounts were, well, different" (p. 24). Over the next few months, Bernanke, Paulson, and Geithner formed a united front around the view that they did not have the legal authority to save Lehman Brothers, which is what Geithner and Bernanke explained to the Senate in their confirmation hearings in January 2009 and January 2010, respectively.

7. Timothy F. Geithner, 2010, "Secretary Written Testimony before the House Committee on Oversight and Governance Reform," January 27. Note, however, that before policy makers circled their wagons around the accident explanation, Geithner held a broader perspective on the sources of the crisis. In March 2008, when he was still president of the New York Federal Reserve Bank, Geithner noted that, "The origins of this crisis lie in the complex interactions of a number of forces. Some were the product of market forces. Some were the product of market failures. Some were the result of incentives created by policy and regulation. Some of these were evident at the time, others are apparent only with the benefit of hindsight." This quotation is from the following speech: Timothy F. Geithner, 2008, "The Current Financial Challenges: Policy and Regulatory Implications," Remarks at the Council on Foreign Relations Corporate Conference 2008, New York, March 6.

8. See Gerard Caprio, Daniela Klingebiel, Luc Laeven, and Guillermo Noguera, "Banking Crisis Database: An update of the Caprio–Klingebiel Database (1996, 1999)," The World Bank, October 2003. http://www1.worldbank.org/finance/html/database_sfd.html.

9. Beyond finance, the political scientist Mark Blyth at Brown University demonstrates that economic ideas have shaped economic policies and institutions throughout the twentieth century. See Mark Blyth's 2002 book, *Great Transformations: Economic Ideas and Institutional Change in the Twentieth Century*, Cambridge, UK: Cambridge University Press.

10. See Simon Johnson and James Kwak, 2010, *13 Bankers: The Wall Street Takeover and the Next Financial Meltdown*, New York: Random House.

11. LTCM was a hedge fund composed of the "best and brightest." In addition to Mullins, their leadership included former star trader (John Meriwether) from Salomon Brothers and two Nobel laureates (Myron Scholes and Robert Merton), but the firm collapsed (and precipitated a crisis) in 1998 due to high leverage, illiquidity, and market movements not anticipated by their models—which sounds like the crisis that began in 2007! See Roger Lowenstein, 2000, *When Genius Failed: The Rise and Fall of Long Term Capital Management*, New York: Random House.

12. For example, see Whalen, Christopher, 2011, "The Revolving Door at the Fed," *The Institutional Risk Analyst*, April 4.

13. For instance, see Atif Mian, Amir Sufi, and Francesco Trebbi, 2010, "The Political Economy of the U.S. Mortgage Default Crisis," *American Economic Review*, December, and their working paper, "The Political Economy of the Subprime Mortgage Credit Expansion," June. Also see Deniz Igan, Prachi Mishra, and Thierry Tressel, 2009, "A Fist Full of Dollars: Lobbying and the Financial Crisis," *International Monetary Fund Working* Paper 287, December. This literature builds on the path breaking research by Edward Kane (https://www2.bc.edu/~kaneeb) on incentive conflicts in financial regulation.

14. For example, the free throw percentage of visiting teams in the National Basketball Association is 75.9 percent, while the free throw percentage of home teams is also 75.9 percent. In Major League Baseball, pitchers throw the same percentage of strikes at home and away, when using a computer-generated assessment of the location of each pitch. Furthermore, in the National Football League, teams from cold weather climates are no more likely to win at home when the weather is cold, and teams from hot weather climates are no more likely to win at home when the weather is warm. Also the home field advantage is the same in soccer in small countries like the Netherlands, where travel is unlikely to be much of a burden as it is in large countries, like the United States, Russia, and Brazil, where travel is a bigger deal.

15. This is a quotation from Tobias J. Moskowitz and L. Jon Wertheim, 2011, *Scorecasting: The Hidden Influences Behind How Sports are Played and Games are Won*, New York: Crown Archetype, p. 157.

16. Again, we obtain this information and insight from the perspicacious book, *Scorecasting*, by Tobias Moskowitz and J. Jon Wertheim.

17. This section draws on Ross Levine, 1997, "Financial Development and Economic Growth: Views and Agenda," *Journal of Economic Literature* 35 (June): 688–703.

18. This paragraph covers a vast history. Some of the salient readings are: Larry Neal, 2000, "How It All Began: The Monetary and Financial Architecture of Europe during the First Global Capital Markets, 1648–1815," *Financial History Review* 7: 117–140; Douglass North and Barry Weingast, 1989, "Constitutions and Commitment: The Evolution of Institutions Governing Public Choice in Seventeenth-Century England," *Journal of Economic History* 49 (December); and Richard Sylla, "The Political Economy of Early U.S. Financial Development," in

Stephen Haber, Douglass C. North, and Barry R. Weingast, eds., *Political Institutions and Financial Development*, 1997, Stanford University Press.

19. See Ross Levine, 2005, "Finance and Growth: Theory and Evidence," in Philippe Aghion and Steven Durlauf, eds., *Handbook of Economic Growth*, Dordricht: Elsevier Science, pp. 866–934; Thorsten Beck, Ross Levine, and Alexey Levkov, 2010, "Big Bad Banks?" *Journal of Finance* 65: 1637–68; Ross Levine and Asli Demirguc-Kunt, 2009, "Finance and Inequality: Theory and Evidence," *Annual Review of Financial Economics* 1 (December): 287–318; Thorsten Beck, Asli Demirguc-Kunt, and Ross Levine, 2007, "Finance, Inequality, and the Poor," *Journal of Economic Growth* 12: 27–49; Thorsten Beck, Asli Demirguc-Kunt, Luc Laeven, and Ross Levine, 2008, "Finance, Firm Size, and Growth," *Journal of Money, Banking, and Finance* 40 (October): 1371–1405; Franklin Allen, and Elena Carletti, 2008, "The Roles of Banks in Financial Systems," in A. Berger, P. Moyneux, and J. Wilson, eds., *The Oxford Handbook of Banking,* Oxford: Oxford University Press.

20. See, for example, Stephen Haber, 2011, "Politics and Banking Systems: Evidence from New World Economies" in Stanley Engerman and Kenneth L. Sokoloff, eds., with contributions by Stephen Haber, Elisa Mariscal, and Eric Zolt, *Economic Development in the Americas since 1500: Endowments and Institutions,* Cambridge: Cambridge University Press; Stephen Haber, Armando Razo, and Noel Maurer, 2003, *The Politics of Property Rights: Political Instability, Credible Commitments, and Economic Growth in Mexico, 1876–1929,* Cambridge: Cambridge University Press; and Charles Calomiris and Stephen Haber, forthcoming, *Fragile Banks, Durable Bargains: Why Banking Is All about Politics and Always Has Been.*

Chapter 2

1. A simple numerical example may help solidify the intuition. Consider both a safe and a risky project, each with the same average payoff of $2.00 in one year. The safe project generates a payoff of $2.00 in one year with 100 percent certainty. The risky project has a payoff of $4.00 half of the time and a payoff of $0 half of the time. So the risky project also has an average payoff of $2.00. Further assume that the debt holder is owed $1.00. The debt holder, on the one hand, would urge the company to invest in the safe asset because it always generates sufficient earnings for the corporation to pay its debt obligations, while the risky project only generates sufficient earnings to pay the debt holder half of the time. The shareholder, on the other hand, will be more attracted to the risky project. With the safe project, after the corporation pays the debt holder $1.00, the shareholder only receives $1.00 after making an initial investment of $1.00. But, if the corporation invests in the risky project and it succeeds, the shareholder receives $3.00. Since the shareholder gets nothing if the risky project fails, the average profit accruing to the shareholder when the corporation invests in the risk project is $1.50 (because he gets $0 half of the time and $3.00 half of the time). This is 50 percent more than the average profit from the safe project ($1.00). While it is not certain that

every owner in all situations prefers the risky project, the owner clearly finds the risky endeavor more appealing than the debt holder.

2. The classic references in this area are Charles Calomiris, and Charles Kahn, 1991, "The Role of Demandable Debt in Structuring Optimal Banking Arrangements," *American Economic Review* 81 (3): 497–513; Douglas W. Diamond and Philip H. Dybvig, 1983, "Bank Runs, Deposit Insurance and Liquidity," *Journal of Political Economy* 91 (3): 401–19.

3. See Calomiris and Kahn (op cit. at note 2), and Charles Calomiris, and Joseph Mason, 2003, "Fundamentals, Bank Panics, and Bank Distress during the Depression," *American Economic Review* 93 (5): 1615–47.

4. For evidence, see the discussion in James R. Barth, Gerard Caprio, and Ross Levine, 2006, *Rethinking Bank Regulation: Till Angels Govern*, New York: Cambridge University Press, and also the insightful papers by Paola Sapienza, 2004, "The Effects of Government Ownership on Bank Lending," *Journal of Financial Economics* 72(2): 357–84; Asim Khwaja and Atif Mian, 2005, "Do Lenders Favor Politically Connected Firms? Rent Provision in an Emerging Financial Market," *Quarterly Journal of Economics* 120 (4): 1371–1411; Atif Mian, Amir Sufi, and Francesco Trebbi, 2010, "The Political Economy of the U.S. Mortgage Default Crisis," *American Economic Review* 100 (5): 1967–98. Furthermore we take the expression "the grabbing hand" from the excellent book by Andrei Shleifer and Robert W. Vishny titled, appropriately, *The Grabbing Hand: Government Pathologies and Their Cures*, Cambridge: Harvard University Press, which was published in 1998.

5. Also see Thorsten Beck, Asli Demirguc-Kunt, and Ross Levine, 2006, "Bank Supervision and Corruption in Lending" *Journal of Monetary Economics* 53(8): 2131–63; James R. Barth, Gerard Caprio, and Ross Levine, 2004, "Bank Regulation and Supervision: What Works Best." *Journal of Financial Intermediation* 13: 205–48; James R. Barth, Gerard Caprio, and Ross Levine, 2008, "Bank Regulations Are Changing: For Better or Worse?" *Comparative Economic Studies* 50 (4): 537–63.

6. This section draws on chapter 5 of James R. Barth, Gerard Caprio, and Ross Levine, 2006, *Rethinking Bank Regulation: Till Angels Govern*, New York: Cambridge University Press.

7. It is our understanding that the first use of the term the "visible hand" as a play on Adam Smith's "invisible hand" was by Alfred Chandler, who was referring to the visible hand of managers in large corporations. His 1977 book *The Visible Hand: The Managerial Revolution in American Business* (Cambridge, MA: Belknap Press) is a classic. But we are following Jerry Z. Muller's use of the term in his extraordinarily insightful book, *The Mind and the Market: Capitalism in Modern European Thought*, 2002 (New York: Knopf). Muller uses the "visible hand" to refer to the government's role in facilitating the functioning of capitalist markets. The remainder of this subsection draws heavily on Professor Muller's chapter on Adam Smith.

8. For example, Smith explains, "It is not from the benevolence of the butcher, the brewer or the baker, that we expect our dinner, but from their regard to their own

self-interest. We address ourselves, not to their humanity but to their self-love." Smith, Adam [1776] (1977), *An Inquiry into the Nature and Causes of the Wealth of Nations*, Chicago: University of Chicago Press.

9. In a famous passage, Adam Smith notes: "People of the same trade seldom meet together, even for merriment and diversion, but the conversation ends in a conspiracy against the public, or in some contrivance to raise prices." Ibid.

10. Beyond the value of education in promoting productivity, Smith focused on the degrading effects of increasingly specialized labor on humanity: "His dexterity at his own particular trade seems, in this manner, to be acquired at the expense of his intellectual, social, and martial virtues. But in every improved and civilized society this is the state into which the laboring poor, that is, the great body of the people must necessarily fall, unless government takes some pains to prevent it." This quotation from *The Wealth of Nations* is taken from Jerry Z. Muller, 2002, *The Mind and the Market: Capitalism in Modern European Thought*, New York: Knopf, p. 78.

11. This quotation by Adam Smith from *The Wealth of Nations* is taken from Muller, 2002, *The Mind and the Market*, p. 79.

12. Muller (op. cit. at note 10), p. 80.

13. These quotations by Adam Smith from *The Wealth of Nations* are taken from Muller (op cit. at note 10), p. 76.

14. This quotation by Adam Smith from *The Wealth of Nations* is taken from Muller (op cit. at note 10), p. 68.

15. For example, Smith argued, "The statesman who should attempt to direct private people in what manner they ought to employ their capitals, would . . . assume an authority which could safely be trusted, not only to no single person, but to no council or senate whatever." This quotation from *The Wealth of Nations* is taken from Muller (op. cit. at note 10), p. 67.

16. See Michalopoulos, Stelios, Luc Laeven, and Ross Levine, 2010, "Financial Innovation and Endogenous Growth," NBER, WP15356, and the references therein.

17. By way of disclosure, one of the authors (Jerry Caprio) was asked to lead (against his will, by the way) the development of the FSAP from the World Bank's side in its initial years and had to watch with dismay the developments described in the text.

18. See Central Bank of Ireland, 2010, "The Irish Banking Crisis: Regulatory and Financial Stability Policy 2003–2008," Report to the Minister for Finance by the Governor of the Central Bank, May 31, http://www.bankinginquiry.gov.ie/The%20Irish%20Banking%20Crisis%20Regulatory%20and%20Financial%20Stability%20Policy%202003-2008.pdf

19. See his paper—first published in 1993—"Sending the Herd off the Cliff Edge: The Disturbing Interaction between Herding and Market-Sensitive Risk Management Practices," *Journal of Risk Finance* 2 (1): 59–65.

20. See Suzanne McGee, 2010, *Chasing Goldman Sachs: How the Masters of the Universe Melted Wall Street Down . . . and Why They'll Take Us to the Brink Again*, New York: Crown Business.

21. This is taken from J. K. Rowling's *Harry Potter* epic. Dementors are creatures that glorify in ". . . decay and despair, they drain peace, hope, and happiness out of the air around them. . . ." This is certainly not our intent!

Chapter 3

1. "Tough Questions for the Credit Rating Agencies," *Time*, June 3, 2010. http://www.time.com/time/business/article/0,8599,1993744,00.html.

2. See Luc Laeven and Ross Levine, 2007, "Is There a Diversification Discount in Financial Conglomerates?" *Journal of Financial Economics* 85 (August): 331–67.

3. See *Report of Anton Valukas, Examiner, into the Bankruptcy of Lehman Brothers Holding Co.,* vol. 1 (March 2010), pp. 43–57, http://lehmanreport.jenner.com/.

4. See Floyd Norris, 2009, "It May Be Outrageous, but Wall Street Pay Didn't Cause This Crisis," *New York Times*, July 30. The study mentioned in that article by René Stulz and Rudiger Fahlenbrach, 2010, "Bank CEO Incentives and the Credit Crisis," Charles A. Dice Center for Research in Financial Economics, WP 2009-13.

5. See Loretta Mester, 2008, "Optimal Industrial Structure in Banking," in the *Handbook of Financial Intermediation*, Arnoud Boot and Anjan Thakor, eds., Amsterdam: North Holland, and Joseph Hughes and Loretta Mester, 2010, "Efficiency in Banking: Theory and Evidence," in *Oxford Handbook of Banking*, Allen Berger, Philip Molyneux, and John Wilson, eds., Oxford: Oxford University Press.

6. See Martin Goetz, Luc Laeven, and Ross Levine, 2010, "The Private Benefits from Controlling Complex Bank Holding Companies," mimeo, Brown University.

7. See Yener Altunbas and David Marqués Ibáñez, 2004, "Mergers and Acquisitions and Bank Performance in Europe: The Role of Strategic Similarities, European Central Bank," WP 398, and http://finance.mapsofworld.com/merger-acquisition/bank/european-banks.html.

8. A hedge fund is a fund open to high-wealth individuals and institutional investors (e.g., pension funds, insurance companies, and bank trust departments) that engage in various investment and trading activities—including shorting (betting on a decline of) currencies or companies' shares. Private equity funds are similar but tend to specialize in less liquid investments, including especially those in firms that are not publicly traded, with the goal of improving their performance and then taking them public.

9. Robert Shiller, 2005, *Irrational Exuberance*, Princeton: Princeton University Press, ch. 3, argues that the capitalist explosion and spread of the "ownership society" is one of the forces that contributes to market bubbles. The most successful in amassing wealth might become hedge fund clients, and more generally the growth in the numbers of those with the resources to bid on assets might lead to at least a transitory increase in trading. Also Emeritus University of Chicago Professor Robert Aliber pointed out (in discussions with Jerry Caprio) the increase in investment banks' reliance on trading.

10. Hedge Fund Intelligence, 2008, " Global Hedge Fund Assets Rise 27% to $2.6 Trillion," Press Release, April 16, and Marco Avellaneda and Paul Besson, 2007, "Hedge-Funds: How Big Is Big?" mimeo, Courant Institute, New York University. math.nyu.edu/faculty/avellane/HFCapacity.pdf.

11. See Congressional Record, 1998, Proceedings and Debates of the 106th Congress, Second Session, Part I, p. 541.

12. See UBS, 2008, "Shareholder Report on UBS's Write-Downs," April 18, p. 42. www.ubs.com.

13. Ibid., p. 33.

14. The authors are thankful to Joseph Mason for pointing them toward articles by Nomura Fixed Income Research, *Rating Shopping: The Consequences*, February 16, 2006, and *Bond Rating Confusion*, June 29, 2006. Both publications in turn cite earlier research dating back to the late 1990s, such as R. Skora, 1998, "Correlation, the Hidden Risk in CDOs," in *Derivatives Strategy*, November, confirming that these aspects of mortgage related securities had been known for some time.

15. Allen Frankel, 2009, "The Risk of Relying on Reputational Capital: A Case Study of the 2007 Failure of New Century Financial," WP 294, Bank for International Settlements, p. 4.

16. Ibid., p. 8.

17. Louise Story, 2008, "On Wall Street, Bonuses, Not Profits, Were Real," *New York Times*, December 18. http://www.nytimes.com/2008/12/18/business/18pay .html.

18. Ibid, p. 33.

19. ProPublica, 1020, "The Magnetar Trade: How One hedge Fund Helped Keep the Bubble Going." http://www.propublica.org/article/all-the-magnetar-trade-how-one-hedge-fund-helped-keep-the-housing-bubble. There is also an excellent show on *Planet Money*, "Inside Job," that explains the way that insiders who thought that the who CDO process was insane could encourage the process of creating securities likely to default and then bet against them (http://www. thisamericanlife.org/radio-archives/episode/405/inside-job). See further Michael Lewis, 2010, *The Big Short: Inside the Doomsday Machine*, New York: Norton.

20. Thomas Philippon and Ariell Reshef, 2009, "Wages and Human Capital in the U.S. Financial Industry: 1909–2006," NBER WP 14644.

21. See Norris (op. cit. at note 4), and Stulz and Fahlenbrach (op. cit. at note 4).

22. Lucien Bebchuk, Alma Cohen, and Holger Spamann, 2010, "The Wages of Failure: Executive Compensation at Bear Stearns and Lehman, 2000–2008," *Yale Journal on Regulation* 27: 257–82. It would be useful to look beyond the top five executives, who are not necessarily the most highly paid and do not "cash out" the most, to include the principal staff running the buy and sell side of the securitization business, those managing the proprietary trading of a bank, and so forth. However, these data are not generally available.

23. See Story (op. cit. at note 17).

24. See Gretchen Morgenson, 2010, "How Countrywide Covered the Cracks," *New York Times*, October 16.

25. In the interest of full disclosure, one of the authors left the Federal Reserve Board of Governors to take a job at JP Morgan—though then it was still known as Morgan Guaranty, and he (lamentably) was paid on a commercial banking pay scale, just as Morgan was leaving behind both its dowdy former name and plunging into a more universal banking model. Still, in contrast to other job changes, when his compensation more frequently declined (but his satisfaction increased!), his pay more than doubled. Many times larger percentage increases for those moving from a regulatory body to the financial sector were seen in recent years.

26. Thorvaldur Gylfason, 2010, "From Boom to Bust: The Iceland Story," in Thorvaldur Gylfason, Bengt Holmström, Sixten Korkman, Hans Tson Söderström, and Vesa Vihriälä, eds., *Nordics in Global Crisis:Vulnerability and Resilience*, Taloustieto Oy: Research Institute of the Finnish Economy (ETLA) Publisher, p. 149.

27. Testimony of Mark Froeba, 2010, before the Financial Crisis Inquiry Commission, June 2, pp. 3–4. http://fcic-static.law.stanford.edu/cdn_media/fcic-testimony/2010-0602-Froeba.pdf.

28. Statement of Eric Kolchinsky, 2010, before the Senate Permanent Subcommittee on Investigations, Hearing on Wall Street and the Financial Crisis: The Role of Credit Rating Agencies, April 23.

29. Lewis (op. cit. at note 19), p. 98, has an unflattering but accurate sounding depiction of ratings agencies staff working in this area.

30. Raghuram Rajan, 2010, *Fault Lines: How Hidden Fractures Still Threaten the World Economy*, Princeton: Princeton University Press.

31. Gillian Tett describes in *Fool's Gold: How the Bold Dream of a Small Tribe at J.P. Morgan Was Corrupted by Wall Street Greed and Unleashed a Catastrophe* (New York: Simon and Schuster, 2009) how Morgan invented a product ("Bistro") that would allow banks to use derivatives to move assets to off-balance sheet entities. However, she argues (in chapter 4) that Morgan's management hesitated to apply this to the mortgage market due to the difficulty in getting data on the extent to which underlying loans were correlated (the possibility, as seen in the crisis, that they could deteriorate in quality simultaneously). By the time they were about to overcome these concerns—in part due to the success of their competitors—housing prices began to decline and led to a halt of the planned expansion in this area.

32. See Andrew Ross Sorkin, 2009, *Too Big to Fail: The Inside Story of How Wall Street and Washington Fought to Save the Financial System—and Themselves*, New York: Viking, ch. 6.

33. Ibid.

34. See Table Rock Films, 2009, *American Casino*, directed by Leslie Cockburn, produced by Andrew Cockburn. http://www.americancasinothemovie.com.

35. See Tett (op. cit. at note 32), ch. 4 in particular.

36. For an accessible discussion of this "peso problem," as it is labeled in economics, see Keith Sill, 2000, "Understanding Asset Values: Stock Prices, Exchange Rates, and the "Peso Problem," Federal Reserve Bank of Philadelphia *Business Review*, September–October.

37. On risk modeling, Patrick Honohan's, 2008, "Bank Failures: The Limitations of Risk Modeling" (Institute for International Integration Studies Discussion Paper 263), and Robert Shiller's, 2005, *Irrational Exuberance* (Princeton: Princeton University Press), provide an excellent discussion of "new era" thinking. Joseph Stiglitz, 2010, *Freefall: America, Free Markets, and the Sinking of the World Economy* (New York: Norton), discusses how models and other innovations have posed dangers to financial systems.

Chapter 4

1. This is taken from Board of Governors of the Federal Reserve System, 2005, *Purposes and Functions*, Washington, DC: Federal Reserve. And, to be very precise, the Dodd–Frank Act of 2010 somewhat augmented these responsibilities, as we discuss in chapter 7.

2. Given the transfer of some of OTS functions into the OCC, the numbers in the text combine the 2009 values for OCC and Office of Thrift Supervision that form the new OCC.

3. The Fed's structure is complex. The Board of Governors in Washington has sole authority in setting regulation. The supervisors with the responsibility to oversee the banks in each district sit in that district Federal Reserve Bank, and they report to the head of supervision at the Board, though senior management in the bank in which they sit certainly might influence them.

4. According to Dodd–Frank, presidents of the Federal Reserve Banks will be elected by class B directors, which are elected by district member banks to represent the public, and by class C directors, which are appointed by the Board of Governors to represent the public. Class A directors, which are elected by member banks to represent member banks, will no longer vote for presidents of the Federal Reserve Banks. There are three of each class of director on the board of directors of each Federal Reserve Bank. This explains the numbers in the text.

5. Simon Johnson and James Kwak, 2010, *13 Bankers: The Wall Street Takeover and the Next Financial Meltdown*, New York: Pantheon.

6. Both of these descriptions are from David Wessel, 2009, *In Fed We Trust: Ben Bernanke's War on the Great Panic*, New York: Crown.

7. Ibid., p. 50.

8. This is from a *60 Minutes* interview with Ayn Rand as quoted in "The Warning," *Frontline*, Public Broadcasting System, October 20, 2009. http://www.pbs.org/wgbh/pages/frontline/warning.

9. Alan Greenspan, 2007, *The Age of Turbulence: Adventures in a New World*, New York: Penguin Press, as quoted in "The Warning," *Frontline*, Public Broad-

casting System, October 20, 2009. http://www.pbs.org/wgbh/pages/frontline/warning.

10. Ibid.

11. Wessel (op. cit. at note 6). For information about the philosophy of SEC chairman Christopher Cox and its connection with Ayn Rand, see Stephen Labaton, 2005, "Bush S.E.C. Pick Is Seen as Friend to Corporations," *New York Times*, June 3.

12. See chapter 2 and our book, *Rethinking Bank Regulation: Till Angels Govern*, which was published by Cambridge University Press in 2006.

13. Gillian Tett, 2009, *Fool's Gold*. New York: Free Press, p. 49.

14. Ibid., p. 64.

15. James R. Barth, Tong Li, Wenling Lu, Tiphon Phumiwasana, and Glenn Yago, 2009, *The Rise and Fall of the U.S. Mortgage and Credit Markets*, Hoboken, NJ: Wiley.

16. Tett (op. cit. at note 13), pp. 17–18, 39–40.

17. See Barth, Li, Lu, Phumiwasana, and Yago (op. cit. at note 15), pp. 184–93; Michael Lewis, 2009, "The Man Who Crashed the World," *Vanity Fair*, August; and Lawrence G. McDonald and Patrick Robinson, 2009, *A Colossal Failure of Common Sense: The Inside Story of the Collapse of Lehman Brothers*, New York: Crown.

18. Tett (op. cit. at note 13), pp. 160–63.

19. See Barth, Li, Lu, Phumiwasana, and Yago (op. cit. at note 15).

20. See his books *F.I.A.S.C.O.: The Inside Story of Wall Street Trader* (New York: Norton, 1997) and *Infectious Greed: How Deceit and Risk Corrupted the Financial Markets* (New York: Holt, 2003).

21. Quoted from Anthony Faiola, Ellen Nakashima, and Jill Drew, 2009, "What Went Wrong." *Washington Post*, October 15.

22. Commodity Futures Trading Commission, 1998, "CFTC Issues Concept Release Concerning Over-the-Counter Derivatives Market," Release Number 4142–98, May 7.

23. Michael Kirk, 2009, "The Warning." *Frontline*, Public Broadcasting Service, WGBH Boston.

24. Ibid.

25. Ibid.

26. Ibid.

27. Faiola, Nakashima, and Drew (op. cit. at note 20).

28. Kirk (op. cit. at note 22).

29. Faiola, Nakashima, and Drew (op. cit. at note 20).

30. Ibid.

31. The astute reader will recognize the influence of Sergeant Schultz from the late-1960s sitcom *Hogan's Heroes*.

32. Stephen Labaton, 2008, "The Day the S.E.C. Changed the Game," *The New York Times*, video, September 28. http://www.nytimes.com/interactive/2008/09/28/business/20080928-SEC-multimedia/index.html.

33. Ibid.

34. Return on equity (ROE) is the product of leverage times the return on assets, so as leverage grows so does the ROE. So even the dullest financial clod, who can only earn a meager return on his assets, can appear to be a financial wizard with leverage, at least for a while.

35. Robert Colby, 2007, "Testimony Concerning the Consolidated Supervision of U.S. Securities Firms and Affiliated Industrial Loan Corporations." US House of Representatives Financial Services Committee, April 25.

36. Office of Inspector General, SEC, 2008, "SEC's Oversight of Bear Stearns and Related Entity: The Consolidated Supervised Entity Program." *Securities and Exchange Commission*. September 25, and John C. Coffee Jr., 2008, "Analyzing the Credit Crisis: Was the SEC Missing in Action? *New York Law Journal* 5 (December).

37. Stephen Labaton, 2008, "Agency's '04 Rule Let Banks Pile Up New Debt," *New York Times*, October 3.

38. Office of Inspector General, 2008, "SEC's Oversight of Bear Stearns and Related Entities: The Consolidated Supervised Entity Program," September 25. http://www.sec-oig.gov/Reports/AuditsInspections/2008/446-a.pdf.

39. Labaton (op. cit. at note 36).

40. Scot J. Paltrow, "S.E.C. No Evil," *Portfolio.com*, September 18. http://www.portfolio.com/executives/features/2008/09/18/Profile-of-SEC-Chief-Christopher-Cox.

41. Ibid.

42. Richard J. Hillman, 2009, "Testimony on SEC: Greater Attention Is Needed to Enhance Communication and Utilization of Resources in the Division of Enforcement." US Government Accounting Office, May 7.

43. Some of the reduction in fines is probably explained by the earlier increase in fines associated with the accounting scandals.

44. The SEC did not even follow its own rules in conducting consolidated supervision. The SEC's Inspector General Report notes that the SEC (1) conducted internal audits when external audits were required under rules of the CSE program and (2) SEC approved the admittance of some investment banks into the CSE program before the inspections of the broker-dealers had been completed, violating its own procedures.

45. US Securities and Exchange Commission, Office of the Inspector General, Office of Audits, 2008, "SEC's Oversight of Bear Stearns and Related Entities: The Consolidated Entity Program," Report 4446-A, September 25, pp. viii–ix.

46. Ibid, p. 25.

47. A. R. Valukas, 2010, "Lehman Brothers Holdings Inc. Chapter 11 Proceedings Examiner's Report," US Bankruptcy Court Southern District of New York, March 11. http://lehmanreport.jenner.com.

48. Wessel (op. cit. at note 6).

49. On Christopher Cox and Ayn Rand, see Labaton (op. cit. at note 11).

50. E. Wyatt, 2010, "SEC Puts Wall St. on Notice," *New York Times*, April 19.

51. Quoted from Gretchen Morgenson, 2008, "Debt Watchdogs: Tamed or Caught Napping?" *New York Times*, December 7.

52. We relied heavily on Frank Partnoy, 1999, "The Siskel and Ebert of Financial Markets: Two Thumbs Down for the Credit Rating Agencies," *Washington University Law Quarterly* 77(3): 619–712, which is a brilliantly insightful examination of credit-rating agencies. For the empirical evidence on the performance of credit-rating agencies, see G. E. Pinches and J. C. Singleton, 1978, "The Adjustment of Stock Prices to Bond Rating Changes," *Journal of Finance* 33 (1): 29–44.

53. Regulators have relied on credit-rating agencies for a long time, which has given the agencies a privileged position in financial markets. As discussed by Mechoir Palyi in 1938, "Bank Portfolios and the Control of the Capital Market," *The Journal of Business* 11(1): 70–111, the Comptroller of the Currency in 1936 prohibited banks from purchasing speculative securities, where speculative was, in essence, defined by the ratings agencies, especially Moody's ("Law and Summary of Regulations and Rulings Governing the Purchase of Investment Securities," October 27, 1936, p. 4.). Thus regulatory authorities gave rating agencies market power. As expressed by L. L. Watkins in the *American Economic Review Papers and Proceedings* in 1940, "Neither is it important to discuss the alleged merits or faults of the concept of ratings. The important thing which is emphasized here is that rating agencies, without solicitation on their part, have been endowed with power to determine into which channels investment funds will flow." Also see Nathan L. Silverstein, 1940, "Some Considerations on the Management of Commercial Bank Investments," *Journal of Business* 13 (2): 136–45.

54. Morgenson (op. cit. at note 50).

55. Lowenstein, Roger. 2008. Triple-A Failure. The *New York Times*, April 27.

56. Morgenson (op. cit. at note 50).

57. S. Chan, 2010, "Documents Show Internal Qualms at Rating Agencies," *New York Times*, April 23.

58. Ibid.

59. Michael Lewis, 2010, *The Big Short: Inside the Doomsday Machine*, New York: Norton, p. 157.

60. See, for example, United States Securities and Exchange Commission, 2003, *Report on the Role and Function of Credit Rating Agencies in the Operation of Securities Markets* (as Required by Section 702(b) of the Sarbanes–Oxley Act of 2002), January, and the references to early SEC documents and letters therein. See also United States Securities and Exchange Commission, 1994, "Nationally Recognized Statistical Ratings Organizations: Concept Release," File S7–23–94.

61. The "Partnoy's Complaint" phrase is an example of financial economics humor that could explain the limited social lives of most financial economists. Frank Partnoy, 1999, "The Siskel and Ebert of Financial Markets: Two Thumbs Down for the Credit Rating Agencies," *Washington University Law Quarterly* 77 (3): 619–712.

62. The Sarbanes–Oxley Act of 2002 set new and enhanced standards for all US public company boards, management, and public accounting firms. The bill was enacted as a reaction to a number of major corporate and accounting scandals including those affecting Enron, Tyco International, Adelphia, Peregrine Systems, and WorldCom. These scandals, which cost investors billions of dollars when the share prices of affected companies collapsed, shook public confidence in the nation's securities markets. Among other goals, the bill is designed to make corporate behavior more transparent and reduce potential conflicts of interest.

63. Chan (op. cit. at note 56).

64. In 1978, Congress created the Federal Financial Institutions Examination Council, which also coordinates with state agencies on important regulatory issues.

65. The Inspector General performs a Material Loss Review for each insured institution that causes a material loss to the FDIC's Deposit Insurance Fund. A loss is material if it exceeds the greater of $25 million or 2 percent of an institution's assets.

66. See www.fdicoig.gov/MLR.shtml. We examined the 61 reports on failed banks, 22 from 2009 and 39 from 2010. We completed our review on June 21, 2010.

67. These quotations are from MLR 09_017.

68. The quotation is by Jon Rymer, and it is taken from "FDIC Failed to Limit Commercial Real-Estate Loans (Update 1)," *Bloomberg.com*, April 8, 2010.

69. See the Fannie Mae publication, *2008 Q2 10-Q Summary*, the Freddie Mac publication from August 2008, *Freddie Mac Update*, and the calculations by Peter J. Wallison and Charles W. Calomiris, 2008, "The Last Trillion-Dollar Commitment: The Destruction of Fannie Mae and Freddie Mac," *Financial Services Outlook*, American Enterprise Institute for Public Policy Research, pp. 1–10.

70. See Steven A. Holmes, 1999, "Fannie Mae Eases Credit to Aid Mortgage Lending," *New York Times*, September 30, and Alex Berenson, 2003, "Fannie Mae's Loss Risk Is Larger, Computer Models Show," *New York Times*, August 7.

71. See Zachary A. Goldfarb, 2008, "Affordable-Housing Goals Scaled Back," *Washington Post*, September 24, Stephen Labaton, 2003, "New Agency Proposed to Oversee Freddie Mac and Fannie Mae," *New York Times*, September 31, and Alan Greenspan, 2004, "Proposals for Improving the Regulation of the Housing Government Sponsored Enterprises," Testimony before the Committee on Banking, Housing and Urban Affairs, US Senate, February 24.

Chapter 5

1. Patrick Honohan, 2009, "Euro Membership and Bank Stability, Friends of Foes? Lessons from Ireland," paper presented at the Fifteenth Dubrovnik Economic Conference, June 2009.

2. This popular saying in finance apparently is owed to Johann Wolfgang von Goethe, *The Autobiography of Goethe: Truth and Poetry from My Own Life*, translated by John Oxenford, London: Bell and Daldy, 1872, p. 388.

3. See Philip Lane, 2011, "The Irish Crisis," IIIS Discussion paper 356, Trinity College, Dublin, and Luc Laeven and Fabian Valencia, 2010, "Resolution of Banking Crises: The Good, the Bad, and the Ugly," International Monetary Fund WP/10/XX.

4. The two reports are: "The Irish Banking Crisis: Regulatory and Financial Stability Policy 2003–2008," Report to the Minister for Finance by the Governor of the Central Bank, May 31, 2010, http://www.centralbank.ie/data/NewsFiles/The%20Irish%20Banking%20Crisis%20Regulatory%20and%20Financial%20Stability%20Policy%202003-2008.pdf, and "A Preliminary Report on the Sources of Ireland's Banking Crisis," by Klaus Regling and Max Watson, May 2010, http://www.bankinginquiry.gov.ie/Preliminary%20Report%20into%20Ireland%27s%20Banking%20Crisis%2031%20May%202010.pdf.

5. See Morgan Kelly, 2009, "The Irish Credit Bubble," UCD Centre for Economic Research WP 09/32.

6. Ibid., pp. 1–2.

7. Subprime loans as the term is formally used usually refer to borrowers with weak credit histories, often included periods of payment delinquencies and even bankruptcies, which result in a low credit score. On the FICO scale from 350 (poor credit) to 850 (excellent credit), the cutoff for subprime usually is around 620 to 640. Alt-A loans are those in between subprime and prime and usually include borrowers who do not fully document their income, so this category includes some of the so-called NINJA loans—loans made with no verification of income, jobs, or assets. See Barth et al. (2009, ch. 3) for more information. However, in keeping with more common practice, we use the term subprime as referring to anything less than prime mortgage loans, understanding as Barth notes that there is a gray area, and credit score alone does not define a clear cutoff point.

8. Barth et al. (2009, ch. 6).

9. Patrick Honohan, 2004, "Response to Dr. Allan Kearns—Are Irish Households and Corporates Over-indebted and Does It Matter?" Barrington Lecture 2003/04, *Journal of the Statistical & Social Inquiry Society of Ireland* 33: 180–82.

10. Report to the Minister for Finance by the Governor of the Central Bank, 2010 (op. cit. at note 4), p. 16.

11. The Irish Financial Services Regulatory Authority was an independent entity and the regulator of the financial system between 2003 and late-2009 (thereafter it merged back into the Central Bank of Ireland, where it previously had been located).

12. Report to the Minister for Finance by the Governor of the Central Bank, 2010 (op. cit. at note 4), p. 69.

13. See "Banking Supervision: Our New Approach," Central Bank and Financial Services Authority of Ireland, June 21, 2010. http://www.centralbank.ie/frame _main.asp?pg=nws%5Farticle%2Easp%3Fid%3D523&nv=nws_nav.asp.

14. See "The Turner Review: A Regulatory Response to the Global Banking Crisis," U.K. Financial Services Authority, March 2009.

15. See "The Run on the Rock: Fifth Report of Session 2007–08," House of Commons Treasury Committee, vol. 1, pp. 11–12.

16. Ibid., p. 25.

17. "The Supervision of Northern Rock: a lessons learned review," Financial Services Authority Internal Audit Division, March 2008.

18. We are indebted to Charles Littrell for pointing out this incident. See John Palmer and Caroline Cerruti, 2009, " Is there a need to rethink the supervisory process," mimeo, World Bank and the Banco De Espana paper presented at the international conference, Reforming Financial Regulation and Supervision: Going Back to Basics, June 15, 2009, Madrid.

19. See p. 38, paragraph 3.19, HM Treasury, "Reforming Financial Markets," Presented to the Chancellor of the Exchequer by Command of Her Majesty, July 2009.

20. According to Richard Portes ("The shocking errors behind Iceland's meltdown," *Financial Times*, October 13, 2008), "But Iceland has excellent institutions and human capital, as well as sophisticated service enterprises." Also in according to a World Bank database on governance in 212 countries) Daniel Kaufman, Aart Kraay, and Massimo Mastruzzi, 2008, "Governance Matters VII: Aggregate and Individual Governance Indicators, 1996–2007," World Bank Policy Research WP 4654), Iceland ranked first in its control of corruption, this based on survey data.

21. Robert Z. Aliber, 2011, "Monetary Turbulence and the Icelandic Economy," forthcoming in *Prelude to the Icelandic Financial Crisis*, edited by Robert Aliber and Gyfli Zoega, London: Palgrave.

22. Willem Buiter and Anne Sibert, 2008, "The Icelandic Banking Crisis and What to Do about It: The Lender of Last Resort Theory of Optimal Currency Areas," Centre for Economic Policy Research, Policy Insight 26.

23. Ibid., pp. 149, 153–54.

24. A great note by Thorvaldur Gylfason, 2010, "Iceland's special investigation: the plot thickens," *VOX*, April 30, http://www.voxeu.org/index.php?q=node/4965, drew our attention to the Report of the Special Investigation Commission, http:// sic.althingi.is. We use some of the quotes that he finds revealing, as well as other parts of the report.

25. Ibid., ch. 2, p. 1.

26. Ibid., pp. 2–3.

27. Ibid.

28. Ibid.

29. Gylfason (op. cit. at note 24).

30. Ibid., p. 149.

31. Carmen Reinhart and Ken Rogoff's excellent volume, *This Time Is Different: Eight Centuries of Financial Folly* (Princeton: Princeton University Press, 2009) is a great source for a review of such episodes.

32. See "The Pain in Spain Falls Mainly on the Cajas," *Bloomberg Businessweek*, February 25, 2010.

33. See our earlier book, James R. Barth, Gerard Caprio Jr., and Ross Levine, 2006, Rethinking Bank Regulation, Till Angels Govern, Cambridge: Cambridge University Press, ch. 2.

34. "Froth and Stagnation: House Prices in Parts of Asia Continue to Soar, despite Efforts to Slow Them," *Economist*, July 8, 2010.

35. See House Price Indexes: Eight Capital Cities, June 2011, Australian Bureau of Statistics. http://www.abs.gov.au/ausstats/abs@.nsf/mf/6416.0.

36. See Steven Davis, 2010, *Effective Bank Regulation and Supervision: Lessons from the Financial Crisis*, London: Searching Finance Ltd., ch. 7. Note that a frequent criticism of stress tests is that they examine the impact of a mild shock, such as a modest increase in the default rate. However, after significant economic booms, a substantial jump in defaults is more likely as credit is found to have been extended far too generously during boom times.

37. John Kiff, 2009, "Canadian Residential Mortgage Markets: Boring but Effective?" IMF WP/09/130.

38. These data come from Statistics Canada and the US Census Bureau.

39. Peter Boone and Simon Johnson, in their blog on "The Canadian Banking Fallacy," http://baselinescenario.com/2010/03/25/the-canadian-banking-fallacy/, argue that Canadian banks were more leveraged than US counterparts, seeming to ignore that US banks had moved many of their assets off balance sheet.

40. Jason Allen and Walter Engert, 2007, "Efficiency and Competition in Canadian Banking," *Bank of Canada Review*, Summer. We also benefited from email correspondence from John Chant of Simon Fraser University, for information about the Canadian banking system.

Chapter 6

1. As quoted in the New York Times, July 21, 2010. http://www.nytimes.com/2010/07/22/business/22regulate.html.

2. See Frederic Mishkin, 2006, *The Economics of Money, Banking, and Financial Markets*, 8th ed., chapter 12 (New York: Pearson-Addison Wesley), for a brief description of the structure of the Federal Reserve, and Allan Meltzer, 2002, *A History of the Federal Reserve, Volume 1: 1913–1951* (Chicago: University of Chicago Press).

3. Many bank runs, even in the Great Depression, were runs from higher risk banks, and the unambiguously systemic run, including on healthy banks, was in

1933, when people anticipated that President Roosevelt was going to cease to honor the convertibility of dollars into gold, so they tried to take their funds out of the banking system. For more, see Charles Calomiris and Joseph Mason, 2003, "Fundamentals, Panics and Bank Distress during the Depression," *American Economic Review* 93, (December): 1615–47, and in *Financial Crises*, edited by Franklin Allen and Douglas Gale (Cheltenham, UK: Edward Elgar Publishing, 2007).

4. For a good discussion of the role of financial factors in the Great Depression, see Charles W. Calomiris, 1993, "Financial Factors in the Great Depression," *Journal of Economic Perspectives* 7 (spring): 61–85.

5. See James R. Barth, Joseph J. Cordes and Anthony M. J. Yezer, 1980, "Federal Government Attempts to Influence the Allocation of Mortgage Credit: FHA Mortgage Insurance and Government Regulations," *Proceedings on the Conference on the Economics of Federal Credit Activity.* Washington, DC: US Congressional Budget Office.

6. This section draws very heavily on various co-authored works by James R. Barth and R. Dan Brumbaugh Jr., who first introduced Barth to the problems of the savings and loan industry. For more detailed information on savings and loans, see James R. Barth, 1991, *The Great Savings and Loan Debacle* (Washington, DC: AEI Press) and R. Dan Brumbaugh Jr., 1988, *Thrifts under Seige* (New York: Ballinger Publishing). Barth and Brumbaugh, working at the time at the Federal Home Loan Bank Board (FHLBB), were the first to point out in a 1985 report that was approved for public release on the condition of the savings and loan industry that the insurance fund for these institutions was insolvent. Once the full implication of their analysis was realized after being reported in various news media, however, the conclusions were rejected for a time by the top officials of the FHLBB. But within a few months, the FHLBB admitted that the insurance fund was indeed insolvent. This suggests that sometimes individuals within an agency may reach conclusions that top officials at the agency may not wish, at least initially, to make public, re-enforcing the need the Sentinel fully discussed in chapter 8.

7. See William Heisel and Ralph Vartabedian, 2008, "Regulator Provided Cover for IndyMac," *Los Angeles Times*, December 23.

8. See Brumbaugh Jr. (op. cit. at note 6).

Chapter 7

1. For a good and detailed discussion of the various provisions of the new law, see Mayer Brown, 2010, "Understanding the New Financial Reform Legislation," July. www.mayerbrown.com/public_docs/Final-FSRE-Outline.pdf.

2. See Gary B. Gorton and Andrew Metrick, 2010, "Regulating the Shadow Banking System," October 18. SSRN:http://papers.ssrn.com/sol3/papers.cfm?abstract_id=1676947.

3. For example, the Secretary of Treasury is given the discretion to exempt foreign-exchange swaps from the regulation.

4. See chapter 4 for a discussion of OTC derivatives.

5. See Duff McDonald, 2011, "How to Lose Friends in Washington: Be Tarp Cop," *CNNMoney.com*, April 5.

6. As quoted in Andrew Ackerman, 2011, "A Bailout Watchdog Says TARP Fell Short," *Wall Street Journal*, March 31.

7. See Markus Brunnermeier, Andrew Crockett, Charles Goodhart, Avinash D. Persaud and Hyun Shin, 2009, "The Fundamental Principles of Financial Regulation, Geneva Reports on the World Economy," ICMB (International Center for Monetary and Banking Studies), as well as Charles Goodhart, 2009, *The Regulatory Response to the Financial Crisis*, Northampton, MA: Edward Elgar.

8. It should be noted that a more straightforward and non–risk-based measure like tangible common equity (or the market value of equity) provides a quite different, and in some cases a more accurate, indication of the financial condition of the institutions. It may therefore be a far better approach to set a relatively high and non–risk-based required capital ratio, such as one based on tangible common equity, since during the crisis this was only measure most people paid attention to in assessing the financial condition of financial institutions. But, in our view, even this will not be enough. Why? Because there is still no assurance that regulators will perform better without being held accountable for their actions.

9. See Jonathan Stempel, 2009, "Federal Reserve Loses Suit Demanding Transparency," *Rueters*, August 24, and Robert MacMillan, 2009, "Fox Business Sues Fed for Information on Bailouts," *Rueters*, January 12.

10. See Jesse Eisinger, Postcrisis, 2011, "A Struggle over Mortgage Bond Ratings," *New York Times*, January 5, and Gretchen Morgenson, 2011, "Hey, S.E.C., That Escape Hatch Is Still Open," *New York Times*, March 5.

11. Tett, Gillian, 2009, *Fool's Gold*, New York: Free Press, p. 49.

12. For a discussion of these institutions, see James R. Barth, Yuan-Hsin (Rita) Chiang, and Tong Li, 2011, "The Industrial Loan Corporation: Dinosaur—or Financial Phoenix?" *Milken Institute Review* (April, first quarter): 38–45, and James R. Barth, Tong Li, Apanard Angkinand, Yuan-Hsin Chiang, and Li Li, 2011, "Industrial Loan Companies: Supporting America's Financial System," Special Report, *Milken Institute*, April.

13. For an excellent discussion of the mixing of banking and commerce, see Joseph G. Haubrich and João A. C. Santos, 2003, "Alternative Forms of Mixing Banking with Commerce: Evidence from American history." *Financial Markets, Institutions and Instruments* 12 (2): 121–64. Also see James R. Barth, R. Dan Brumbaugh Jr., and James A. Wilcox, 2000, "Glass–Steagall Repealed: Market Forces Compel a New Bank Legal Structure." *Journal of Economic Perspectives* 14 (2): 191–204.

Chapter 8

1. Joe Nocera, 2011, "Letting the Banks Off the Hook," *New York Times*, April 18.

2. *Wall Street Journal*, December 2, 2010, "The Fed's Bailout Files."

3. See Bloomberg research on the Federal Reserve FOIA release timeline. http://www.bloomberg.com/chart/ini3jl5OaEuw.

4. See Edward Kane, 1990, "Principal-Agent Problems in S&L Salvage," *Journal of Finance* 45 (3): 755–64, and Arnoud Boot and Anjan Thakor, 1993, "Self-interested Bank Regulation," *American Economic Review* 83 (2): 206–12.

5. These examples are from the Asher Hawkins article, "The SEC's Revolving Door," which was published in *Forbes* on July 19, 2010.

6. The Senate in fact recently called for an investigation of the SEC's revolving door—even though, we would add, Congress increases the importance of the revolving door by holding down pay (and overall budgets) at the SEC. See Tom McGinty, 2010, "SEC Lawyer One Day, Opponent the Next," *Wall Street Journal*, April 5, and Tom McGinty, 2010, "SEC 'Revolving Door' under Review," *Wall Street Journal*, June 16.

7. See *New York Times, Week in Review*, August 1, 2010, p. 2.

8. Thomas K. McCraw, 1984, *The Prophets of Regulation*, Cambridge: Harvard University Press.

9. While using high salaries to attract to attract first-rate experts into public sector jobs is highly unusual, it is not unprecedented. In Ireland, the National Treasury Management Agency head has received close to €1 million—about $1.35 million—including a bonus, another sixteen staff receive over €200,000 (as discussed in, "Salaries top €200,000 for 16 staff at treasury in the Irish Times," http://www.irishtimes.com/newspaper/ireland/2010/1223/1224286170836.html, December 23, 2010.) And Singapore is also notable for high public sector salaries. The average pay for a government minister is about US $1.3 million and the prime minister is paid about $2 million (5 times the salary of the US president (as discussed in "Singapore announces 60 percent pay raise for ministers," *New York Times*, April 9, 2007, http://www.nytimes.com/2007/04/09/world/asia/09iht-sing.3.5200498.html).

10. True, within the Federal Reserve System, the Board of Governors and not the Reserve Bank presidents determine regulations within the discretion provided by Congress. However, the district bank presidents have such access to the Board members and lines are so blurred to many outsiders (even Treasury Secretary Geithner has suggested that as NY Fed president he had regulatory authority) that the appearance of a conflict of interest is damaging to public perceptions.

11. See "Economist William White Predicted Crisis in 2003," *Der Spiegel* online, July 8, 2009. http://www.midasletter.com/news/09070802_Economist-william-white-predicted-crisis-in-2003.php.

12. Andrew Lo, a professor of finance at MIT, has suggested that just as an expert team is assembled after each plane crash to produce a report on what happened, and their report has no force of law—they just reveal information—the same should be done in finance (as discussed in Eric Fielding, Andrew Lo, and Jian Helen Yang, 2011, "The National Transportation Safety Board: A Model for Systemic Risk Management," MIT mimeo). We agree with his reasoning, but many financial crises are so devastating, and in contrast to plane crashes, are more directly traceable to regulators not doing their jobs. So we think that it is morally and fiscally irresponsible to wait for another crisis, and thus want a Sentinel agency to issue regular reports with the goal of increasing the pressure on the Guardians

to act in a timely manner. Effective post-crisis reports were issued in Iceland, Ireland, and the United Kingdom, and it is likely that the taxpayers' reactions were characterized by rage that their regulators had not taken effective steps to stop the dangerous activities of those in the financial sector and by dismay that they had to wait until after the costs of the crisis had already been incurred to find out about them. And at least those post-crisis reports were relatively timely—appearing in 2009 or early 2010—compared with the report of the Financial Crisis Inquiry Commission, which issued divided reports by the ten members in February 2011. The FCIC also differed from those just cited in including former politicians and some with polarized views as commissioners.

13. Edward Kane has written extensively in this area. See his 2011 paper, "The Importance of Monitoring and Mitigating the Safety-Net Consequences of Regulation-Induced Innovation," mimeo, Boston College.

14. We also disagree with those that suggest that even with reasonable pay, the Sentinel will be unable to attract sufficiently skilled staff because private institutions can always pay more. We disagree. The prominence and significance of the institution will help attract first-rate staff. Those working for the Sentinel would attain considerable stature, esteem, and influence. The opportunity to promote the public interest, achieve career aspirations, work within a multi-disciplinary team, and earn a market-based wage would attract talented individuals to the Sentinel. Even though many highly skilled, talented individuals will, and should, choose to work in the private sector, we are confident that every country has talented individuals with a strong understanding of the financial sector who would choose to devote themselves to the mission of the Sentinel, especially if the salary differences between the private and public sector jobs were not several orders of magnitude different.

15. See James Barth, Gerard Caprio, and Ross Levine, 2006, *Rethinking Bank Regulation: Till Angels Govern,* New York: Cambridge University Press; Thorsten Beck, Ross Levine, and Alexey Levkov, 2010, "Big Bad Banks? The Winners and Losers from Bank Deregulation in the United States," *Journal of Finance* 65(5): 1637–67; Asli Demirguc-Kunt and Ross Levine, 2009, "Finance and Inequality: Theory and Evidence," *Annual Review of Financial Economics* 1 (December): 287–318; Thorsten Beck, Asli Demirguc-Kunt, and Ross Levine, 2007, "Finance, Inequality, and the Poor," *Journal of Economic Growth* 12 (1): 27–49; Thorsten Beck, Asli Demirguc-Kunt, and Ross Levine, "Bank Supervision and Corruption in Lending," *Journal of Monetary Economics* 53(8): 2131–63.

Index

About the Authors

James R. Barth is the Lowder Eminent Scholar in Finance at Auburn University and a Senior Finance Fellow at the Milken Institute. His research focuses on financial institutions and capital markets, both domestic and global, with special emphasis on regulatory issues. He has served as leader of an international team advising the People's Bank of China on banking reform and traveled to China, India, Russia, and Egypt to lecture on various financial topics for the US State Department. He was interviewed about the financial crisis of 2007 to 2009 by the Financial Crisis Inquiry Commission and the Congressional Oversight Panel.

An appointee of Presidents Ronald Reagan and George H. W. Bush, Barth was chief economist of the Office of Thrift Supervision and previously the Federal Home Loan Bank Board. He has also held the positions of professor of economics at George Washington University, associate director of the economics program at the National Science Foundation, and Shaw Foundation Professor of Banking and Finance at Nanyang Technological University. He has been a visiting scholar at the US Congressional Budget Office, Federal Reserve Bank of Atlanta, Office of the Comptroller of the Currency, and the World Bank.

Barth has testified before the US House and Senate banking committees on several occasions. He has authored more than 200 articles in professional journals and has written and edited several books, including *The Rise and Fall of the U.S. Mortgage and Credit Markets: A Comprehensive Analysis of the Meltdown, China's Emerging Markets: Challenges and Opportunities, The Great Savings and Loan Debacle and The Reform of Federal Deposit Insurance*. Other recent books are *Rethinking Bank Regulation: Till Angels Govern* and *Financial Restructuring and Reform in Post-WTO China*. Barth is the co-editor of *The Journal of Financial Economic Policy* and overseas associate editor of *The Chinese Banker*. He has been quoted in news publications ranging from *The New York Times, The Financial Times*, and *The Wall Street Journal* to *Time* and *Newsweek*. In addition he has appeared on such broadcast programs as *Newshour, Good Morning America, Moneyline*, Bloomberg News, Fox Business News, and National Public Radio. Barth is also included in *Who's Who in Economics: A Biographical Dictionary of Major Economists, 1700 to 1995*.

Gerard Caprio Jr. is the William Brough Professor of Economics at Williams College and the Chair of the Center for Development Economics. Until January 2006 he was the Director for Policy in the World Bank's Financial Sector Vice Presidency and previously served as head of the financial sector research team in the Bank's Development Research Group. Past positions included: Vice President and Head of Global Economics at JP Morgan, economist at the Federal Reserve Board and the IMF, and adjunct professor at George Washington University. He received his PhD in economics from the University of Michigan. Jerry has researched and written extensively on financial sector policy, financial reform, and banking crises, including *Financial Reform: Theory and Experience*, and *Financial Liberalization: How Far, How Fast* (all Cambridge University Press). He co-authored *Finance for Growth: Policy Choices in a Volatile World,* with Patrick Honohan, and with Jim Barth and Ross Levine, co-authored *Rethinking Bank Regulation: Till Angels Govern.* He is editor of the forthcoming online *Encyclopedia of Financial Globalization* (Elsevier) and also a co-editor of *The Journal of Financial Stability.* His current research is on the links between financial sector regulation and supervision and the development and stability of the financial sector.

Ross Levine   is the Willis H. Booth Chair in Banking and Finance at the Haas School of Business at the University of California, Berkeley, Director of the William R. Rhodes Center for International Economics and Finance, a Research Associate at the National Bureau of Economic Research, and a member of the Council on Foreign Relations.

Levine's work focuses on the links between financial sector policies, the operation of financial systems, economic growth, and income distribution. Professor Levine co-authored *Financial Structure and Economic Growth* with Asli Demirguc-Kunt and *Rethinking Bank Regulation: Till Angels Govern* Jim Barth and Jerry Caprio, while publishing over 100 articles, including papers in the leading finance and economics journals. His work and opinions have been discussed and quoted in major news outlets and he is ranked as one of the ten most cited scholars in economics and finance.